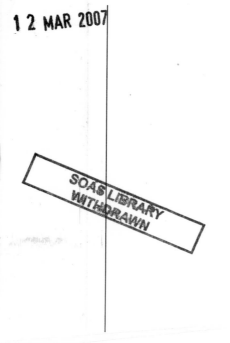

PENGUIN BOOKS

Free Expression is No Offence

Free Expression is No Offence

EDITED BY LISA APPIGNANESI

An English PEN Book

PENGUIN BOOKS

PENGUIN BOOKS

Published by the Penguin Group
Penguin Books Ltd, 80 Strand, London WC2R ORL, England
Penguin Group (USA) Inc., 375 Hudson Street, New York, New York 10014, USA
Penguin Group (Canada), 90 Eglinton Avenue East, Suite 700, Toronto, Ontario, Canada M4P 2Y3
(a division of Pearson Penguin Canada Inc.)
Penguin Ireland, 25 St Stephen's Green, Dublin 2, Ireland
(a division of Penguin Books Ltd)
Penguin Group (Australia), 250 Camberwell Road,
Camberwell, Victoria 3124, Australia (a division of Pearson Australia Group Pty Ltd)
Penguin Books India Pvt Ltd, 11 Community Centre,
Panchsheel Park, New Delhi – 110 017, India
Penguin Group (NZ), cnr Airborne and Rosedale Roads, Albany,
Auckland 1310, New Zealand (a division of Pearson New Zealand Ltd)
Penguin Books (South Africa) (Pty) Ltd, 24 Sturdee Avenue,
Rosebank, Johannesburg 2196, South Africa

Penguin Books Ltd, Registered Offices: 80 Strand, London WC2R ORL, England

www.penguin.com

First published 2005
1

Editor's Preface copyright © Lisa Appignanesi 2005
Individual contributions copyright © the authors 2005
p. ix constitutes an extension of this copyright page
All rights reserved

The moral right of the authors has been asserted

Set in 11/13 pt Monotype Dante
Typeset by Rowland Phototypesetting Ltd, Bury St Edmunds, Suffolk
Printed in England by Clays Ltd, St Ives plc

ISBN-13: 978-0-141-02473-8
ISBN-10: 0-141-02473-9

8760A

Publisher's Note

This book is published in association with English PEN, a vital part of an international organization that champions freedom of expression everywhere and the right of writers, artists and indeed anyone to say whatever they feel without fear of persecution or penalty.

It appears in the seventieth year of Penguin's life, and we are delighted to be publishing it as a part of our birthday celebrations. It is also a part of our ongoing commitment to English PEN and all of its activities, including its objections to a law criminalizing 'religious hatred' – a modification to this country's justice system which puts all writers, artists and performers at risk, and limits all of our fundamental rights to free expression. Following the London bombings of July 2005, before which these essays were completed, this issue is of more importance than ever.

In 1960 Penguin fought, successfully, an obscenity trial to publish D. H. Lawrence's *Lady Chatterley's Lover* in Britain, thirty-two years after it was first printed (privately) in Florence. Forty-five years on, we are proud to be publishing this exceptional collection of essays and contributions in support of our crucial and continuing right in Britain to express ourselves freely.

Our thanks go to all of the contributors and to the book's editor, Lisa Appignanesi.

You can find out more about English PEN at www.englishpen. org.

Contents

Contents

Acknowledgements

PEN/Penguin is grateful to all contributors for their articles. We also gratefully acknowledge permission to reprint from the following sources:

Timothy Garton Ash's 'Save Our Raphael' appeared in an earlier, shorter version in the *Guardian* on 17 February 2005.

Gurpreet Kaur Bhatti's 'This warrior is fighting on' ['A Letter'] © Gurpreet Kaur Bhatti first appeared in the *Guardian* on 13 January 2005.

Gurpreet Kaur Bhatti's foreword to her play *Behzti* © Gurpreet Kaur Bhatti 2004 is reprinted by kind permission of the publisher Oberon Books (www.oberonbooks.com).

Ian Buruma's article 'Final Cut' originally appeared in a longer form in the *New Yorker* of 3 January 2005.

Frances D'Souza's speech comes from Hansard, Columns 1116–1118, 14 March 2005. Parliamentary copyright material is reproduced with the permission of the Controller of Her Majesty's Stationery Office on behalf of Parliament. The quotations from the debate on 7 February are from Hansard of that date.

Pervez Hoodbhoy's article 'Science and Islam' first appeared, in a longer version, as 'Returning Science to Islam – The Rocky Road Ahead' in *Trust Me, I'm a Scientist*, one of ten volumes of essays first published as *Birthday Counterpoints*, for the British Council's seventieth anniversary. The other titles are available via the website of Counterpoint, the British Council's think-tank on cultural relations (www.counterpoint-online.org).

Hanif Kureishi's 'Loose Tongues' was first delivered at the Hay Festival and appeared in the *Guardian* on 7 June 2003.

Editor's Preface

Lisa Appignanesi

'If liberty means anything at all it means the right to tell people what they do not want to hear.'

Like so many of the greatest writers, George Orwell was good at telling people what they didn't want to hear. In this quotation from his unpublished preface to *Animal Farm*, the 'people' are, perhaps surprisingly, neither State, nor Church, nor any other formal authority whose censorious powers he targeted elsewhere. They are, instead, what he perceived as a left-leaning establishment, an 'English intelligentsia', who had during the antifascist struggle developed 'a nationalistic loyalty towards the USSR'. For them, doubting 'the wisdom of Stalin was a kind of blasphemy'.

Orwell understood the jealousy of power. He portrayed the murderous totalitarian kind in his fictions; here, he was worried by the power of prevailing orthodoxy, those bearers of the time's political correctness who could silence unpopular ideas and keep inconvenient facts in the dark.

Authoritarian regimes have always been alive to those troublesome viruses that ideas can be. A radical journalist before he came to power, Lenin, once ensconced, asked, 'Why should freedom of speech and freedom of the press be allowed? . . . [A government] would not allow opposition by lethal weapons. Ideas are much more fatal things than guns.' Hitler burned books before burning people. The Inquisition had paved the way well before him. Religions are particularly sensitive to competing ideas, which they label offensive or attacks on that purity central to so much religious thought. In 1832, Pope Gregory XVI declared that freedom of the press was heretical vomit. Fiction, which appeals to the heart as well as the mind, which transports the reader directly into the everyday life of another individual, can prove even more dangerous in its seductions. Indeed, if the Papal Index had had its way, the entire canon of French literature from Rabelais to Voltaire, Diderot, Baudelaire, Flaubert and even Simone de Beauvoir would have been prohibited. Nazi views on purity and corruption were not so very different. One of the tactics of authority is to label its ways pure and ring-fence its power by excluding the impure other.

The Universal Declaration of Human Rights grew out of the world waking to the horror that had been Nazism and its perversions. The final draft emerged from a committee which had a broad cultural and geographical mix. Article 19 states: 'Everyone has the right to freedom of opinion and expression; the right includes freedom to hold opinions without interference and to seek, receive and impart information and ideas through any media regardless of frontiers.' In Britain, the struggle against censorship and for free expression has a long and honourable, if chequered, history. From 1559 all serious books had to be approved by the Queen, her Archbishops or the Chancellor of Oxford or Cambridge University, before being licensed by the Stationers' Company. When Cromwell brought censorship back in 1643 after a brief hiatus, Milton penned his *Areopagitica*, a passionate plea for free expression. He argued that promiscuous reading was necessary to the constituting of human nature. To keep out evil doctrine by 'licensing' was:

. . . like the exploit of that gallant man who thought to keep out the crows by shutting his park gate . . . Lords and Commons of England, consider what nation it is whereof ye are the governors . . . a nation not slow and dull, but of a quick, ingenious and piercing spirit . . . It must not be shackled or restricted . . . Give me the liberty to know, to utter and to argue freely according to conscience, above all liberties.

Not until the Glorious Revolution and the Bill of Rights in 1689 were liberties extended; not far enough, however, to prevent the political radical John Wilkes from being thrown into the Tower in 1763 and the printers and publishers of his 'seditious and treasonable paper', the *North Briton*, from being arrested. After Wilkes won his case, it was indirectly assumed that the press had the right to comment on and criticize Parliament, as well as report debates. Ever since, Britain has rightly been proud of its long history of liberties. But freedom of expression was still bound in various ways, whether by politics, obscenity, or blasphemy – as the cases of Thomas Paine, D. H. Lawrence and most recently, in 1978, *Gay News* make clear.

Censorship in the theatre – that form of imaginative expression in which ideas are embodied in live actors who perform in front of a collective public, not unlike politicians in Parliament or barristers in court – continued assiduously until 1968 when the Lord Chamberlain was finally divested of his power to vet all plays before production. The 1737 Theatre Licensing Act had given the Lord Chamberlain sufficient powers to prevent satire undermining the authority of Walpole's contested Government. It had created a 'legitimate' theatre. The Theatre Act of 1843 went further. All plays had to be vetted before production. The Chamberlain now had the power not only of the blue pencil, but of prohibiting entire scenes or performances. Aristophanes' *Lysistrata* went, along with Shaw's *Mrs Warren's Profession*, Oscar Wilde's *Salomé*, and, in 1892, all of Ibsen, whose characters, the censor claimed, were 'morally deranged', the heroines 'dissatisfied spinsters . . . or dissatisfied married women in a chronic state of rebellion'. It is hardly coincidental that through the nineteenth and first half of the twentieth centuries, so many of the plays to bear the brunt of censorship were to do with women, and, as the twentieth century moved on, with homosexuality.

Today, in many countries around the world, censorship continues. Books are banned, their writers arrested. In 2004 PEN listed just under 1000 writers worldwide who were in prison for their writing. Twelve had been killed; still more had disappeared. Where religious and state power coincide, restrictions on free expression are particularly intense. Iran and Bangladesh have issued fatwas against writers. In Saudi Arabia it is illegal to distribute the Bible; in Myanmar, where writers are regularly silenced and imprisoned, it is forbidden to translate the Bible into local languages. Ironically, for some six hundred years after the Council of Toulouse in 1229, the Roman Catholic Church felt the same about the Bible's translation into the vernacular or indeed about its possession by ordinary reading people, for whom it was evidently dangerous. Meanwhile, in America in our own time, certain circles are prone to think that the Bible is the only 'good-for-you' book, while evangelical Christians work energetically to ban Darwin and any notion of evolution from schools, not to mention Imax cinemas. Creation stories have long been contested by different beliefs: now they even float across to the life of embryos.

Here, in Britain, we thought we were free from such infringements on our freedoms. After all, a Tory Government had defended Salman Rushdie through the years of the Ayatollah Khomeini's fatwa; and the case for extending the law of blasphemy to *The Satanic Verses* had failed in the courts. PEN, with its mission to protect writers under threat, focused its attention abroad, on China or Myanmar, Iran or North Africa.

Then the Labour Government decided to try and make a crime of 'incitement to religious hatred'.

The Offence of Religious Hatred

David Pannick, QC, summed up the Government's legislation in *The Times*:

The relevant provisions are contained in Schedule 10 to the Serious Organized Crime and Police Bill. They seek to amend the Public Order

Act 1986, which already makes racial hatred a criminal offence. If the Bill is enacted, the same scheme would apply to religious hatred. So it would be a criminal offence to use threatening, abusive or insulting words or behaviour if you 'intend to stir up religious hatred', or if religious hatred is 'likely to be stirred up'. Prosecutions could be brought only by the Attorney-General. A convicted person would face up to seven years in prison.

(*The Times*, 11 January 2005)

The Muslim Council, a lobbying umbrella group which claims to represent some two hundred Muslim grassroots organizations, had long called for such a law. There is an element of historical irony in the fact that the Council had itself been partly spurred into being by a concerted attack on a book – Salman Rushdie's *The Satanic Verses*, which earned the writer who had long campaigned against racism the vitriol of the very people whose condition he had so brilliantly described. Indeed, the controversy over *The Satanic Verses*, its attendant riots and iconic book-burning helped to consolidate not only the public presence of British Muslims, but the notion, always arguable, that they form a unified 'community' of interests.

In 2004, the Labour Government, recognizing that British Muslims had suffered from the war on terrorism after 9/11, its control orders, Guantanamo, and the Iraq war, decided to give with one hand what it had patently taken away with another. There was a spirit of political correctness in the way Fiona Mactaggart, then Parliamentary Under-Secretary for Race Equality, Community Policy and Civil Renewal, championed the proposed offence of Incitement to Religious Hatred. Even if the legislation talked of all religions generally, it was openly intended for a group who had been discriminated against and would now be helped.

This law was devised by the Home Office, but its Government advocates seemed blind to the wider implications of their proposed legislation. The authoritarian and hierarchical bias of so many religions, their global reach and funding, let alone their reactionary stance on women, never seemed to cast a shadow over the Government's public utterances. They were also unpardonably cavalier about freedom of expression. This would inevitably suffer as publishers and broadcasters chafed under the worries of possible prosecution and nudged writers down the dangerous slopes of self-censorship Orwell had so well described.

The law banning incitement to religious hatred received its first reading in the House of Commons on Wednesday, 24 November 2004, the day after the Queen's Speech. Its earliness in the agenda, alongside other Home Office legislation, stressed its importance for the Government. By the time of the first debate in the Commons on 7 December, response was already strong and critical. It came from writers and stand-up comedians, from civil rights groups and barristers. Some said that if the law had existed during the time of the Rushdie affair, the Government instead of protecting Rushdie would have prosecuted him themselves. Legal notables advised that the law was unnecessary and badly framed. Journalists and writers pulled apart the meaning of 'hatred', 'insult', 'offence' and warned that it would be better to let 'sleeping dogmas lie'. They didn't.

Sikh protests against Gurpreet Kaur Bhatti's *Behzti* (*Dishonour*) erupted as if released by the proposed legislation on hatred. They grew to a climax on 18 December 2004, when a crowd of over 1000 Sikhs smashed windows, hurled eggs, injured three police officers, and stormed the Birmingham Repertory stage. They claimed the play by a young Sikh woman was sacrilegious and insulting to their religion. The violence, the danger to audience, actors and staff, forced the play to be closed by the management. Here was a clear signal of the intolerance of religious groups to artistic expression – particularly, perhaps, when the artist, who represents the community in less than a perfect light, is one of their own.

Fiona Mactaggart, in her media comments, was hardly charitable to the writer's case. Nor did she condemn the intimidation and threats made against Bhatti's life, which she equated with free speech: 'The free speech of the protesters is as important as the free speech of the artist,' she declared (*Daily Telegraph*, 22 December 2004). To some of us, it seemed to be rather *more* important, given that Gurpreet Bhatti was forced into hiding, while no prosecutions were brought on public order offences against the rioters.

While the *Behzti* controversy rumbled, a new protest had been building in the wings. The BBC had announced the screening on 8 January 2005 of *Jerry Springer – The Opera*, a gripping satire of the louche American television talk show here transformed into a sung morality play. Originally mounted by London's National Theatre, the *Opera* had moved into the West End after a critical and box office success. For the BBC to screen a contemporary opera was a risky and adventurous artistic undertaking. But any fear of low ratings was transformed by the mass attention Christian evangelical protest focused on the venture. Over 45,000 emails blocked the BBC lines. Many of them came from American sites. On the night, 1.7 million viewers watched the *Opera*. Christian Voice, which led the demonstration in front of the BBC headquarters, promised to bring a private prosecution against the BBC for the common law offence of blasphemy. Threats were made to key BBC employees whose addresses were posted on the Christian Voice website. Security guards were deployed. Despite all this, the BBC stood firm against what some called attempts by religious bullies to dictate what could and couldn't be seen in Britain.

The Campaign

It was in the midst of all this that English PEN launched its campaign against the Government's incitement legislation: Free

Expression is NO OFFENCE. Salman Rushdie, whose life has been so enmeshed with this very issue, was fortuitously in London. He addressed English PEN members at the Adam Street Club:

It seems we need to fight the battle for the Enlightenment all over again in Europe too. That battle was about the Church's desire to place limits on thought. The Enlightenment wasn't a battle against the State but against the Church. Diderot's novel *La Religieuse*, with its portrayal of nuns and their behaviour, was deliberately blasphemous: it challenged religious authority, with its indexes and inquisitions, on what it was *possible* to say. Most of our contemporary ideas about freedom of speech and the imagination come from the Enlightenment. We may have thought the battle won, but if we aren't careful, it is about to be 'un-won'.

In the first week of 2005, over four hundred writers, as well as contacting their own MPs, signed a PEN letter addressed to the Home Secretary, Charles Clarke.

Dear Charles Clarke,
The proposed offence of 'incitement of religious hatred' in the Serious Organized Crime and Police Bill.
On behalf of the members of English PEN and their affiliates abroad, we wish to state our opposition to the proposed legislation which would make it illegal to express what some might consider to be provocative views on religion.

Although we applaud the Government's wish to make everyone in our multicultural, multi-faith nation feel that they have an equal stake in Britain, the proposed amendment to the Bill is misguided. It is emphatically not the way forward. It creates a climate which engenders events such as the recent Sikh riot in Birmingham. Here a violent mob, on the grounds that a play offended their religion, successfully prevented its performance, acted as censors, and threatened the life of its author.

Fiona Mactaggart, the Home Office Minister, has contended that the remit of the proposed legislation is narrow. However, the signal the offence clause sends out to religious leaders is broad. It serves as a sanction for censorship of a kind which would constrain writers and impoverish our cultural life. Rather than averting intolerance, 'it would', as the Southall Black Sisters have pointed out, 'encourage the culture of intolerance that already exists in all religions.' To gag criticism is to encourage abuse of power within religious communities. The proposed legislation could also backfire on those very groups the Government is keen to placate: some of their own literature could readily be prosecuted under the law's aegis.

We contend that under the proposed legislation the necessary freedoms of a mature democracy will be curtailed. The freedom to practise and believe for all religions can only be maintained within secular states. Religious leaders, alongside legislators, might like to take note of the historical fact that nowhere have so many different religions co-existed peacefully as in a democracy where freedom of expression is a right. Looking beyond Britain will quickly show that where the State intervenes in religious matters, there is no possibility of a plurality of equals.

Finally, as writers of many faiths and none, we must emphasize that if religious leaders had their way, we would have little literature, less art and no humour. The religious can be quick to take offence. The Papal Index makes salutary reading: it has banned every great offender from Voltaire to Flaubert to James Joyce. On their side, some Jews have objected to Philip Roth and to Joseph Heller; while some Muslim clerics have been so severely offended by the fictions of Salman Rushdie and the Egyptian writer Naguib Mahfouz as to issue fatwas against them – much to the distress of other Muslims. Now British Sikhs have succeeded in censoring the play Behzti *and forcing Gurpreet Kaur Bhatti into hiding.*

The new legislation encourages rather than combats intolerance. We do not need it. What we need is a signal from Government that it wishes to defend true democracy and its many virtues, including those of dissent and the freedom of expression.

> *If the Government feels more legislation is essential in this area,*
> *then it would achieve more of its ends by repealing the law on*
> *blasphemy, a relic of pre-multicultural times. Less, here, is more.*
>
> *The times are such that we need to champion the freedoms our*
> *democracy has fought hard to secure alongside the cultural riches we*
> *have the liberty to enjoy and create.*
>
> *We hope the Government will join us in this.*

The response to this letter from Fiona Mactaggart invited Salman Rushdie and PEN to meet with her so that she could explain the Government's position. Rushdie, Geoffrey Robertson, QC, and I attended the meeting, together with Rowan Atkinson who had fought the legislation from the very start. Ms Mactaggart sought to reassure us by stating that the new offence had a narrow remit: it was there to plug a loophole; to give Muslims the protection other faiths, such as Sikhs and Jews, already had under the rubric of incitement to 'racial hatred'. It would only target that hate speech which is a precursor to violent action (though there had been no Government prosecution of the violent action by religious extremists in the *Behzti* case). Prosecutions would take place at the discretion of the Attorney-General.

We were not reassured. Geoffrey Robertson pointed out that there was enough legislation on the statute books to protect Muslims from the kind of incitement the new clause addressed.[1] Rushdie spoke of how, whatever the Government intended, the law was misunderstood by many Muslims and held to have a wide brief. He wryly noted that good intentions had paved the road to hell before this. Rowan Atkinson talked of the crushing impact the law would have on comedy and satire: even if *prosecutions* didn't ultimately result from material that religions

---

[1] Several articles in the book deal with existing legislation (cf. Anthony Lester, p. 211) so I don't detail it here.

construed as offensive, the long-drawn-out process of police investigation would destroy lives. I was certain that this misguided law would send a signal of approval to religions and have them prosecuting imaginative expression as well as each other.

After the meeting, Ms Mactaggart wrote to us to put the Home Office case once more, and also to announce that, in the light of our worries, the name of the legislation had been changed. A change of name but not of substance was hardly enough. We received the letter on Friday, 4 February. The following Monday, 7 February, the Bill went to the House of Commons. Despite opposition and an amendment carefully delimiting the powers of the incitement legislation from the Liberal Democrats, the legislation secured a second reading. On Labour's own back benches, there was evident misunderstanding of the Bill as drafted: here, the new legislation appeared as a blasphemy bill for Muslims, something the head of the Muslim Council had also in the early days of the Bill's history contended. The next day we replied to the Home Office Minister.

Dear Fiona Mactaggart,
Thank you for your long and considered response to our meeting on the religious hatred offence in the Serious Organized Crime and Police Bill. We are pleased that, in order to allay our very real worries, you have decided to change the title of the offence to 'Hatred against persons on racial or religious grounds'. We wish, however, that the change were not only in name.

We understand, as we have previously stated, that the Government's intentions are to plug a loophole and protect Muslims specifically in the way that others are protected under racial legislation. But a law which draws a wide brief in order to protect a specific instance seems misguided from its outset.

Despite your arguments, and whatever the guidelines that will attend the clause when it becomes law, it will inevitably aggravate tensions amongst the various faiths, clog up the courts, and induce (self)-censorship in our artistic, broadcasting and publishing establishments. It will also, we fear, create a climate in which expression is constrained for those who might wish to criticize some of the palpable ills associated with religious hierarchies, while encouraging those who want to use the courts and media for self-aggrandizement.

Some of us attended the debate in the House on 7 February. Others of us have read Hansard. We trust that you have taken note of the confusion on your own benches about the breadth of the proposed Offence. That confusion exists within the very group you are purportedly setting out to protect. Mr Mahmood, MP for Birmingham, Perry Barr, is happy to defend free speech in its generality, but as soon as he is asked a direct question, a very real intolerance is evident and a wish to see the law applied to precisely the instances you say it doesn't cover.

Just to remind you, here is the point in Hansard.

Ms. Abbott: My hon. Friend says that nobody in the Muslim community denies that people should be able to make valid criticisms of the religion, but I was a Member of Parliament at the time of 'The Satanic Verses', and there were thousands and thousands of Muslims who believed emphatically that people were not entitled to criticise their religion.
Mr. Mahmood: I am sorry, but I take issue with that. It was not a question of making a valid criticism of the religion. In the context of Salman Rushdie, the issue was the abusive words that he deliberately used, which were written in phonetic Urdu, criticising –
[Interruption.] Actual swear words were used within that text.
Mrs. Alice Mahon (Halifax) (Lab): Who decides?
Mr. Mahmood: The decision is taken in the courts, if it comes to that. As my right hon. Friend the Member for Holborn and St. Pancras (Mr. Dobson) said, there will be an opportunity for some of those cases and issues to be tested. In a sense, that is what the judicial system is about and what this democracy is about: giving people that opportunity.

If even your own backbenchers have false expectations of this new Offence, is it too much to imagine how widespread these expectations will be outside the House and what serious constraints on expression will follow, let alone heightened strife amongst the disparate groupings in Britain today?

You say, quite emphatically, in your letter, that writers and artists like ourselves 'are rightly concerned about freedom of expression'. You go on to say, 'The Government's prime concern is the safety and security of our communities.' Would it not be more correct to say that it is the Home Office which is chiefly concerned with security and therefore finds itself blind to other and equally pressing matters? The Government as a whole, we would argue, must be concerned with far more than security – and freedom of expression must indeed be part of that more general concern. After all, if the Government isn't concerned with that freedom, it may soon find the very parliamentary system from which it is formed, let alone its own politics, under serious threat.

The fact that the various groups you name want this new Offence is not particularly reassuring. (There are other groups which aren't being listened to, after all.) Nor is the fact that an ICM poll backed it to 57%. The call for capital punishment or hanging for paedophiles might have less than 43% of a poll against it: we trust the Home Office won't instantly see fit to propose this. A Government that considers the general good over a term beyond elections should, we feel, put forward laws which work for the benefit of all. Religiously biased constraints on free expression do not.

The Home Office blind spot is evident, too, in the way you talk about the Behzti case. The fact that the Police did not ultimately find grounds for prosecution under the incitement to racial hatred legislation does nothing to alter the fact that the performance of the play was stopped, its expression forcibly constrained, the person of its author threatened and forced into hiding. Nor did the Government decide to prosecute those who had issued threats against the author's life, certainly worth saving, whatever the offence felt by her co-religionists.

So, while we are pleased that you have seen fit to re-title the

*proposed Offence, we cannot say that we are reassured. We trust that
the Lords won't be either. It is a sadness to us that we now have to
look to the Upper House for the protection of our basic rights.*

Letters to the press and a variety of articles, notably one by
Timothy Garton Ash in the *Guardian*, took up the case for free
expression in the light of the debate in the Commons.

On 14 March, Serious and Organized Crime Bill went to the
House of Lords, latterly a bastion of our civil liberties. Forceful
arguments against the incitement legislation were put by many,
including Lord Lester and Baroness Frances D'Souza, the former
head of Article 19, the organization which campaigns for free
expression.

Given the opposition to the legislation and the pending election, the Government decided to put through the Serious Organized Crime Bill without Schedule 10. For a brief moment, we had
the illusion of triumph. But the contested matter made its way
into the Labour Party manifesto. Charles Clarke wrote to the
nation's mosques promising that the legislation would come back
early in the new term. 'It remains our firm and clear intention to
give people of all faiths the same protection against incitement
to hatred on the basis of their religion.'[2] Letters from Charles
Clarke and the Labour Party did not go out to Catholic churches
nor the temples of other faiths. Meanwhile, Fiona Mactaggart
told *Muslim News*[3] that, if need be, the Parliament Act would be
invoked to bring the legislation into being. We wrote once more
to the Home Office:

Dear Charles Clarke,
*English PEN and its wide-ranging membership were distressed to see
that the proposed legislation on 'incitement to hatred on religious*

2 Letter of Tuesday, 12 April 2005 from the Office of Charles Clarke and signed.
3 *Muslim News* press release, 15 April 2005.

grounds' appeared in the Labour Party manifesto and did so in the most ambiguous terms – ones which might lead interested parties to believe that a promise to criminalize provocative writing was indeed on the agenda.

When we went to see Fiona Mactaggart, she adamantly denied that there was any intention in the proposed legislation to conflate criticism of religious belief with criticism of the person of the believer. We know, however, that there is confusion about this on your own back benches (see Mr Mahmood, in Hansard for 7 February 2005, who is ready to prosecute The Satanic Verses*). Now, it seems that for election purposes, you are willing to make that confusion more general. This seems to be a case where expectations of a law if not fulfilled will cause grave disquiet in one community, whereas if they are fulfilled, our basic freedoms will suffer a constraint disastrous to the culture of this country.*

You have now compounded the problem by writing to mosques around the country, once more promising legislation which could easily be construed to have a broad rather than narrow remit. Have you written to other faith groups? The conflation of religion, which is a set of beliefs and hierarchies, and race, a question of history and ethnicity, is inflammatory in our multicultural society. Your letter pits Jews and Sikhs against Muslims. Is it Labour policy to aggravate tensions here?

Are you seriously setting out to create a climate in which expression is constrained for those who might wish to criticize some of the palpable ills associated with religious hierarchies, while encouraging those who want to use the courts and media to entrench their authority?

The letter to mosques seems to us to be an attempt to exploit the religious and race card in marginal seats. It goes directly against the assurances given us by the Home Office, is objectionable in principle and dangerous in practice.

As writers of many faiths and none, who care about our liberties as well as our civil society, and who might indeed, like mosque- and

> *churchgoers, be stirred to vote Labour, we trust you can provide us*
> *with some clearer indication of your intentions.*

Needless to say, PEN received no pre-election response to the letter. In the May 2005 election, one of our basic freedoms was being bartered for a few marginal seats Labour thought the Muslim vote could swing. With the new Parliament, criminalizing religious hatred made it into the Queen's Speech and rapidly got its own Bill. What matter a few protesting writers, stand-ups, civil libertarians . . . though it became increasingly clear to us that a large section of the public, once properly informed about the potential impact of the Bill, cared deeply about established freedoms. Then came the bombs . . .

The contemporary globalized world is riven with confusions about where protection can collide with repression; where worries about security and respect for others bump into and topple liberties by becoming fixed in law. The essays in this book confront some of these confusions.

The Wider Picture

In Britain, rather more than in the rest of Europe – where still-remembered dictatorial states have engendered a tougher adherence to hard-won freedoms – writers sometimes feel ambivalent about championing free expression on their own turf, as if it were a display of self-interest. Some may even feel 'offensive' artists deserve what they get and that sensitivities, particularly of minority groups and faiths, have to be respected at all costs. The rights of groups, from this perspective, outweigh the rights of individuals.

This is the argument that was played out in the hate-speech debates on American campuses in the eighties. It resulted in university codes which enshrined respect for groups who had undergone a history of discrimination. The codes had some benefits. But their prescriptive weight quickly grew disciplinary and constricting. This was true even for the members of the group themselves. It may be that the benefits of free expression do indeed outweigh those of purified speech – purged for whatever politically or religiously correct ends. The experience of history, as well as a glance at current regimes around the world, under-lines what the Nobel Prize-winning economist Amartya Sen has pointed out: that freedom of speech is a marker for other kinds of freedom. Its lack is always linked to repressive regimes, to the 'unfreedoms' of poverty and famine, as well as to the oppression of women.

Imaginative writers, no matter how responsible, no matter what groups they may affiliate themselves to, always write as individuals: this is both our strength and our weakness. Fiction, including theatre, is the playground of individuals, of heroes and anti-heroes. Plagued by doubts (or those certainties Voltaire thought far more absurd), subject to the conflicting demands of lovers or wives or church or work, driven by dreams and desires and duplicities, their plight becomes a key to understanding the disorders of the world. How could the narrow, 'cloistered' virtue of authority find such 'individuals' anything other than 'offensive', indeed dangerous?

'Suspending moral judgement is not the immorality of the novel; it is its *morality* . . .' Milan Kundera wrote, in making a case for the European arts. And it is these very arts which have helped to constitute the individuality at the heart of our society of human rights.

That said, a good number of the articles in this book are not written by champions of absolute free speech. I was interested in drawing together essays which would allow us to confront some of the tangled matter which life in the contemporary world forces on us. Never before has communication across continents worked instantly, has news sped across national boundaries with the tap of a button. Never before have so many radically different cultures born of different histories, let alone so many pious adherents of so many religions, lived side by side with believers in the stringently secular. Never before has so much difference been subject to the same laws, whether national or, in some religious instances, global. In such a heterogeneous world, writers, particularly of fiction, can hardly predict the way in which readers will respond to their work, what seeds it may plant in imaginations, exactly how it might provoke. In our multi-ethnic culture where skins can be thin, offence can be found both where it is and isn't intended.

It is clear that, in this new century, Enlightenment rights of freedom of expression are in tension with religious sensitivities. It is also clear that relatively small conservative Christian groups or self-elected representatives of faith lobbies can hold far larger and more liberal populations to ransom by using lobbying techniques married to internet and email 'attacks'. The challenge that I put to writers in this volume – some of the best minds of our time – was to consider how, given this environment, we are to understand the competing freedoms of imagination and religion; how we might negotiate the demands of individual imagination and collective cohesion, of personal conscience and public need.

Some of the articles in this book spring immediately from the Government's legislation and respond to it in various ways. I thought it would prove illuminating to include Gurpreet Kaur Bhatti and one of the actors in *Behzti*, Madhav Sharma, to convey a sense of how people feel when their established rights are suddenly threatened by the force of a mob. Nicholas Hytner, who, as Director of the National Theatre, knows what it means to receive protests from the offended, reflects on theatre in the light of the new legislation. Monica Ali begins with a sense that a law which makes hate speech an offence is good and then, weighing the evidence, finds herself on the opposition benches. Timothy Garton Ash recognizes that 9/11 began a process which needs to be remedied, but argues that the incitement legislation isn't the way.

Other essays take us further afield. Philip Pullman reflects on identity politics; Ian Buruma on the situation in Holland, which shares with Britain a history of tolerance, now disturbed by the tensions of multiculturalism. Michael Ignatieff wonders whether our secular emphases need to learn at least some form of respect towards religious thinking. Hari Kunzru prods at the laziness of state versions of multiculturalism and supine, liberal responses to the New Age of Faith. Howard Jacobson and Julian Evans turn us towards history and what it reveals about religion and its fundamental antipathy to the artistic imagination. Two pieces – one by Hanif Kureishi, the other an interview with Adam Phillips – explore what it means from the inside for speech, if it can, to be free.

At the other end, Pervez Hoodbhoy brilliantly articulates the fate of science under Islam, a story which brings to mind certain moments of contention between the Catholic Church and the emergence of modern science. Andrew Berry charts the triumphs and dangers of creationism in the United States and warns of its influence in Britain. Finally, two eminent legal minds: Anthony Lester, QC, navigates the choppy waters of human rights law and its impact on Britain's common law, while giving us some of the history and possible future of what in our multi-ethnic nation is a historic relic, the blasphemy law; Helena Kennedy, QC, brings her passionate clarity and her vibrant independence to bear on civil liberties in our time.

I am deeply grateful, as is PEN, to all the contributors who have produced these riveting essays; they have done so purely because the subject of this book is a crucial one, constitutive of the kind of world we want. They have, I think, provided us with an intellectual armoury which will be useful in coming battles.

My thanks as well to Simon Prosser at Hamish Hamilton and the Penguin Group, who took this book on when it was not much more than an idea and a promise, but one he felt was integral to Penguin's own publishing history. Juliette Mitchell, his associate editor, has been of great help, as has Richenda Todd, and Derek Johns of AP Watt, who is a member of the PEN executive. Alastair Niven, President of English PEN, Susie Nicklin, its Director, and Tanya Andrews, Simon Birt and the English PEN staff also did a great deal for this volume and the campaign. Finally John and Katrina Forrester put up with my endless commentary on free expression, Home Office obtuseness, and religious intolerance. Occasionally, the latter grumbled a 'Mum, no offence, but could you just keep quiet?'

May–July 2005

Coming After Us

Salman Rushdie

I never thought of myself as a writer about religion until a religion came after me. Religion was a part of my subject, of course; for a novelist from the Indian subcontinent, where the supernatural and the mundane coexist in the streets and are considered as being of the same order of reality, how could it not have been? But in my opinion I also had many other, larger, tastier fish to fry. Nevertheless, when the attack came, I had to confront what was confronting me, and to decide what I wanted to stand up for in the face of what so vociferously, repressively, and violently stood against me. At that time it was often difficult to persuade people that the attack on *The Satanic Verses* was part of a broader, global assault on writers, artists, and fundamental freedoms. The aggressors in that matter, by which I mean the novel's opponents, who threatened booksellers and publishers, falsified the contents of the text they disliked, and vilified its author, nevertheless presented themselves as the injured parties, and such was the desire to appease religious sentiment even then that in spite of the murder of a translator in Japan and the shooting of a publisher in Norway there was widespread acceptance of that topsy-turvy view. In spite of all the public calls for violence to be done, not a single person – in Britain or anywhere else – was arrested or charged with any offence. I revisit these bad old days with extreme reluctance, but I do so because now, sixteen years later, religion is coming after us all, and even though most of us probably feel, as I once did, that we have other, more important concerns, we are all going to have to confront the challenge. If we fail, this particular fish may end up frying us.

For those of us who grew up in India in the aftermath of the Partition riots, the shadow of that slaughter has remained as a dreadful warning of what men will do in the name of God. There have been too many recurrences of such violence, in Meerut, in Assam, most recently in Gujarat. Communalist politics have become a powerful force, in the form of the extremist Hindu nationalists of the thuggish Vishwa Hindu Parishad, whose cadres destroyed the Babri Masjid in Ayodhya because of the supposed presence of the birthplace of the god Ram below its foundations, and the Maharashtrian Shiv Sena, whose orange-bandannaed gangs of youths brought terror to the once-tolerant streets of my home town of Bombay; and this new religious fanaticism has regularly targeted the world of the arts and scholarship, destroying paintings by distinguished artists and libraries full of old texts. In the last Indian general election the politics of Hindu radicalism were, for the moment, defeated; but one wonders whether any lessons have been learned.

Nor should Europeans feel too smug. European history, too, is littered with proofs of the dangers of politicized religion: the French Wars of Religion, the bitter Irish troubles, the 'Catholic nationalism' of the fascistic Spanish dictator Franco, and, longer ago, the spectacle of the rival armies in the English Civil War going into battle, both singing the same hymns.

People have always turned to religion for the answers to the two great questions of life: where did we come from? And how shall we live? But on the question of origins, all religions are simply wrong. No, the universe wasn't created in six days by a superforce that rested on the seventh. Nor was it churned into being by a sky-god with a giant churn. And on the social question, the simple truth is that wherever religions, with their narrow moralities, get into society's driving seat, tyranny results. The Inquisition results. Or the Taliban.

And yet religions continue to insist that they provide special access to ethical truths, and consequently deserve special treatment and protection. And they continue to emerge from the world of private life, where they belong, like so many other things that are acceptable when done in private between consenting adults but unacceptable in the town square, and to bid for power. The emergence of radical Islam needs no redescription here; but the resurgence of faith is a larger subject than that.

In today's United States, for example, it's possible for almost anyone – women, gays, African-Americans, Jews – to run for, and be elected to, high office. But a professed atheist wouldn't stand a popcorn's chance in hell. Hence the increasingly sanctimonious quality of so much American political discourse: the President, according to Bob Woodward, sees himself as a 'messenger' doing 'the Lord's will', and 'moral values' has become a code phrase for old-fashioned, anti-gay, anti-abortion bigotry. The defeated Democrats also seem to be scurrying towards this kind of low ground, perhaps despairing of ever winning an election any other way. Perhaps, in time, unlikely as it now seems, they will come to understand that in today's fifty-fifty America they may actually have more to gain by standing up against the Christian Coalition and its fellow travellers and cohorts, and refusing to let the Mel Gibson view of the world shape American social and political policy. But if, as seems far more probable, America continues to allow religious faith to control and dominate public discourse, then the Western alliance will be placed under ever-increasing strain, and those other religionists, the ones against whom we're supposed to be fighting, will have great cause to celebrate.

According to Jacques Delors, ex-president of the European Commission, 'The clash between those who believe and those who don't believe will be a dominant aspect of relations between the US and Europe in the coming years.' In Europe, the bombing of a railway station in Madrid and the murder of the Dutch film-maker Theo van Gogh are being seen as warnings that the secular principles that underlie any humanist democracy need to be defended and reinforced. Even before these atrocities occurred, the French decision to ban religious attire such as Islamic headscarves had the support of the entire political spectrum. Islamist demands for segregated classes and prayer breaks were also rejected. Few Europeans today call themselves religious (just 21%, according to a recent study); most Americans do (59%, according to the Pew Forum). The Enlightenment, in Europe, represented an escape from the power of religion to place limiting points on thought; in America, it represented an escape into the religious freedom of the New World – a move towards faith rather than away from it. Many Europeans now view the American combination of religion and nationalism as frightening.

The exception to European secularism can be found in Britain, or at least in the Government of the devoutly Christian and increasingly authoritarian Tony Blair, which tried to steamroller Parliament into passing a law against 'incitement to religious hatred' before the May 2005 general election, in a cynical vote-getting attempt to placate British Muslim spokesmen, in whose eyes just about any critique of Islam is offensive. Lawyers, journalists and a long list of public figures warned that such a law would dramatically hinder free speech and fail to meet its objective – that religious disturbances would increase rather than diminish. But Mr Blair's Government seems to view the whole subject of civil liberties with disdain – what do freedoms matter, hard-won and long-cherished though they may be, when set against the requirements of a Government facing re-election?

The danger is there for all to see. During the House of Commons debate, a Labour MP, Mr Khalid Mahmood, suggested that the unique awfulness of what I wrote in my novel *The Satanic Verses* would make me liable for prosecution under the new legislation.

Mr Mahmood's remarks were disturbing for three reasons. Firstly, they revealed a startling intolerance to criticism, allied to an ignorance of the nature of literature. Must it really still be explained, sixteen and a half years after the publication of this novel, that the prophet in the book is not called Muhammad, the religion is not called Islam, the city in which the action occurs is not called Mecca, that the whole sequence takes place inside the dreams of a man who is losing his mind, and that this is what we call fiction?

Secondly, he was clearly at odds with his own Government's (highly suspect) position, which is that books, films, jokes, and the like will not be victimized under the new law.

And thirdly, he ridiculously misrepresented my work, saying, 'In the context of Salman Rushdie, the issue was the abusive words that he deliberately used, which were written in phonetic Urdu . . .' I have re-examined the text of the novel and can confirm that in the two supposedly contentious chapters of the novel a single Urdu swear-word, *bhaenchud*, occurs precisely once, and is not aimed at the character of the fictional prophet ('a *bhaenchud* nightmare' is the phrase). Elsewhere in the chapter, however, there occurs the following passage: 'Mother-fucking dreams, cause of all the trouble in the human race, movies too, if I was God I'd cut the imagination right out of people and then maybe poor bastards like me could get a good night's rest.' Which strikes me, give or take a non-Urdu, non-phonetic swear-word, as representing Mr Khalid Mahmood's position pretty well.

As I tried to explain to Fiona Mactaggart when I met her at the Home Office, the lurking intolerance of the likes of Mr Mahmood, combined with their belief that the new legislation will be on the side of the intolerant, is a recipe for future mayhem. I urged her to abandon her efforts to introduce this foolish law, and adopt the eminently sensible Liberal Democrat amendment instead. She did not agree.

The legislation did not pass, because the House of Lords

demonstrated that it still cared about the principles of free expression which the Commons had so signally failed to safeguard; but the Blairites remain intransigent. The Labour Party's election manifesto contains a clumsily worded promise to reintroduce the legislation, and Fiona Mactaggart has threatened to use the Parliament Act to force such legislation through.

Meanwhile, and very revealingly, the Home Secretary Charles Clarke has written a letter to every mosque and religious 'leader' in the country (who actually follows these self-styled 'leaders', one sometimes wonders?) to apologize for the failure of the legislation to pass, and promising, like a good schoolboy standing abashed before his masters, to do better in future. This letter exposes the untruth of Labour's argument that their proposed legislation will protect us all. Were any other religious or community leaders sent the letter? They were not. Were secularists concerned about the hate speech so often heard from the pulpits of British mosques personally reassured? They were not. Would Clarke or Mactaggart send the police into mosques on Fridays to arrest firebrand Islamists under their proposed new law? Don't make me laugh. New Labour is playing with the fire of communal politics, and in consequence we may all be burned.

Religion is everywhere on the march, but that does not mean we should not confront it. Victor Hugo wrote, 'There is in every village a torch: the schoolmaster – and an extinguisher: the parson.' We need more teachers and fewer priests in our lives; because, as James Joyce once said, 'There is no heresy or no philosophy which is so abhorrent to the church as a human being.' But perhaps the great American lawyer Clarence Darrow put the secularist argument best of all. 'I don't believe in God,' he said, 'because I don't believe in Mother Goose.'

A Letter

Gurpreet Kaur Bhatti

As a writer I lead a quiet life, so nothing could have prepared me for the furore and intense media interest of the past few weeks. I am still trying to process everything that's happened – my play, *Behzti*, has been cancelled. I've been physically threatened and verbally abused by people who don't know me. My family has been harassed and I've had to leave my home.

I have chosen not to speak until now, but not because I have been frightened into silence. However, dealing with the practical issues around my own safety and that of those close to me has been my priority.

Firstly, I have been deeply angered by the upset caused to my family and I ask people to see sense and leave them alone.

I am very grateful for the overwhelming support I have received nationally and internationally from the artistic world, from fellow Sikhs and many others. At a time when the power of words is under the closest scrutiny, please know that your words have kept my spirit strong.

My play and the foreword to my play are in the public domain, and I wholeheartedly stand by my work. I was very saddened by the decision to stop the play but accepted that the theatre had no alternative when people's safety could not be assured. Contrary to some reports, nothing in *Behzti* was ever altered as a result of pressure from anyone. As any drama practitioner knows, new writing evolves during rehearsal; any changes made were simply part of the usual creative process between writer, director and actors. Nor, as has been suggested, did I ever veto any attempts to restage *Behzti*. And I will, when the time is right, discuss the play's future with relevant parties.

The closing of the play has triggered a series of timely and valuable discussions. However, there can never be any excuse for the demonization of a religion or its followers. The Sikh heritage is remarkable; I am proud to come from this people and do not fear the disdain of some, because I know my work is rooted in honesty and passion. I hope bridges can be built, but whether this prodigal daughter can ever return home remains to be seen.

Unfortunately the contents of *Behzti* seem to have been taken out of context by many. Surely it is only by reading or seeing the whole thing that anyone can usefully comment on the decisions made and the play's merits or flaws?

I certainly did not write *Behzti* to offend. It is a sincere piece of work in which I wanted to explore how human frailties can lead people into a prison of hypocrisy. In my view, the production was respectful to Sikhism. It is only a shame that others have not had the chance to see it and judge for themselves.

Religion and art have collided for centuries and will carry on doing battle long after my play and I are forgotten. The tension between who I am, a British-born Sikh woman, and what I do, which is write drama, is, I think, at the heart of the matter. These questions of how differences in perspective and belief are negotiated in Britain today will I hope continue to bring about a lively and essential debate.

I believe that it is my right as a human being and my role as a writer to think, create and challenge. Theatre is not necessarily a cosy space, designed to make us feel good about ourselves. It is a place where the most basic human expression – that of the imagination – must be allowed to flourish.

As for the threats and hate mail – these have stirred only tolerance and courage within me. My faith remains strong and I pray that these days pass peacefully, that my life will normalize and that I can get back to working on my other commissions for theatre and television. Finally, I want to pay tribute to the Birmingham Rep, which has supported my work for the past six years and to the show's fantastic cast and crew who showed great fortitude under the most oppressive conditions. You can all rest assured – this warrior will not stop fighting.

Foreword to *Behzti*

Gurpreet Kaur Bhatti

Truth is everything in Sikhism, the truth of action, the truth of an individual, God's truth. The heritage of the Sikh people is one of courage and victory over adversity. Our leaders were brave revolutionaries with the finest minds, warriors who propagated values of egalitarianism and selflessness.

But sometimes I feel imprisoned by the mythology of the Sikh diaspora. We are apparently a living, breathing success story, breeding affluence through hard work and aspiration. There is certainly much to be proud of and our achievements and struggles have been extraordinary. They are a testament to our remarkable community – energetic, focused and able. But where there are winners there must be losers. And loss.

I find myself drawn to that which is beneath the surface of triumph. All that is anonymous and quiet, raging, despairing, human, inhumane, absurd and comical. To this and to those who are not beacons of multiculturalism, who live with fear and without hope and who thrive through their own versions of anti-social behaviour. I believe it is necessary for any community to keep evaluating its progress, to connect with its pain and to its past. And thus to cultivate a sense of humility and empathy; something much needed in our angry, dog-eat-dog times.

Clearly the fallibility of human nature means that the simple Sikh principles of equality, compassion and modesty are sometimes discarded in favour of outward appearance, wealth and the quest for power. I feel that distortion in practice must be confronted and our great ideals must be restored. Moreover, only by challenging fixed ideas of correct and incorrect behaviour can institutionalized hypocrisy be broken down. Often, those who err from the norm are condemned and marginalized, regardless of right or wrong, so that the community will survive. However, such survival is only for the fittest, and the weak are sometimes seen as unfortunates whose kismet is bad. Much store is set by ritual rooted in religion – though people's preoccupation with the external and not the internal often renders these rituals meaningless.

My play reflects these concerns. I believe that drama should be provocative and relevant. I wrote *Behzti* because I passionately oppose injustice and hypocrisy. And because writing drama allows me to create characters, stories, a world in which I, as an artist, can play and entertain and generate debate.

The writers whom I admire are courageous. They present their truths and dare to take risks whilst living with their fears. They tell us life is ferocious and terrifying, that we are imperfect and only when we embrace our imperfections honestly can we have hope.

In order for a story to be truly universal I think it is important to start with what is specific. Though the play is set in a gurdwara, its themes are not confined to Sikhism, and it is my intention that a person of any faith, or indeed of no faith, could relate to its subject matter.

Over the years there have been many robust dramas about world religions. Sikhism is a relatively new entrant to this arena and I am aware of the sensitivity around such discussion.

The human spirit endures through the magic of storytelling. So let me tell you a story.

December 2004

A View from Inside

Madhav Sharma

'NOW SIKH RIOT THEATRE RAISES CURTAIN ON MUSLIM BROTHELS' scream the tabloid headlines reporting protests this Easter about *Bells*, a new play by a woman about the secret world of Britain's Muslim courtesans, at the Birmingham Rep. It brought back distressing memories of my personal experience at that same theatre, when violent demonstrations by Sikhs resulted in the closure last Christmas of another new play (now the winner of an international award), also by a woman. What is going on?

The reassuring plop of a large envelope landing in my hall-way heralded my first acquaintance with *Behzti* (*Dishonour*) by Gurpreet Kaur Bhatti. It reminded me of how I felt when I first saw Munch's painting *The Scream*, and I found myself deeply moved by the overwhelming sense of pain underlying the poetry of unmistakable truth.

And so it was that I agreed to take on the challenge of trying to portray the head of a gurdwara (Sikh temple) renovation committee who abuses the psychological hold he has by raping, within the confines of his office, the devout daughter of his former homosexual lover. He is murdered, and our heroine ultimately finds some salvation thanks to her abiding faith in God and the love of a younger Afro-Caribbean man.

In the first week of rehearsals, we were instructed by our employers to give a reading of the play to members of the Sikh community. The objections to the play, as stated then and since by their so-called representatives, all male, seemed to boil down to:

'It is unacceptable and insulting to all Sikhs to have a black man kissing a Sikh woman.'

'It is unacceptable for a Sikh to be shown as a homosexual.'

'While the play is brilliant artistically, it is unacceptable for it to be set in the environs of a gurdwara.'

My unease grew during the remaining short rehearsal period, not least because of threats of a campaign to stop all public funding to the theatre unless the play was withdrawn or altered.

One afternoon, the theatre arranged for me and some colleagues to be driven to the main Sikh gurdwara in Birmingham. When we arrived, we were informed that we were not welcome there, and that we should leave immediately.

We then drove to another, smaller gurdwara nearby where we received the usual warm welcome that I have otherwise always experienced in places of worship. The Giani, being one who devotes himself to the study of the holy book of Sikhism, talked to me about the fallibility of all human beings, and about the unfortunate hypocrisy of many 'suit wallahs' who abuse their positions of trust and who exist in all religions. He reminded me that the ninth Guru of Sikhism, because he exercised freedom of speech, had been executed by a Muslim emperor. He then, in a touching act that felt like a blessing, tied my turban for me – the same turban that I wore at every performance of the play that was to be allowed to take place.

During the rehearsals we had decided, for artistic reasons, that neither the rape nor the murder would actually be depicted on stage. All references in the play to Sikhism were positive, and none of that faith's fundamental principles or its revered Gurus was being attacked. Also, the devotion of the playwright to God and to her particular religion was plain for all to see. I myself have an irrational belief in God, believing as I do that faith, like happiness, is an ideal not of reason but of the imagination. Therefore, I believed the objections to the play were like the proverbial storm in a teacup. How very wrong I was.

After the dress rehearsal, a chilling, outwardly calm voice speaking in Punjabi could be heard clearly berating the playwright with hurtful abuse and extraordinary threats.

Just before the half-hour call for our first performance to a paying audience, we were informed that before every performance a statement written by lawyers for the Sikhs would be read out and that every member of the audience would also receive, on entrance to the theatre, a document about Sikhism. Further, 'small' groups of Sikhs were to be permitted to protest outside and distribute their own leaflets. Apparently, in return the 'leaders' of the Sikhs would do their best to control the 'hot heads' in their community and to dissuade them from any disruption to the lawful business of the theatre.

After each one of the performances, I spoke to many members of the audience, quite a few of them Sikhs. It was very noticeable that women were the most vocal in support of the play, although one Sikh woman said to me rather wistfully after she had apparently seen the play for the second time: 'Everything in this play rings true but I can't discuss it with my father, my husband or my son, and if I can't discuss it with the people I love and share my life with, what hope is there? Gurpreet Kaur must be a very brave woman, obviously a true Sikh, but she has taken a very big risk.'

I made a particular effort to speak to many of the protestors. Some of the comments made to me included:

'It is a matter of Sikh pride, innit.'

'We won our right to wear turbans instead of helmets because we are special. We can even carry kirpans [daggers], yeah? The police can't touch us, right, because they are too scared of us.'

'The British Empire owes us Sikhs too much to meddle with us. Look what happened to Indira Gandhi when she tried.'

'We will stop this white man's theatre, you wait and see, we are organizing and it will all kick off sooner than you may think.'

The tenth performance of the play was a Saturday matinée, and the police had warned the theatre to expect some trouble that evening. I sat overlooking the all-glass frontage of the build-ing, and observed the Sikh demonstrators arriving and steadily growing in number. Several hundred were now gathered outside, standing behind police barricades.

What started as a carnival-like atmosphere was slowly but surely turning into something quite ugly to behold. Groups of young men were standing around in balaclavas and black gloves. There were some in orange turbans – I have since been told that they believe in a separate nation state for the Sikhs called Khalistan. There were men openly wearing long swords, admit-tedly in their sheaths, contributing to the atmosphere of intimi-dation. There were older men in black or blue turbans rushing around talking into mobile telephones. There were elderly men in white turbans and beards, on both sides of the barricades, some with video cameras, and there was orchestrated, rhythmic chanting. Soon eggs and other objects were being thrown at the theatre building.

Going through the foyer, I saw young men at the front of the mob trying to storm the building, some breaking in and lashing out at the police trying to restrain them. There was a lot of noise including that of shattering glass, and both entrances to the front of the theatre were under siege. In the pandemonium, I tried to help the other theatre staff to shepherd terrified people, many of them children, up the stairs. When I got backstage, I saw and heard more chaos. One female actor was trying to calm another who was hysterical, worried about the unborn child that she was carrying.

After what seemed like an interminably long time, we were told that it was now safe for us to leave the building. Obviously it was impossible to perform that night, members of the public had been evacuated by the police, and I was advised to check into a secure hotel for my own safety that weekend.

Birmingham suddenly no longer felt like a beacon of multi-culturalism, but a place full of separate communities all uncom-prehending and resentful of each other. I thanked some policemen and policewomen for risking injury in our protection and wondered what pressures the lone Sikh policeman, whom I had seen earlier, was under. Later that night, a Sikh woman, introducing herself as a 'Brummie born and bred', apologized to me for the thugs in her community, begged me not to think unkindly of Sikhs in general, and expressed the fear that this was going to make race relations worse in Britain. The drumming and the chanting, now muted, were still going on outside the Symphony Hall.

On the Monday, the Artistic Director told us the leaders of the Sikh community were unable to guarantee that there would be no repetition of what had happened on Saturday night, when eight hundred people – members of the public on their Christmas outing, and staff – in the theatre felt bullied and threatened by the violent acts of some Sikh demonstrators who had also committed criminal trespass and damage. The police were unable to guarantee total security in the circumstances. Therefore the Board had been forced to call off all the remaining scheduled performances of *Behzti*.

The public debate since then seems to have concentrated on the one question of freedom of speech versus religious sensibility. Isn't the limitation on speech designed to lead to violence, affray or public disorder already supposed to be enshrined in British law?

As one Sikh male playwright has suggested, does it not inevitably lead one to wonder what the religious 'leaders' of the Sikhs are trying to hide?

Am I alone in thinking that arts organizations should re-examine their policies of contemporary multiculturalism? Is 'separate development' sometimes a convenient excuse to discriminate against and segregate those from ethnic minority backgrounds in a form of cultural apartheid, while appearing piously liberal at the same time?

Are some liberals trying to have their cake and eat it, by proclaiming that free speech is necessary in principle while arguing that, in practice, one should give up that right because of the need to appease minority religious sensibilities? This has been described with exquisite politeness as tiptoeing around, doing our best not to irritate other people by disagreeing with their opinions. Does freedom of speech not include the right to irritate, annoy, dismay and shock anyone who listens?

Are people unable these days to walk away from a play they dislike, or turn off any offending TV programme, by using their God-given gift of free will, or do we need yet another piece of ill-thought-out pragmatism from the nanny state?

But was the violence actually about perceived religious offence, or was it really about politics and power? Was there a lack of political will, due to 'cultural sensitivity' within Birmingham City Council, to ensure that bullying must not be allowed to succeed over law and order?

If religious leaders can cite the will of God as determining what individuals can or cannot do in a multi-faith society, can they pick those interpretations of His Will they find politically expedient? Cannot such leaders then invoke the most horrendous retribution on those who don't comply, especially women – the parameters of whose lives, morals, even clothing can be set out by religious decree?

Meanwhile, Gurpreet Kaur Bhatti has been forced to live in hiding for a while, on police advice, after threats against her personal security and her very life, and I gather that her nearest and dearest have had to endure intolerable pressures.

Should we now be tolerant of intolerance, or should we be calling for more voices from the rational majority of Sikhs, Muslims, Hindus, Parsees, Christians, Jews, Humanists and others, whatever their race, gender, creed, sexual or political orientation, to speak out in support of what Gurpreet Kaur Bhatti symbolizes? Should we not answer the curtailment by religious bigots of her right to free speech with more speech about our cherished values and the many issues arising from this brave Sikh woman daring to write what is, ironically, a profoundly moral play? Or shall we be stereotypically British about the whole thing, sweep all the facts under the proverbial carpet so as not to inflame a section of a religious minority like the Sikhs, and hope that it will all simply go away?

No Limits: The Business of Theatre[1]

Nicholas Hytner

Gurpreet Bhatti's play *Behzti* had been running for some two and a half weeks before the Birmingham Repertory Theatre was stormed. It should have been a straightforward law and order issue. But the police, though they arrested three people, prosecuted none of the rioters. Nor was the theatre given the guarantee that it was entitled to: namely that audience, workforce and premises would be protected. They had no alternative but to cancel the play. What is particularly depressing is that theatre and play seem to have been the victims of political jostling between a local Labour minority and a Tory–Lib Dem coalition. All of them, since elections were on the horizon, were out to curry favour with ethnic minorities, so none of them stepped forward to condemn lawlessness for what it was. There was a deplorable lack of support for the theatre at Westminster. No one from the Home Office was prepared to defend the playwright, even after she was threatened. No defence was made of *her* right to invent a world and to people that world with invented characters in order to convey a clash of ideas and a clash of generations. That's the business of theatre and it always has been.

There is a difference between the statements: 'This play should not be staged' and 'I do not think people should see this play. It's a terrible play. It's offensive.' I don't have a problem with the latter. I deal all the time with letters telling me that the work we do at the National Theatre is offensive, terrible, a misrepresentation

1 This article is based on an interview with the editor.

of Shakespeare or a misrepresentation of Christianity. I am happy to respond to such complaints.

But I'm perplexed by the inability to distinguish between fiction and documentary. I'm obviously not in a position to know whether the things the play imagines happening in a gurdwara have ever happened or not, and I have no particular opinion on the matter. That's not what's at issue. A play is not a documentary. It's a work of the imagination. It seems to me that there literally should be no limit to what the creative imagination can imagine. And there should be no limit to what the creative artist is allowed to imagine or to publish or perform.

It's clear that what's at play here is a conflict between two great liberal causes. I have been struck by the equivocation of some liberals when confronted with the challenge of free expression in the face of what I guess we can call inter-cultural respect and understanding. They back away from an adherence to the principles of free speech.

Of course, I recognize that an adherence to free speech does not include a commitment to defend incitement to any kind of violence. But I would say that there is a huge difference between inciting harm or hatred of people and hatred of their ideas or beliefs. Very simply: you can threaten the writer with violence and force her into hiding; or you can protest against her play or write a foul review of it. These are two very separate things. The first is an offence. The second isn't. Nor is writing the play. It's dangerous for us as a society to start restricting what the work of the imagination can say, or to condone those who would force an artist into silence.

It's in the very nature of the theatre, it's the business of theatre and always has been, to disturb and provoke. That's the theatre's power. It's startling to be reminded quite so dramatically that it still does have that power. The fundamentalist's insistence that offensive ideas should be suppressed has to be resisted. We need to remember, by the way, that fundamentalism is not confined to those of religious faith. There are *political* fundamentalists and there are *liberal* fundamentalists who are equally intolerant of the publication or even the fictional elaboration of ideas which they find profoundly offensive.

I genuinely believe that the exchange of offensive ideas and the confrontation of offensive ideas is what produces powerful theatre. This is where theatre finds its origins. The analogy may not be altogether precise, but the purpose of Athenian tragedy was indeed to confront on stage that which was *most* terrifying, *most* appalling. And by confronting it, to exorcize or purge our fear of it: that's what catharsis is.

The Greeks, of course, had a great advantage over us: their theology did not insist on a wholly benign deity. So their theology embraced their worst fears – the fear that their lives were governed by entirely capricious and sometimes malignant deities. The last of the great tragedians, Euripides, was consistently and violently cynical, and often sacrilegious. His treatment of the gods is regularly dismissive. He's equally cynical about his political masters, contemptuous in particular about the conduct of the Peloponnesian War. In fact he's utterly disrespectful of the authorities.

From its beginnings Western theatre has been a safe place for argument and for extremes of emotion. Here ideas which were sometimes too dangerous to be uttered *naked* – such as misgivings about the official religion, however profound or contemptuous – were explored through their cloaked fictional embodiments. Renaissance drama seems to me to be inherently provocative, the most eloquent manifestation of the first great flowering of Western humanism. The theatre actively promoted the humanist point of view to a society still gripped by religious absolutism. The theatre was, and is, a secular space demonstrably interested in the fate of man, in *this* life. Shakespeare is always grappling with it, with the relation of human beings to one another. When he confronts the deity, the question he asks is whether there is one; and if there is, then why does he appear to kill us for his sport?

The theatre seems to be the form that the authorities fear above others. There is something potentially dangerous about a large number of people, a communal group, charged by a live performance enacted in the same space. They might be moved by the performance of a story that has the power to go beyond reason, to affect them emotionally, to send them out changed, to release them inspired by the love of an idea subversive of the State, or by the hatred of an idea dear to the State. Or, simply, they may come out of the experience with their priorities reordered in a way that is threatening to the stability of the State.

A fiction acted out live in front of a group has an emotional power, an atavistic power, that the printed word can't match. This has always been threatening to the authorities: state censorship was abolished in Britain only in 1968.

And theatre doesn't happen, isn't dramatic, unless there are characters in conflict with each other. There's always going to be some idea embodied in that fictional conflict that is going to be offensive to someone. If any idea that has the potential to hurt is suppressed, the theatre will die. Drama doesn't happen without ideas being tested, pitted against each other.

My basic proposition is that nobody has the right not to be offended. It is only through the clash of ideas, through intellectual and emotional conflict, that the theatre happens. And in the public arena, intellectual, social and political progress only emerges when offensive ideas are proposed, tested, knocked back and forth, amended and changed in the process.

When I took over the job of Director of the National Theatre, it never occurred to me that almost forty years after the abolition of the Lord Chamberlain's power to censor plays, we'd have to reassert our right to put things on stage that might offend. Must we defend once again from the censor plays like *Lysistrata* by Aristophanes, George Bernard Shaw's *Mrs Warren's Profession* and

Ibsen's *Hedda Gabler*? You don't have to work hard to list the great fictional works that derive their power from seducing you into identifying with terrible positions and terrible acts. Is *Macbeth* offensive? *Richard III*? Of course they are. And that's where their power lies.

We've got ourselves into the position, or at least the Government has got itself into the position, where the demands of faith communities that we should be silenced are treated as negotiable. They're not negotiable. In the plural, secular and democratic state we inhabit – a hard-won liberal and enlightened polity – it's the theatre's duty to explore the edges of public taste, to push and prod at those edges. There is no idea so sacred that it deserves protection from robust artistic attack.

The Enemy Within

Yasmin Alibhai-Brown

'You are the most gifted nuisance I know,' the veteran writer and journalist Edward Pearce told me. It was a compliment I shall treasure. I don't write to whip up needless irritation. Some columnists deliberately generate fury; they are celebs, cocky, playful, rich provocateurs, but insiders all the same. I am not one of them. I loiter and observe from the periphery. Occasionally I am allowed close to power, and then it isn't easy for either side. The rules of engagement, so evident to them, are incomprehensible to me.

I write what I believe as honestly as possible. I change my mind. At times, I have been spectacularly wrong or naïve, and my views are unpredictable except on a few issues where I have remained steadfast – immigration above all.

Loyalty is much in demand in the world today. It is an insistent, tyrannical stipulation, calling on people to give an absolute, unquestioned approval to this group or that. I feel no such unconditional loyalty to *all* members of my family, my 'community', faith, nation, political party, culture or continent. Yet there is a menacing mood growing where one is denounced for so-called transgressions and betrayals. New Labour, multicultchi Tories, the Monarchy, Zionists, Muslim apologists, British nationalists, Black and Asian appeasers, have all described me as the 'enemy within'.

Britain is evolving, constantly shifting. That is what happens to accessible islands. The tides of change keep hitting the shores. This is an inescapable reality. Trading with difference, domination, conquests, the ceaseless wash of migration, mongreliz-ation, cultural pollution and transformations is part of the contested identity of this complicated country.

The mélange inevitably leads to endless conflicts, tribal battles, quarrels over rights and entitlements, and value clashes. National and community narratives cannot agree on versions of the truth, past or present.

Politics and policies need continuous evaluation. White racism is still a blot on our landscape, and since *The Satanic Verses*, white liberals have revealed their deep, sometimes psychotic prejudices against 'the other'. But it would be dishonest to claim things have not substantially improved since the dark days of the sixties and seventies.

Our country is raucous, disorderly but yet rubs along; irrever-ent and reverent, questioning but too easily placated by the powerful.

Ordinary Muslims worldwide are today caught in the middle of two ruthless forces; we are squeezed and crushed in the war between them. The US and its satellites are embarked on international and domestic policies without rules, without a moral compass and the targets are Muslim people and Muslim states, these days frequently described as 'terrorists'. The 9/11 attack has created a madness which will not subside. Muslim states and too many individuals are corrupt and violent, often towards their own. Islamic networks are proliferating and some have an anti-Western and a Stalinist agenda. And every time they blow up places and people, all Muslims stand accused. This collective culpability drives too many young Muslims into the arms of fanatics. They ask – and they have a point – why are suicide bombers worse than sophisticated US, UK and Israeli weapons which pulverize babies and their mothers?

In this landscape threats flow daily for voices like mine.

John's one. He longs to rip my clothes off and do me over:

45

'You Pakis with your shaved-off clits need to be fucked senseless by English patriots and thrown to the sharks, like in those James Bond films.'

There's no stopping Sharon or Michael either, oh no. Since I wrote I was going to boycott Israeli goods I have been branded a Jew-hater. Egocentric Americans continue furiously to demand a blind and unconditional approval of their nation.

I should also mention the 'Odwyers' and Maureen and Milo (who likes to call me a 'trashy girlie') who are hysterically opposed to black immigration and repelled by my uppitiness.

Then there's Shahin, who distributes lofty thoughts around the world from his website.

Moderates like Yasmin Alibhai-Brown are our eternal enemies. Allah hates these people . . . her face is like a dog's backside . . . Wake up Ms Apostate Brown. Allah shows us how to recognize these traitors. Alibhai-Brown has even supported the adulteress in Nigeria when all true Muslims know fornicators must be punished. She supports sodomites, she has Jewish and Christian friends. The only reward for these people will be death, crucifixion. We must undermine and silence these 'Moderate' reformers. Burn them without mercy.

Add to these the Friends of the USA who also want people like me or Robert Fisk or Mark Steel first tortured then dead, the Russians who warned me off after my piece on their treatment of Chechens, the Hindu fundamentalists who want me never to set foot in India and you begin to understand the chaos of the twenty-first century.

To speak at all these days, to attempt to tell any kind of truth, means offending someone. The words which carry no offence of any kind may carry as little meaning.

Do We Need Laws on Hatred?

Monica Ali

We do not have to go very far back to recall the days in which our cities were disfigured by slogans demanding that 'Niggers Go Home' and proclaiming 'White Power'. It is less than forty years since it was perfectly acceptable for public figures as well as political extremists to call for repatriation of non-white immigrants. We know that this kind of physical and verbal vandalism led to the practices of so-called 'Paki-bashing' and 'nigger-hunting' – both of which are well documented by the CRE and its predecessor bodies.

> (Commission for Racial Equality Briefing on Incitement to Religious Hatred Provisions, Serious Organized Crime and Police Bill)

It is clear and it is simple. We need this new law. Attacks on religious groups are on the rise. They – particularly Muslims – are not protected under existing legislation. Sikhs and Jews are. This is mighty unfair. Forty years ago it was not uncommon for people to say 'niggers go home'. Now hardly anyone would. There are many reasons for this but one is certainly that it became unlawful to incite racial hatred. Who would complain about the impact on free speech in this context? Why should they when 'racial' is replaced with 'religious'?

According to a Joint Statement issued by the representatives of a number of faiths including the Board of Deputies of British Jews, the Churches Commission on Inter-Faith Relations, and the Muslim Council of Britain:

. . . the current gap in the law is not only inequitable; it is also dangerous. It leaves the way open for extremists to incite hatred of religious groups . . . setting one group against another in ways which could significantly undermine the good community relations painstakingly developed by ethnic and faith communities in Britain over recent decades. Where this happens it is not just specific communities who are vulnerable – the bonds of our common society are put under strain.

There is something deeply compelling in this. We can legislate for a better, more bonded society. Extremists repent – your days are numbered.

I have to say I am tempted. I am not unmoved by these arguments. Nobody should be persecuted for their faith (or lack of faith). Belonging to any religious group should not turn you into a second-class citizen. Muslims are too often at the bottom of the pile, and they have lobbied hardest for this new provision.

Looking back over the decades at the evolution of laws on hate crimes, equal opportunity and discrimination it seems fitting – a natural next step – to close the 'legal loopholes' where religious affiliation is concerned. Viewed in a certain light this is progress; there is a momentum which has built up that takes on the hues of historical inevitability. (Viewed in another light it's base politics and a desperate attempt at vote-buying, but let's leave that aside for now.)

We can trace our way back to the Public Order Act of 1936 passed in the wake of the British Union of Fascists' east London rallies, and join the dots through to the present Government's first attempt at the incitement to religious hatred provisions in 2002 in the wake of the BNP's offensive campaigning which had led, at least in part, to the disturbances in Bradford and Leeds and elsewhere in the previous year. When we've finished the picture, it is a portrait of Enlightenment.

And so it is. With a pox on its face. Because though I feel passionately that certain groups in our society are disadvantaged and that more should be done to help them, and though I am instinctively drawn to anything that purports to banish harassment and discrimination, this draft law is anything but enlightened.

What's the problem here? I think there are many but I want to set them down into three broad areas. The first concerns the differences between race and religion as far as free speech is concerned. There is certainly a freedom of speech argument to be made that 'incitement to racial hatred' should not be a criminal activity, that if people hate and urge others to hate that is repugnant but a matter for the individual conscience, that the only way to kill an idea is with a better idea, that it is nonsense to criminalize a state of mind. But to attack another person on the grounds of his or her ethnicity, even if 'only' in speech or in writing, is to attack their 'human dignity and common humanity', as Anthony Lester, QC, and Alison Hayes have put it, in their jointly authored article.[1] It is not in the faintest way plausible to vilify a particular race and to claim that no harm is intended towards members, individually or collectively, of that racial group.

Religions, on the other hand, are sets of ideas and beliefs. They should not be privileged over any other set of notions. I am not bound to respect the idea that I may be reincarnated as an insect or a donkey or that Jesus is the son of God or anything else that I regard as mumbo-jumbo. Indeed if there are aspects and practices of a religion which conflict with my own notions and beliefs (of fairness and justice and so on) then the moral onus is on me to speak up against them. If I loathe the fact that Islam has been used to deny the right of women in Saudi Arabia to vote then I ought to say so.

There is an argument, advanced with liberal intentions, that there is not so great a distinction as might be supposed between race and religion because some people are born into tight-knit

1 *Runnymede's Quarterly Bulletin*, No. 340, December 2004.

religious communities. The costs of exit are so high as to be prohibitive. It is undeniably true that the obstacles may be enormous to some individuals. But the inference – that therefore the religions should remain beyond critical analysis, or in the fashionable mode 'respected' – is wholly wrong.

The Government, the CRE and other supporters of the proposals maintain, in any case, there is no threat to freedom of expression here. The prohibition will be on distributing or possessing words or material that might 'stir up hatred of a *group of persons*' defined by reference to their religious beliefs. The *content* of what they believe may be opposed, attacked, ridiculed, with impunity. So, there is a clear separation between the believer and the belief. Hate the sin, love the sinner.

But is this plausible? Is it plausible to members of faith groups?

For many believers, particularly of the Muslim faith, religion has come to be a signifier as strong as, if not stronger than, ethnicity in their personal identities. Many people who would once have identified themselves as British Asian, or Bangladeshi and so on, now refer to themselves primarily as Muslim. In these circumstances, they may and do feel an attack on their religion as an attack on the followers of the religion.

Indeed, they will be encouraged – how could they not be? – by the very existence of a law to view the two as inextricably intertwined. The crucial tenet (and wording) of the Bill is that the believer is *defined* by reference to the religious beliefs they hold. If you criticize a belief which I hold very deeply and I am defined by that belief then how could a criticism of the belief not be a criticism of me?

If the law were to be passed as it is currently worded expectations will be raised and most likely frustrated. This is not a recipe for good community relations. There are certainly instances, on the other hand, where vitriol poured on Islam is a thinly disguised attack on a community. For example, a BNP leaflet distributed in Dewsbury was headlined 'The Truth About

Islam: Intolerance, Slaughter, Looting, Arson, Molestation of Women'. In Dewsbury there is a sizeable Pakistani community, locally referred to as 'the Muslims'. There is an eminently sensible amendment to the Government's proposals, put forward by Lord Lester of Herne Hill, under which this kind of material would be dealt with for what it actually is: a kind of incitement to racial hatred by proxy.[2]

My second area of difficulty concerns the broad sweep, vagueness and, as I see it, general impracticality of the law as it is currently written. The Bill says that an offence will be deemed to have been committed if 'having regard to all the likely circumstances the words, behaviour or material . . . are likely to be heard or seen by any person in whom they are . . . likely to stir up religious hatred'.

Those with a mind to complain are given an extraordinarily wide remit. A seven-year jail term or a fine or both await those who use threatening, abusive or insulting words or behaviour, or display or publish written material which is threatening, abusive or insulting, or publicly perform a play or distribute, show or play a recording or broadcast a programme involving the use of such words or behaviour.

At first glance perhaps this doesn't sound bad. None of us wants threatening behaviour or words to be directed against us. But there already exist a number of offences which incur even higher penalties if they are motivated or aggravated by religious hostility. Section 4A of the Public Order Act 1986 describes an offence of using threatening, abusive or insulting behaviour, or displaying any writing, sign or other representation of the same, with the intention and effect of causing harassment, alarm or distress. The Protection from Harassment Act 1997 also covers the same area and indeed a successful prosecution has already

2 It should be pointed out that it is as 'races' that Jews and Sikhs are afforded 'special' protection.

been brought (and upheld on appeal) against a BNP member, under its terms, for displaying a poster calling for Islam to be kicked out of the UK.

Insult, of course, particularly in religious terms, is always in the eye of the beholder but freedom from harassment is the right of every citizen.

But the new Bill goes much further than this. Offences could be committed not only with *intent* to 'stir up racial hatred' but also when religious hatred 'in all the likely circumstances' is 'likely' to be stirred up.

Good grief! What does this mean? Who is going to decide on which circumstances are relevant and whether or not it is 'likely' that hatred will be 'stirred up'?

Proponents of the Bill, including the CRE, insist that 'serious' comment and analysis, and also satire and so forth, will be exempt. That is not what it says in the Bill. The way, therefore, is clear for mischief.

Going back to my previous example, if I say that I loathe the way that Islam is practised in Saudi Arabia because it denies the democratic rights of women, what are the relevant circumstances of my utterance? Are they that I also believe that Muslims should be free from arbitrary arrest and detention (even if that detention will be inside their own homes), that the underachievement of Muslims within our educational system should be urgently addressed, and that the French were wrong to ban the wearing of the hijab within schools? Or are the relevant or 'likely' circumstances that in Britain today hostility against Muslims is on the increase, that any strongly worded criticism is going to inflame those feelings still further and that someone who already has deep-seated prejudice and hatred towards Muslims is 'likely' to have that existing hatred thus 'stirred up'?

Perhaps that sounds a little far-fetched. But when I add a reminder that Polly Toynbee, a serious commentator and longstanding equal rights campaigner, was recently labelled as

Islamophobe of the Year at an award ceremony run by an Islamic group, it sounds nothing of the sort.

Let's be clear about this. Truth, before this law, would be no defence. Lord Mackay of Clashfern in a recent article in *The Times* cited Tony Blair's speech to his constituency. Blair justified his war on terror after 9/11 by saying that those actions were the work of religious fanatics. He said they were pleased that they had killed 3,000, they would have been more pleased if they had killed 30,000 and they would be still more pleased if they had killed 300,000.

It's hard to think up a situation or statement in which, in all the likely circumstances, hatred is more likely to be stirred up. It's equally hard to think that what he was saying was actually untrue. Lord Mackay, a former Lord Chancellor, is on the record as saying, 'I have looked carefully at the words of the provision and I would find it difficult to mount a defence [of the Prime Minister].'

The wording of the clause is alarmingly vague. When, for instance, does antipathy turn to hatred? What does 'stir up' actually mean? Everything in the provisions can be interpreted in myriad different ways. For Labour MP Khalid Mahmood it was clear that Salman Rushdie could be prosecuted under the new law. Fiona Mactaggart, Home Office Minister, insists that few prosecutions would be brought under its terms. But this is nothing more than assertion and it would be grave folly to rely on the views of a minister to safeguard our fundamental freedoms.

What is certain is that the legislation is being put forward at a time when censorship is on the march. Eleven regional theatres have pulled out of the showing of *Jerry Springer – The Opera* after campaigning by a Christian pressure group. Another play, *Behzti*, was closed after the Birmingham Repertory Theatre was stormed by Sikhs. One of the leaders of the Muslim Council of Britain is on the record as saying, 'Defamation of the character of the

Prophet Muhammad is a direct insult and an abuse of the Muslim community.' In this atmosphere it seems wholly improbable that the invocation of this law would fall only within the very restricted and serious sets of circumstances which the Home Office Minister envisages.

'Hang on,' say the supporters of the Bill, 'people may bring complaints, but if they are not worthy complaints they will be thrown out. Plenty of safeguards apply, including European Human Rights legislation.'

If a complaint is brought, the police have a duty to investigate. If they decide to proceed then it is the Attorney-General who has to make a decision about whether the prosecution should be brought to trial. Here is another 'safeguard'. The Attorney-General, argue the proponents, will act as bulwark and buffer to protect our freedom of speech.

This argument misses the point in two very important ways. The first is that the very bringing of the complaint with the attendant publicity will tend to increase tensions between communities. If the trial goes ahead, irrespective of conviction or acquittal, the likely outcome is a stirring up of antipathy if not outright hatred. It is not hard to imagine that if a few Islamic zealots attempted to get a writer, journalist, playwright or broadcaster prosecuted, the tabloids would have a field day and sizeable swathes of Middle England would be reinforced in their mistaken beliefs about the 'threat' from Islam.

The second is that, given the combination of the current climate of calls for censorship and the bewildering vagueness of the law, the very prospect of a police investigation will have a chilling, not to say freezing, effect on freedom of expression. Gurpreet Kaur Bhatti went into hiding after receiving death threats from individual Sikhs. Who could blame her? In contrast with such a dramatic situation, how much trouble could a mere police investigation be? Surely writers and dramatists and journalists are not such a feeble lot that they would in any way be affected by such a tame prospect, knowing (or hoping) that in the end their words would be justified by reason of serious enquiry or artistic endeavour?

I sincerely wish to say of course not, not a single one. But I must be realistic. Considering myself in such a position, where a complaint has been made against me, when the police open investigations and enter my home and seize files and documents and perhaps my computer, and take a series of statements from witnesses which may or may not be accurate and where there will inevitably be leaks and media coverage, I begin to think I would rather write about gardening or fashion or some other subject in which I have no interest.

Actually, it won't work quite like that. No one wants to feel themselves a coward and no one likes to think they will pipe down or be diverted from a legitimate interest. But for all that, writers, publishers, broadcasters will be deflected, put on guard. The effects of this law will be subtle and all the more invidious for it.

Where you stand on this law depends on a wide range of factors, not least your own personal idea of what a 'good' society looks and feels like. I opened with the CRE's observations about the enormous changes that have happened over the last few decades in terms of what is and isn't acceptable language and behaviour with regard to race. Those changes, I say, have been for the good, and while there are a few (or perhaps not so few) who lament that things have 'gone too far', that 'it's all got too PC', I for one do not sit in a haze of nostalgia saying, 'Do you remember the days when you could start a joke with "A Paki, an Irishman and a Jew . . ."'

What I fear is a future where I sit here thinking, I remember the days when it was still possible for the BBC to screen a show starring a gay Jesus in a nappy, and the debate about all religions was open and vigorous and entirely legitimate.

I have to admit though that my idea of a 'good' society is not the same as every other person's idea of a 'good' society. There are certainly people who would say that it is better not to offend people within the different faith communities in these ways. If everyone exercises 'self-restraint' and 'respects' each other's religions then there is a price to be paid in terms of freedom of expression, but that price is well worth it because the result will be that we all live in peace and harmony.

At the risk of selling out on my principles I say that sounds like a terrific idea. What are high ideals, anyway, when compared to the practical outcome of peace on earth?

But it can never work like that. Not least because it is inherent in every proselytizing religion that unbelievers and followers of other faiths are in for something pretty nasty if they don't change their minds sharpish. To give just one example of what can and does follow, on 14 March, in the House of Lords debate on the Serious Organized Crime and Police Bill, Lord Chan read an excerpt from a letter he had received from a minister of religion at a multicultural church in Rochdale. The church distributes Christian literature to local households, some of which are Muslim. Two policemen, having received a complaint, visited church officials and attempted to tell them that it was a 'serious racial offence' to distribute the literature, one which carried a seven-year jail term.

The passing of this new law as it stands would, surely, tend to encourage this kind of complaint.

So my final area of difficulty is this: leaving aside all thoughts about the damage to freedom of expression, which for the time being we'll pretend we don't care about, just how efficacious would the law be in bringing about harmony?

All the evidence suggests not at all. We can only look to examples abroad to inform ourselves. Supporters point out eagerly that in 1987 Northern Ireland introduced a local law against incitement to religious hatred. It seems strange that they would even bring that up. Hate-speech laws in Canada, Denmark,

France, Germany and the Netherlands have not resulted in a decrease in insults directed towards Jews, Muslims, Turks, African immigrants or other minorities. In fact there has been growth in support for the extreme Right in those countries. On 22 March the *Guardian* newspaper reported that the number of racist, anti-Semitic and xenophobic attacks in France had soared by nearly ninety per cent last year. Jews and Muslims were the main victims of the threat and acts of violence.

In the Australian state of Victoria, where similar legislation exists, the counterproductive effects have been highlighted by the Executive Director of the Australian Muslim Public Affairs Committee, who fears that tables are being turned against Muslims who themselves advocated the law. In a statement called 'Why I've changed my mind on vilification laws', he says, 'This legislation is undermining those religious freedoms it is intended to protect.'

We would be wise to pay a little less attention to the pronouncements of our own Government and a little more attention to the evidence of other countries. And we would be wisest of all to pay heed when it comes to India. They have some experience of religious strife there. The former Attorney-General Soli Sorabjee states that:[3]

. . . experience shows that criminal laws prohibiting hate speech and expression will encourage intolerance, divisiveness and unreasonable interference with freedom of expression. Fundamentalist Christians, religious Muslims and devout Hindus would then seek to invoke the criminal machinery against each other's religion, tenets or practices. That is what is increasingly happening today in India. We need not more repressive laws but more free speech to combat bigotry and to promote tolerance.

3 Quoted in the report of the House of Lords Select Committee on Religious Offences in England and Wales, HL Paper 95–1, 10 April 2003, paragraph 52.

And, after all and on reflection, even if the evidence had pointed the other way I find that I could not sign up. For, as Rahila Gupta of Southall Black Sisters has pointed out, it would not only be the artistic community paying the price. Whose voices will be silenced, she asks? Writers and so on, certainly, 'but also the more vulnerable groups within religious communities, like women, who may find the newly strengthened group rights weaken their own position'. Gurpreet Kaur Bhatti wrote about a rape in a Sikh temple, a gurdwara. Her play deals with sexual abuse within a religious community and this is a real issue. Less highly charged but no less real is the way in which women find they 'cannot leave oppressive homes because of the stranglehold of culture, religion and enforced mediation by religious leaders'.

The price of putting this kind of curb on freedom of expression may seem like loose change to some; to others it is a king's ransom. It must be wholeheartedly opposed.

The Opposition's Case
Speech to the House of Lords

Rowan Atkinson

I am here to plead the case in opposition to a law of Incitement of Religious Hatred on behalf of those who make a living
from creativity: those whose job it is to analyse, criticize, or
satirize – authors, journalists, academics, actors, politicians and
comedians – all of whom, the Government claims, need have
no concerns about the legislation. But as the arguments both
for and against the measure have evolved, I have found these
reassurances to lack conviction.

I question the legislation and the thoughts behind it for the
following reasons.

Firstly, the Government's belief that the measure will promote
racial tolerance. Racial tolerance may sound a pretty inarguable
notion. Unfortunately, what is very arguable is the definition of
the term – the definition of a tolerant society. Is a tolerant society
one in which you tolerate absurdities, iniquities and injustices
simply because they are being perpetrated by or in the name of
a religion, and out of a desire not to rock the boat you pass no
comment or criticism? Or is a tolerant society one where, in the
name of freedom, the tolerance that is promoted is the tolerance
of occasionally hearing things you don't want to hear? Of reading
things you don't want to read? A society in which one is encouraged
to question, to criticize and if necessary to ridicule any ideas and
ideals and then the holders of those ideals have an equal right to
counter-criticize, to counter-argue and to make their case? That is
my idea of a tolerant society – an open and vigorous one, not one
that is closed and stifled in some contrived notion of correctness.

I question also the ease with which the existing race-hatred legislation is going to be extended simply by the scoring out of the words 'racial hatred' and the insertion of 'racial or religious hatred', as if race and religion are very similar notions, when it is clear to most people that race and religion are fundamentally different concepts, requiring completely different treatment under the law. To criticize people for their race is manifestly irrational but to criticize their religion – that is a right. That is a freedom. The freedom to criticize ideas – any ideas, even if they are sincerely held beliefs – is one of the fundamental freedoms of society and a law which attempts to say you can criticize or ridicule ideas as long as they are not religious ideas is a very peculiar law indeed. It promotes the idea that there should be a right not to be offended, when in my view, the right to offend is far more important than any right not to be offended, simply because one represents openness, the other represents oppression.

Thirdly, I question the inarguable nature of the phrase 'religious hatred', afforded by the use of the highly emotive word 'hatred'. We can change the terminology but retain the meaning by using the dictionary definition of the word hatred, which is 'intense dislike'. Incitement of Religious Intense Dislike. Isn't it strange how that small change makes it seem a much less desirable or necessary measure? I then found myself asking a strange question. What is wrong with encouraging intense dislike of a religion? Why shouldn't you do so, if the beliefs of that religion or the activities perpetrated in its name deserve to be intensely disliked? What if the teachings or beliefs of the religion are so outmoded, hypocritical or abusive of human rights that not ex-pressing criticism of them would be perverse? The Government claims that one would be allowed to say what one likes about beliefs because the measure is not intended to defend beliefs but believers. But I don't see how you can distinguish between them. Beliefs are only invested with life and meaning by believers. If you attack beliefs, you are automatically attacking those who believe the beliefs. You wouldn't need to criticize the beliefs if no one believed them.

I also take issue with the consultation process. After the initial failure to get the law passed in 2001, the Government then engaged in a consultation process, involving a House of Lords select committee and I believe another forum in which it was discussed, to arrive at a new version of the measure that was launched last autumn. What I find extraordinary is that the Government is so wedded to the notion that nobody other than the most rabid fascists could possibly fall foul of this legislation, that the consultation process didn't include anyone from the creative community. Many organizations were consulted in the drafting of this legislation: religious organizations, civil liberties groups, law-enforcement people; but not one writer, not one journalist, not one academic, television producer, theatrical producer, no actor, no comedian, basically nobody whose work could be affected.

How weird this denial of those concerns, when the incident that most inspired those who have been seeking the introduction of this legislation was the publication of a book. And the most vociferous religious protests we have seen in Britain in the last few months have been against a play and a televised opera. Again, the Government will say that these creative works are not the intended targets of this legislation but it is only able to say, with irrational optimism in my view, that creative endeavours *would not* be subject to this legislation. Note, however, that it does not say *could not* be subject to it. And the reason they can't give that degree of reassurance is because creative endeavours clearly could. Comedy could. Newspaper articles could. Theatrical plays could. The legislation is very simple, very clear and all-encompassing.

The Government is relying entirely on the wisdom of the Attorney-General to protect people like me. It is this discretionary nature of the legislation which is arguably the most disturbing thing about it. It allows the Government to rubbish the concerns of the creative community without offering any concrete reassurances other than that the Attorney-General will look after you. What kind of reassurance is that? The Attorney-General is not an independent adjudicator. He is an instrument of government: what is politically expedient will be his guide. As the 9/11 attacks in the United States showed, the political agenda in any country can change in a matter of hours. Who's to say what his priorities are going to be in five days' time, or five hours' time, or in five years' time?

The Government's belief that religious hatred legislation will work just like that of racial hatred is optimistic in the extreme: the pressures in relation to religious hatred are going to be on a completely different scale to that for race – the present spread of fundamentalism across a whole range of religions is going to make the issue politically far more highly charged. And even if I had faith that the Attorney-General would bail me out in the end, at what stage in the process will he ride to my rescue? I don't particularly want to discover that my comedy revue has not, after all, fallen foul of the legislation sitting in an interview room in Paddington Green police station. I would like to know that I could not possibly be put in that situation because of my criticism or ridicule of religious ideas and, by implication, those who follow those ideas. And we now know that even the Attorney-General's judgments can be subjected to judicial review. Where would it end?

However, we have to address the issues that have driven the Government to their current position. We have to sympathize and empathize with the most conspicuous promoters of this legislation, British Muslims, and I appreciate that this measure is an attempt to provide comfort and protection to them. Unfortunately, it is a disproportionate response. The Government could easily introduce legislation to address those concerns that have inspired the measure, viz. the expressing of racial hatred against certain minorities disguised as religious criticism, particularly by the British National Party, but they have chosen not to do so. Something far more broad and sinister is proposed. As a result, those caught in this bigger net are reluctantly going to have to fight to defend intellectual curiosity, the right to criticize ideas, whatever form they take, and the right to ridicule the ridiculous, in whatever context it lies. These ramifications are being denied by the Government because it is politically expedient for them to do so but I personally have been reassured by nothing I have seen, heard or read.

I don't doubt the sincerity of those who are seeking this legislation but I do question the Government's enthusiasm for it so close to a general election, an enthusiasm that must be rooted in their belief that this measure could help their cause in some marginal constituencies with large religious populations, many of whom are critical of the Government's prosecution of the war in Iraq. It seems a shame we have to be robbed permanently of one of the pillars of freedom of expression because it's needed temporarily to shore up a political edifice elsewhere.

25 January 2005

From the Debate in the House of Lords

Frances D'Souza

My lords, I, too, want to speak briefly about the amendments set out in Schedule 10. Words are powerful; they cause injury, often as hurtful as physical attack. Equally, they form the best defence against ignorance, bigotry and intolerance. In those countries where hate-speech laws – whether directed at religious or racist hate speech – prevail, the underlying conditions of discrimination and hatred do not seem to have improved.

The noble lord, Lord Lester of Herne Hill, has, with his customary clarity, exposed the confusions in the Bill as it stands, in particular pointing out the anomalies in the current blasphemy laws. I should like to refer briefly to the wider experience of such laws and the real dangers to freedom of expression that they pose.

Schedule 10 rests on at least three assumptions: that offence and even insult are measurable forms of expression; that the suppression of ideas and communication, however outlandish and/or unacceptable to others, will make for greater peace and harmony – in other words, that laws alone will make for a more gentle and humane society – and that broadly defined laws will not adversely affect the expression of difficult and controversial views inherent in democratic society. I believe those assumptions to be wrong. Offence and feelings of insult are subjective states of mind and feeling. What is offensive to me may not be at all offensive to you, so why should I be able to prevent you from seeing or hearing what is not offensive to you?

Of course, there are conditions to that kind of freedom, the most important being that we are able to avoid offence. That introduces the whole question of context. We must be free not to see the play or film, not to buy or read the book or not to turn on or hear the broadcast. If we are unable to avoid seeing, hearing or reading insulting material, as has already been pointed out by several speakers, existing laws on the statute book, such as the Protection from Harassment Act 1997 and the 1986 Act, provide protection.

There is no attempt to define religion precisely but, instead, to regard a group sharing common beliefs to be legitimate targets of insult. There is here the opportunity for mischievous cases to be brought and for some disreputable cult groups to claim the status of religion and for extreme factions to speak in its name. The phrase in the Bill 'material . . . is likely to be heard or seen by any person in whom . . . it is . . . likely to stir up racial or religious hatred' is chilling. For example, who is qualified to define culturally sensitive notions of threat, abuse or insult? When does dislike or antipathy become hatred, and who defines that turning point?

Unwitting denigration of a particular religious belief or practice on, let us say, a public-broadcast system could well fall foul of the law. The lack of clarity will undoubtedly increase self-censorship, which is already practised by journalists and in the arts.

Although the Home Office Minister Fiona Mactaggart considers it unlikely that many prosecutions would occur, that is not good enough. We cannot rely on the view of one minister in a letter to safeguard fundamental freedoms. Broadly defined and restrictive laws, once on the statute book, have a tendency to be used by authority to maintain power, to stifle criticism and to dampen undercurrents of discontent. An exhaustive study, admittedly carried out in the 1990s, demonstrated how hate-speech laws, where enacted, have had a chilling effect on freedom of expression and, even more seriously, have in some cases been a barrier to public debate on how best to resolve tensions within society.

For example, hate-speech laws in Canada, Denmark, France, Germany and the Netherlands are based on the premise that human dignity, quite apart from any question of safeguarding public order, must be protected. It cannot be argued that those laws have resulted in a decrease in insult directed towards Jews, Muslims, Turkish workers, immigrants from the Maghreb and the rest of Africa or other minorities. In fact, there has been a growth in support for extreme Right-wing parties in those countries. In France, it has been suggested that M. Le Pen, who was convicted of hate speech under the 1972 Act, was forced to temper his message. Recruitment to his party increased significantly in subsequent years – some say because he was prevented from preaching his real aims and policies and came across as less extreme than he actually was and is.

Also in Schedule 10 there is an unhelpful blurring of the distinction between advocacy and incitement. The latter is generally taken to imply both the intention and means to commit a criminal act such as race hatred. Advocacy, on the other hand, is a tool for persuading others – even with the use of hostile language – of a cause, religious or ethnic, and as such is a vital aspect of free speech.

A society that has a more civil tone to its discourse is pleasant and welcome, but some of the issues in society are unpleasant and difficult. We cannot afford to ignore those tensions. I shall cite a distinguished Sri Lankan lawyer, whose country has been torn by racist violence for decades, but who still argues: 'Dissent and indeed hate will eventually be expressed; sadly in Sri Lanka we have witnessed far too much evidence that censoring hate from public discourse only banishes it to more deadly fora.'

Liberty is better protected by less legislation. A focus on laws to curtail expression surely distracts attention from the vital need to invest in education and debate to address the root causes of religious discrimination. In my view, the Bill should proceed without the existing Schedule 10 which, if it ever reached the statute book, would constitute a serious hostage to fortune for many years to come.

15 March 2005

Save Our Raphael

Timothy Garton Ash

Like a man trying to stop a leaking wastepipe with a priceless Raphael drawing, the Government is preparing to do great damage in the cause of averting damage. This impending folly is its attempt to introduce a broadly drawn offence of 'incitement to religious hatred'. Everyone who cares about free speech, the oxygen of so many other freedoms, must shout to stay the Government's hand, and prevent it pushing through Parliament this ill-conceived, badly worded, dangerous piece of legislation.

But first of all, let's acknowledge that there is a problem with that leaking wastepipe. Particularly since the 11 September 2001 terrorist attacks, the effluent of human hatred in Western societies, including Britain, has flowed more strongly against people stigmatized as 'Muslims'. This ranges from casual remarks ('it's terrible on the buses these days – all these Muslims trying to get on') to serious agitation by the xenophobic Right. Police and community-relations officers say such sentiments contributed to the riots in Britain's northern towns in 2001.

The law has already been strengthened to address this problem. Mark Norwood, an activist of the British National Party, was tried for displaying in the window of his flat in Gobowen, a small town in Shropshire, a poster proclaiming 'Islam out of Britain' next to a photograph of the World Trade Center in flames. Norwood was convicted under a 2001 amendment to the 1998 Crime and Disorder Act, which extended the offence of causing alarm or distress to include cases that are 'racially *or religiously*

68

aggravated' (my italics). The conviction was recently upheld by the European Court of Human Rights.

However, as Home Office Minister Fiona Mactaggart stressed in a conversation with me, while the law prevents people like Norwood from publicly offending or harassing Muslims, it does not yet stop them from inciting their followers to do so. Indeed, leaders of the BNP have been reported as gloating to their members that they can say things about 'Muslims' which they can't say about 'blacks'. In a curious anachronism, the British legislation on incitement to racial hatred protects Jews and Sikhs, but not Muslims. That inconsistency is a source of understandable grievance to British Muslims.

Unfortunately, the Government's proposed solution to this real problem will only make things worse. Its proposed amendment to the Serious Organized Crime and Police Bill, as drafted before the 5 May 2005 election, specifies a much broader new offence of incitement to religious hatred. This would criminalize a speech, publication or performance which 'is likely to be heard or seen by any person in whom they are . . . likely to stir up racial or religious hatred'. 'Religious hatred' is defined as 'hatred against a group of persons defined by reference to religious belief or lack of religious belief'. That would seem to cover all the bases, especially since 'religious belief' is nowhere otherwise defined.

This loose talk cast as law is dangerous in several ways. While the Government insists that the law is intended only to prevent incitement against persons, not against religions, the line between criticizing believers and criticizing beliefs is quite unclear. Race and religion are quite different in this respect. There is no possible rational objection to blackness. There are many possible rational objections to religion, whether Christianity, Judaism, Hinduism or Islam, and some of the greatest thinkers in modern history have held them.

Moreover, the legislation does not require proof of the intent to 'stir up' religious hatred, merely the effect. But one could credibly argue that the effect (though obviously not the intention) of the publication of Salman Rushdie's *Satanic Verses* was to stir up religious hatred, first among and then against British Muslims. 'Oh no,' cries the Government. '*Of course* this law would never be used against something like *The Satanic Verses*.' But challenged on this point in a House of Commons debate, Mr Khalid Mahmood, a Labour MP from Birmingham, said, 'In the context of Salman Rushdie, the issue was the abusive words that he deliberately used, which were written in phonetic Urdu . . .' Such issues, he suggested, should be tested in the courts.

The effect of this law, if passed, would be to deter writers, actors or film-makers from risking offensive portrayals of Islam and other religions. Indeed, as Kenan Malik has pointed out in an article in *Prospect* magazine, it might even encourage offended groups to mount riotous protests like those that closed down the Sikh play *Bezhti*. For such public disorder would be evidence in court that religious hatred had, in effect, been stirred up. While ministers hasten to assure us that prosecutions under this legislation are likely to be few and far between, a single case could produce a martyr for the far Right. If, however, there are no prosecutions, the Government will have raised expectations among Mr Mahmood's constituents which will then be disappointed.

Why is the Government doing this? A cynical interpretation is that New Labour is trying to woo back Muslim voters alienated by Blair's stance on the Iraq war, the detentions without trial of British Muslims in Belmarsh prison and Guantanamo, and so on. Fiona Mactaggart argued to me, with passion, that it is about the historically vital task of making the Muslim community feel secure, included and at home in Britain. One can see how, for a committed Labour minister, the two things could merge in the mind.

Yet it is unfair to discredit a serious argument by imputing motives for which one has no hard evidence. So let us take the Government's case on its own terms. It's still wrong. In a letter addressed to Salman Rushdie, as the lead voice in a powerful group of objectors put together by English PEN, Ms Mactaggart wrote 'writers and artists, like yourself, are rightly concerned about freedom of expression. The Government's prime concern is the safety and security of communities.' But no! That may be her prime concern, as the minister for 'Race Equality, Community Policy and Civil Renewal', but the task of the Government, as in all liberal democracies, is to strike a balance between two great public goods, freedom and security. Here they are proposing too great a risk to freedom, for too uncertain a gain in security.

The folly of it all is that there's a simple solution to hand. Before the announcement of the last election halted parliamentary proceedings on the proposed law, the Liberal Democratic MP Evan Harris proposed an amendment, originally drafted by the distinguished human rights lawyer Anthony Lester, which would change the law on incitement to racial hatred to include 'reference to a religion or religious belief or to a person's membership or presumed membership of a religious group as a pretext for stirring up racial hatred against a racial group'. *Basta*. Problem addressed.

If New Labour wants to go further, then in its historic third term it can take two larger steps towards building a society that is both free and multicultural. It can abolish the ludicrously outmoded blasphemy law, rather than tantalizing British Muslims with the prospect of extending it (notionally) to protect other faiths beside the Church of England. And it can disestablish the Church of England, thus allowing Prince Charles to be what he has said he wants to be: defender of faith, not The Faith.

Meanwhile, there's this bad law to be stopped. If the Government decides to reintroduce its proposed change, Parliament should throw it out, and pass instead the practical, careful, precise

71

Lester/Harris amendment. That's an appropriate piece of stout paper to stop the leak in the wastepipe. And we'll save our Raphael.

Free Speech Responsibly

Philip Hensher

There is a phrase one keeps hearing these days, and, in an idle moment, I typed an abbreviated, internet version of it into a search engine. I typed 'Free speech responsibly'. What one hears a great deal is the argument that free speech must be exercised responsibly. The search turned up 168,000 separate entries. These are some of them.

There appears to be a fairly common misperception that freedom equals license; that being free to do something means you possess an irrevocable license to do it. What seems to be lacking is an understanding that our 'rights' also confer an irrevocable responsibility to exercise our freedoms intelligently and responsibly.

That is an internet Campaign for Responsible Speech. A body called Zondervan says, 'If you agree that the true right of free speech is accurately carried out when self-restraint is responsibly exercised, please display the Green Ribbon for Responsibility in Free Speech on your website.'

An American journalist and war veteran says that:

My complaint is not with they [sic] who exercise their right to protest, it is with they who criminally abuse the right to protest. Regrettably, this seems to include the bulk of today's anti-war 'activists.' I submit that all of our sacred American rights carry with them the indivisible mandate to exercise them lawfully and responsibly. Neglect that mandate and you risk forfeiture of the right.

73

A book by Debbie Stanley, *The Right to Free Speech*, is summarized thus: 'This book examines just how much free speech people have and how they must use this freedom responsibly.'

Random examples, but repeated, perhaps 168,000 times, with people of intelligence and those without any echoing the message. Important people, too, are parroting this argument. Fiona Mactaggart, the Home Office Minister in charge of a disgraceful measure currently [2005] proceeding through Parliament that will outlaw anti-religious diatribes, has said that 'wordsmiths' must write and speak with 'responsibility'. Free speech must be used responsibly. Everyone must understand that. Who decides if speech is being used responsibly? Why, the authorities. Home Office ministers. The rule of law. The authorities in the United States will decide whether protest is a responsible use of free speech. So will the authorities in Iran, who have their own views on responsibility. The necrocracy of North Korea would find absolutely nothing to quarrel with in the notion that speech must be exercised responsibly. Nor would any Chinese regime of the last fifty years. Responsibility is in the eye of the Government, the Church, the Roi Soleil, the Spanish Inquisition, and, no doubt, Ivan the Terrible.

Free speech, we generally accept, is subject to reasonable restriction. Criminal libel or racist abuse, for instance, are not generally permitted. The case for 'responsible' exercise of free speech, however, is not talking about reasonable restriction; it is different from a parallel exercise which is taking place at the same time, to draw the lines of 'reasonable restriction' more tightly. What talk of 'responsibility' does is to insist on restrictions which are universally appropriate. A statement may be perfectly legal, and yet – from this point of view – deplorable because 'irresponsible'.

It is absolutely clear that, in most of these cases, the case for 'responsible' free speech is not being made to those who use their power or authority to damage the speechless and the powerless. There might be a case for saying that a powerful newspaper, a government minister, ministers of the Church should not use their voices irresponsibly against those who have no power of response. For instance, it might justifiably be said that the British newspaper which published a story, on no evidence at all, that asylum seekers were killing and eating wild swans was abusing its authority.

Similarly, we might deplore, on the grounds of 'responsibility', the lie spread, without any medical evidence, by the Roman Catholic Church in Africa that the use of condoms is useless against the transmission of HIV. Such bodies, perhaps, do have a duty to consider the weight of their voices, and exercise their right of free speech responsibly. But that is not what is meant here. In almost all cases, what is being addressed is the free and reckless criticism of governments, of religions, of authority of all kinds. The argument that individuals have, individually, a duty to exercise free speech 'responsibly' is not, despite claims, a strengthening of the status of free speech. It is an attack on the idea itself.

When I hear well-meaning people putting forward the completely meaningless formulation that true freedom rests in self-restraint, that free speech is only free speech when it is exercised 'responsibly', I wonder what they know about history. Those who created the conditions of free speech in the West: did they act responsibly? John Wilkes, with his 'Essay on Woman' and the forty-fifth number of the *North Briton*: would his contemporaries have thought that he wrote responsibly? The obituaries on the death of King George IV are reckless abuse, with no responsibility at all; and yet they represent an aspect of the age which created the great Reform Bill of 1832.

Did Shelley write responsibly when he described Castlereagh's tears turning to stone and knocking out the brains of children? Of course not. Free speech does not equal licence, as my useful idiot from the internet has it, but, my God, it comprises it. And the publication of errors, even of disgraceful lies, does not, in itself, damage free speech. There is the Nancy Sinatra defence: if 'you keep lyin', when you oughta be truthin' . . . these boots are gonna walk all over you'. Or, with more dignity, Milton says in *Areopagitica*, the publication even of untruths and errors enables the progress of truth by rebuttal; the statement of the truth combats falsehoods in open debate. But let us see, through debate, which of two positions constitutes the truth. It is not always the statement put out by the more powerful body, or the one more dignified in its expression.

The publication of abuse, of satire, of savage criticism, of irrational mockery is an exercise of free speech, and when directed against our rulers, forces them to defend themselves by some method other than suppression. No wonder they prefer us to censor ourselves; no wonder, from China to Peru, they encourage us to talk in a pretend grown-up manner about 'responsibility'.

My freedom of speech is many things, responsible and irresponsible. It is being able to criticize Government policy, or any country, in the newspapers. It is being able to describe my nature, my race, my beliefs, my sexuality, without fear of physical threat. It is the ability to write about anything I choose to write about, frankly, within the limits of reasonable restriction. But it also encompasses frivolous and irresponsible licence: it includes, in a free country, the licence to shout rude things at a visiting dictator riding down the Mall in the Queen's landau; it includes ridicule of religion and politics; it includes satire and mockery, not just reasoned argument. It extends beyond the pained and civil arguments against religion by, say, Professor Richard Dawkins, to a piece of savage anti-clerical lunacy such as *Jerry Springer – The Opera*. In the face of organized Christian protests against *Jerry Springer*, those involved were forced to insist that their intentions were serious and respectful. They shouldn't have had to: they should have felt free to say, 'We just wanted to take the piss, and, frankly, we think the idea of God, Jesus, the Virgin

Mary and the Devil turning up on a TV chat show is fairly hilarious.'

Both are important statements on the same side of the argument: it is invidious for anyone to decide that only one is 'responsible', and therefore permissible. The progress of free speech has been advanced over the centuries, not just by calm, rational argument, but by excess and irresponsibility. Those who, with increasing noise, are insisting that free speech can only be permitted when it is used 'responsibly' are prescribing, across the board, a range of expression and a range of agreed opinions. That is not free speech at all. If we want to hang on to the free speech of individuals, we must personally insist on continuing the noble and long history of irresponsibility.

Art and Anathema

Howard Jacobson

It is in the nature of art to be offensive. Not accidentally, as one of the democratic freedoms an artist may or may not choose to exercise, and as a condition, or not, of society's willingness to suffer the offence, but in essence – as an expression of its inherent disposition. Art is anathema.

I do not say this in the spirit of transgressive flourish. Indeed, I abhor art which self-consciously trumpets its transgressiveness. Art is anathema not because the artist wishes it to be so but because it has no choice. Etymologically, art and anathema are joined at the navel.

Before it came to mean a thing consigned to damnation, and by extension the act of consigning to damnation, anathema signified the very opposite: an object of sufficient value to be given to a god, a votive offering. Its literal meaning is *placed on high, set up or set aside, suspended*. Thus the temple which Christ scorns in Luke 21: 5 is described as 'adorned with goodly stones and gifts' for which the Greek is *anathemata*; the same *anathemata* with which Antiochus, in 2 Mach. 9: 16, promised to readorn the temple he had despoiled. If these *anathemata* are already subject to ambivalence, that is because gifts to gods are not always distinguishable from idols. A confusion which Deut. 7: 25–26, inveighing against graven images, spells out. 'Neither shalt thou bring an abomination [idol] into thine house, lest thou be a cursed thing [anathema] like it: but thou shalt utterly detest it, and thou shalt utterly abhor it; for it is a cursed thing [anathema].' In this expression of loathing for idolatry we hear that most problematic of all the Commandments: 'Thou shalt not make unto thee any graven image, or any likeness of any thing that is in heaven above, or that is in the earth beneath, or that is in the water under the earth' – the great injunction against the making of art itself, lying like a dead weight across the threshold of Judaeo-Christianity.

And so the pattern for creation and reprisal is laid down – for the making of that which is an anathema, will you be anathematized.

Here is not the place to trace the effect of this prohibition on the Jewish people out of whose imagination the prohibition came. But one consequence can be briefly noted: it has not led to their taking art lightly.

That equivocation between the sacred and the profane which is intrinsic to the idea of anathema, is intrinsic to art. In art we honour the work of the creator and at the same time set out to rival him. No matter how plainly we mean to make a likeness only, and by so doing celebrate what God made and considered good, we cannot avoid an act of criticism. What Wordsworth saw, in Shelley's words, he 'new-created'. And new-creation is a species of impiety.

This is why art is always problematic to believers. There are extreme cases where it is easy to understand, however vehemently we reject, the grounds for the believer's offence. Andres Serrano's *Piss Christ*, for example. Or James Kirkup's 'The Love that Dares to Speak its Name', a poem which, in Mrs Whitehouse's vilifying words, 'vilified Our Lord' by portraying him as homosexual. The case against *The Satanic Verses* and more recently Gurpreet Kaur Bhatti's *Behzti* seemed less clear to me, but that might be because I am educated to measure offence in Judaeo-Christian terms. To those who felt aggrieved enough to express their grievance violently, the offence was evidently clear enough. And just as there are works whose freight of offence is plain to see, so are there works whose apparently overt sacredness very nearly makes aestheticians of the faithful: Bach's B Minor Mass; Haydn's *Creation*. But most of the time the act of believing, even when it does not feel itself beleaguered, has no choice but to find art inimical. 'Why write a book?' a Hassidic person once asked me, Jew to Jew. 'We *have* a book.'

To write another is not only to rival God but to question Him whose word is unquestionable. There would be no jokes, Baudelaire speculates in his essay 'The Essence of Laughter', had things gone as they were meant to go in the Garden. Where there is perfection, there is no laughter. We can push the logic of Baudelaire's thinking further. Where there is perfection, there is no art. Had there been no fall of man, had we gone on as God intended us to go, in the perfection of his plan for us – had we too looked and seen that it was good – no art more subtle than a hymn of praise would ever have been made. Thus art is criticism of God.

Milan Kundera, perhaps no less blasphemously to a religious reader, reversed the tables and saw art, or at least the novel, as God laughing at us. 'There is a fine Jewish proverb,' he said in his address in receipt of the Jerusalem Prize in 1985, 'Man thinks, God laughs. Inspired by this adage, I like to think that François Rabelais heard God's laughter one day, and thus was born the idea of the first great European novel. It pleases me to think that the art of the novel came into the world as an echo of God's laughter.'

The reason God laughs at man's thinking, if we go along with Kundera's fancy, is that man thinks and the truth escapes him – for 'the more men think, the more one man's thought diverges from another's.' This is the great lesson the novel learns from the example of God's laughter: that we are not to seek a truth which will unite us all, because no such truth exists, nor would we find it beneficial to us if it did.

It is not only the religious man, quick to defend what is incontestable and inviolable in his faith, who is guilty of aspiring to bring men's divergent thoughts together. Whoever entertains an ideal view of human nature or of human society, whoever dreams of improving us to the point where all disagreement will vanish, is similarly at fault. And similarly at odds with art. The outlawing of what the Nazis called 'degenerate art' was a natural consequence of their ideology. It followed, as surely as night follows day, from their concept of purity. As did the prohibition under Communism of whatever spoke with a discordant voice. Idealism, which must always tend to absolutism, cannot abide the clash of voices which alone makes art. And we are all subscribing to one form of idealism or another when we censure work – and indeed sometimes wish to censor work – for being, let us say, misogynistic, anti-Semitic, homophobic . . .

It is proper to insist that those disapprobations, however forcibly expressed, and proceeding from no matter how deep an outrage, do not constitute art criticism. This is not fastidiousness, or art elitism, talking. The reason that terms such as 'homophobia' and 'misogyny' do not belong to any branch of aesthetic criticism is that they seek to impose judgements upon art which are external to it. If we reject 'un-Christian' as a criticism of a work of art, we must as soon reject 'anti-Semitic' or 'racist'. Art does not exist to confirm anyone's idea of correct attitudes or behaviour. Or to order thinking into line. Art's first responsibility is to speak, and to be always speaking, a different language. The moment art finds itself in harmony with the prevailing pieties, even the prevailing pieties of the artist, it has lost its function and must either find an alternative language or perish. Art at home in society is not art. Art is anathema.

Pursuing his line of thought about the ungodliness of laughter, Baudelaire invokes Satan. That which denies the realm of God, trumpeting in its place the anarchic joy men take in the consciousness of their superiority, must surely be satanic. Though Kundera in his Jerusalem address – no doubt mindful of what was owing to his hosts – gave God the all-confounding laugh, in *The Book of Laughter and Forgetting* it is the Devil whose laughter 'denies all rational meaning to God's world'. Kundera sees the battle for the domination of our souls as a sort of laughing contest between God's angels and the Devil. Too much uncontested meaning (God's work), and man 'collapses under the burden'. But then again, no meaning at all (the Devil's work), and 'life is every bit as impossible'. If art were simply all the Devil's work, this formulation might spell trouble for it. Art as mouthpiece for the Devil leaves it vulnerable to the charge of nihilism, a charge frequently levelled at it, of course, by those whose certainties art outrages. But art does not do the Devil's work for him. In the spirit of its contrary nature, it rubs the Devil up the wrong way as well, contesting meaning, but not replacing it with chaos. Art can no more believe in nothing than it can, in the religionist's or ideologue's sense, believe in anything.

Yet even if it did, even if it could successfully be argued that art is so completely of the Devil's party that it disorders, and leaves disordered, all it touches, we would still have to be on the side of art.

Kundera talks of the 'greater latitude in living' which the Devil's malicious laughter makes available to us. Leaving the Devil out of it, I recognize that 'greater latitude in living' as a beneficence we come by, imaginatively, only in art. Philip Roth, in his satanic novel *Sabbath's Theatre*, circles around and around this latitude, closing in on it with great swelling paeans of indecorousness, subjecting the obscene puppeteer who is his hero to one liberating indignity after another, refusing, even in the face of death, every consolation of quietude and respectability. Sexually experimenting with women a third of his age, young students of his indecent puppetry workshop, Sabbath sees 'a kind of art' in it, giving 'free play to their budding perversity and to the confused exhilaration that comes with flirting with disgrace'.

Sabbath's Theatre is one long flirtation with exhilaration and disgrace, and in that way reads like a meditation (except that that is far too still and decorous a word) on art itself.

The following is for me a raging *locus classicus* of literary criticism, the most eloquent justification for art's outrages I know.

Yes, yes, yes, he felt uncontrollable tenderness for his own shit-filled life. And a laughable hunger for more. More defeat! More disappointment! More loneliness! More arthritis! More missionaries! God willing, more cunt! More disastrous entanglement in everything. For a pure sense of being tumultuously alive, you can't beat the nasty side of existence.

Not all art, of course, subscribes quite so openly to this liberating tumult. I am conscious that I generalize about art not only from a contemporary situation, but as one in whom desire to hear the laughter in art is unusually marked. Many might agree with Roth that if it's exhilaration of that particular sort you want, then nastiness is without doubt the way to get it, while expressing their own preference for another pitch of exhilaration altogether, or even no exhilaration at all. You can have art which answers to the highest of our expectations, they will insist – art that dissolves all agreement in a dramatic clash of voices, art that speaks for no ideology – but which is nonetheless of a politer cast. Jane Austen, for example. So please explain what it means to say of Jane Austen's art that it is anathema.

Well, the truth is that for every genteel reader of Jane Austen's novels there is another who has anathematized them. To D. H. Lawrence, Jane Austen was a narrow-gutted spinster. To Kingsley Amis, she was mean-spirited and at times morally detestable. There are Marxist critics who charge Jane Austen with a complacent view of society, and post-colonialists who consider her silence in the matter of slave labour a fatal flaw, and historians who boggle at her apparent indifference to the Napoleonic Wars. Many a reader of no political persuasion to speak of is made uncomfortable by the callousness with which Jane Austen, in defiance of Christian charity, will pack a character off to misery or oblivion. Such high-handedness, I have to say, is the very measure of her impiety – a God-like dispensation, sardonic in the extreme, of punishment and reward. Jane Austen might not have formulated a credo of the tumultuous answering to Philip Roth's, but she too can generate exhilarating discomfort. I myself relish the shocking cruelty of such scenes as the throwing of Louisa Musgrove from the Cobb at Lyme Regis, and admit to feeling conscious of a greater latitude of living as a consequence. And this, even as I am agreeing with Anne Elliot's suggestion to Captain Benwick that he forswear Romantic poetry in favour of 'such works of our best moralists as are calculated to rouse and fortify the mind'.

Just when you think your every compunction has been satisfied, Jane Austen throws you with the violence of her wit. And just as you begin to enjoy the consolations of transgression, she shocks you with the primness of her morality. Thus, there is something in Jane Austen to offend everybody.

That protestors do not gather to close down bookshops where her novels are on sale proves only that offence-takers are not close readers. Nor is the fact that no such demonstration has taken place so far any guarantee that it won't hereafter. We grow nicer, more sensitive to insult, by the hour. There is no knowing what we will choose to be offended by next.

The very arbitrariness of offence – cruelly felt one day, and not noticed the next – is reason itself to give it no quarter. Before such whimsicality, free speech, which does not blow whatever way the wind does, can hold its head high. Yet the free-speech argument never quite clinches it for me. By insisting on the artist's right to freedom of expression, we concede too much to those offended by it. We make it a sort of civil matter. We meet the discourse of their offendedness half way. It is not, primarily, freedom of expression that we claim for art, it is *otherness* of expression. To argue that art is anathema is not to beg exemption for it. It is rather to express surprise that human beings would wish to know themselves by any other sort of discourse. Art is deliverance, and yet people go on refusing to leave by the doors which art opens. Because the hurt they feel is nothing but an expression of their continuing enslavement, we have no obligation to it whatsoever.

The obligation artists owe their art, however, not to turn it into an instrument of torture, not to be offensive simply for the boorish fun of it, not to make the mistake of supposing that just because art is anathema, anathema will be art – that is a question of aesthetics, and aesthetics are something else again.

Rabelais: The First Offender

Julian Evans

Humanism, the individual's claim to liberty, the primacy of private enterprise and private conscience in a context of shared human rights – the great surge of new ideas that five hundred years ago became the common stock of European values – began with the learning of a new language. To be more specific, the revival of an old language. The acquisition of classical Greek, moribund till the late fifteenth century, was the key to the Renaissance. The Christian Church understood this power of language well enough to interdict it (as it was soon to interdict the Bible in the vernacular). In France, alarmed by the appearance of Erasmus's commentary on St Luke and by the idea of independent scholars who would read the New Testament in Greek and offer their own interpretations, the Faculty of Theology at the Sorbonne forbade the study of Greek across the country. One of those to fall foul of the decree was a young, highly schooled Franciscan from Indre-et-Loire named François Rabelais – Rabelais, whose wit and incendiary satire on the Church would rapidly see him marked down as the first great offender.

Already respected for his studies in Latin, astronomy, philology and law, around 1520 Rabelais, ignoring the decree from Paris, discreetly found himself a Greek teacher. His superiors found out and confiscated his books. It was the future novelist's first confrontation with a Church he honoured but failed, throughout his life, to agree with. What was at stake? By 1528, when Rabelais finally reached Paris, the Church was confronting the Protestant heresy, with which he sympathized; but the roots of his critique lay deeper, in a boyhood drenched in the natural pleasures of the vineyards and orchards of the Vienne, near Chinon. It had bequeathed to him a paradoxical temperament: spiritually drawn to the Church, intellectually drawn to argument, he was a scholar devoted to scholarship and to laughter. In his personality lies all the coincidence of opposites: the highest meets the lowest, scholarship meets drunkenness, the religious impulse meets the sexual and excretory. And his toy, his supreme pleasure, is language. As the novelist Anatole France writes, 'Rabelais plays with words as children do with pebbles; he piles them up into heaps.'

Why does Rabelais remain significant? Why return to him and not to Erasmus, Ulrich von Hutten, or Martin Luther? Because, beginning with the publication of *Pantagruel* in 1532, he not only willingly exposed himself to mortal risks that more recent writers have been forced to take, but won a first victory for the principle that thought and expression may not be limited by Church or State. Let us not slip into hero-worship: Rabelais was hardly a model of a Renaissance man. He is barely concerned with individuals at all, apart from himself, and he is not, except in the broadest sense, a philosopher. Yet his satirical bandwagon, driven at full tilt at the edifice of religious orthodoxy, is powered by curiosity as much as mischief. He wants to discover *for himself* humankind's place in the world, and find out what a portrait of his age resembles. In the four books of *Gargantua and Pantagruel* (he almost certainly didn't compose the fifth) his exploration is as erudite as it is riotous: we are witness to the scholastic education of the time, the controversies of Paris, the idiocies of students and larcenies of lawyers, the arrogance of militarists and the foolishness of theologians. We are invited to share what would now be the author's misogyny, but which yields an image of relations between the sexes that is sufficiently accurate and funny to be appreciated by Marguerite of Navarre. (And if we believe the Rabelais scholar Madeleine Lazard, women in the sixteenth century were as lascivious, if not more so, than men.)

All this we see from the perspective of giants, whose laughter is the indulgent bellow of complicated recognition, of men who have explored the breadth of life's contradictions.

Retribution was swift. In October 1533 the Sorbonne condemned the bestselling *Pantagruel* on the grounds of obscenity. Rabelais found it prudent to leave for several months for Rome, as physician to his protector Jean du Bellay, then Bishop of Paris. Returning at first cautiously to practise medicine in Lyons, he retaliated with *Gargantua*. Laughter became perilous: the book's systematic satire on the priesthood and monasticism so outraged theologians that Rabelais had to go into hiding. Du Bellay, now Cardinal, took him back to Rome, and probably only powerful patronage and well-timed exile saved him from the stake. Accommodation with the King led to his being forced to make his peace with the Sorbonne, though it refused to lift its ban; and when in 1546 Rabelais published the *Third Book* – miscellaneous in its scholarship and generally blandly avoiding clerical subjects – it was also banned. The story of his disfavour went on: his *Fourth Book* was also condemned and its author named as a heretic first-class for his send-up of the papacy. There were rumours that he was in prison; then, a year later, in April 1553 he died in his early sixties in Paris. 'Tirez le rideau, la farce est jouée' were the dying man's last words. ('Bring down the curtain, the comedy's done.')

Today, in the twenty-first century, Rabelais' work remains intestate but essential. All efforts to rival the scale of his comedy or the exuberance of his language, except, just possibly, those of Laurence Sterne or James Joyce, have failed. The essayist and moralist Jean de la Bruyère notes that: 'His book is a riddle which may be considered inexplicable. Where it is bad, it is beyond the worst; it had the charm of the rabble; where it is good it is excellent and exquisite; it may be the daintiest of dishes.' The Catholic Encyclopaedia continues to declare that: 'As a whole it exercises a baneful influence.' To which one might reply, the

Church rightly notes a continuity of influence. This creator of giants still influences us, because his work is ingrained with authenticity. What he gives to his first readers as comic speculations turns out to be absolutely true: the first to give us descriptions of physical functions as integral to human beings, rather than the lower half of a vertical dichotomy, he is also the first to give us satires on self-serving priests as the truth of an abusive Church. Birth, copulation, death, soul, mind, body, aspiration, anxiety, physical pleasure: he gives us all these together, for the first time offering us the whole human.

Rabelais was the author of a moment that will not return (he was also the first to demonstrate what modern novelists like to call the novel's possibilities, that it can and will do anything its author wants). In social terms, he demonstrated that the novel could reach people with truths that could hardly be conveyed any other way. Most fundamentally of all, perhaps, he showed how, in fiction, there is enshrined a principle (and one that was not enshrined politically for another 150 years): the right to speak without fear of reprisal. In Mme Lazard's words, 'Rabelais' work is an act of confidence in the individual. He has contributed to the emergence of a new idea of what humankind is, of "modern man and woman", [liberating] them from the effects of a paralysing determinism, restoring to them all their human force.'

It was not a foregone conclusion that the Renaissance should turn into a flight from the authority of the Church. To Renaissance thinkers, seeing no contradiction between their humanism and their faith, it did not seem that it should. In the Church's eyes, however, the reformers could not be allowed to come within striking distance of its vast political influence. There is of course a parallel here. It is political power not private faith which is the motor of religious conflict and intolerance in Iraq and Northern Ireland, in Afghanistan and the USA, exactly as in sixteenth-century France. There is always potential conflict between religious hierarchies whose strategies are expansionist

but conservative, and individuals whose faith is potentially subversive. (In case it is of interest, I write here as an Orthodox
Christian.) The historian Norman Davies notes that, even five
hundred years later, Catholic theologians are still prone to view
the Renaissance not as 'the Middle Ages plus Man, but the Middle
Ages minus God', and that American Protestants are no less
forgiving: 'The Renaissance is the real cradle of that very un-
Christian concept: the autonomous individual.'

Yet the West's belief in the individual has survived. Not without some bruising along the way: in the 1890s Oscar Wilde in 'The
Soul of Man Under Socialism' hailed the connection between art
and individualism, but the following century's mass movements,
hailed in their own beginnings, were supremely contemptuous.
Like my fellow writers I suspect I seek balance here – the distance
between a cult of the mass and the eighties individual who asserts
that 'there is no such thing as society' is very short – so it seems
to me that we must take care.

We must take care to defend individuals, and to defend the
threads by which we consider ourselves societies. Democracy
may suffice, though not a democracy with a swollen bureaucracy
and a feverish legislative gleam in its eye, or one with contempt or
ignorance for the necessary balance between humanity's private
sphere – personality, sexuality, faith – and its public – welfare,
plurality, tolerance. Freedom of expression that begins in the
private sphere emerges into the public via whatever medium is
chosen, and is balanced by the right to peaceful protest. As
individuals we too must take care of the balance between the
place where we keep to ourselves and the place where we come
together and where our greatest liberties operate. We must take
care that religious groups, for their reasons, do not try to abolish
the public/private distinction to create, like the sixteenth-century
Church, the world in the image of their laws; and we must take
care that governments, for theirs, do not turn the public space
into their private arena where policy and expediency congregate,

rather than principles. We must take care that, having acquired the language to state our priorities, as Renaissance scholars their Greek, no one is ever forbidden to express his or her opinions about the prevailing structures of power.

At this point, surely, we need a few jokes. Find them in the pages of Rabelais, great offender, draughtsman of the Renaissance, who did not laugh at trivia; you will see that this discontinuous, untrustworthy world is marvellous in its comedy. For Rabelais it is the *agelastoi*, the 'grave, gloomy, sullen', those who do not laugh at the world's badness and madness, who are the unhealthy tendency. 'Le rire est le propre de l'homme.' His words still hold true. 'Laughter is humanity's special attribute.' And five hundred years later the *agelastoi* are still with us. They are the fundamentalists, the bombers and beheaders, but they are no less legion in our political, intellectual, and religious circles. We must take care to laugh, and to defend the right to laughter.

God Save Us from Religion!

Moris Farhi

One of the wisest people I have ever met was an old Turkish gypsy, a horse-groom in a circus. One night he and I chanced upon each other, together with our respective friends, at a tavern in a village by the Bosporus. As often happens in Istanbul, we joined our tables and drank through the night in an intense spirit of brotherhood. Inevitably, we argued about religion and politics, burning issues in a Muslim country that, not long ago, had risen from the ashes of the Ottoman Empire, abolished the Caliphate and embraced secularism.

The old gypsy made no distinction between religion and politics. For him, humanity was divided into two groups: those who wanted to dictate to the masses and, therefore, cuddled up to despots, and those who, seeking to tend their orchards freely, bent their necks to no one. And since both politics and religion sought power over the people, they were the same Devil with two different – and interchangeable – faces, a fact amply proven by their lust for blood.

Then, at first light, we staggered down the cobbled streets to the sea to watch the dawn. The old gypsy, barely holding back his tears, pointed at the emerging sun. 'There is God, our Mother, giving birth to a new day!' He knelt down and scooped up some sand. 'Never forget: just this handful of earth contains the blood of thousands. All killed in the name of some Great Father! But how could a male god have created this soil? And which male God?' He sighed and let the sand trickle out of his hands. 'Yet every religion says: Our God! Our King of the Universe! Our

King over all gods! And to prove it, they send us to kill or get killed!' He turned to the rising sun again. 'So when you next pray to God, pray that She saves us from religion!'

Much as I thought that the old gypsy's conviction of a female God was inspired, it was his view of what religion meant that preoccupied me over the years. As with all nebulous concepts, it would be prudent to define it as clearly as possible. The *Oxford English Dictionary* offers two principal definitions.

1. Action or conduct indicating a belief in, reverence for, and desire to please, a divine ruling power; the exercise or practice of rites or observances implying this.
2. Recognition on the part of man of some higher unseen power as having control of his destiny, and as being entitled to obedience, reverence, and worship; the general mental and moral attitude resulting from this belief, with reference to its effect upon the individual or the community; personal or general acceptance of this feeling as a standard of spiritual and practical life.

At first glance these definitions induce a sense of relief; more importantly, a sense of freedom from individual conscience. Beyond this, they suggest that we have the ability to perceive the ubiquity of 'a divine ruling power', and accept that it is a compassionate presence that will look after us as our birthright.

But a deeper reflection soon disturbs that sense of complacence. Some questions, simple yet as old as humankind, gnaw at our minds. Who or what is this deity? And if He is an 'unseen' power, how do we know He exists? (I use the gender 'He' because ever since patriarchal societies hijacked the affairs of mankind God has always been seen as masculine.)

For those who embrace religion, there is a simple answer to these questions – an answer that constitutes a principal precept of that religion and, therefore, must be accepted as an act of faith.

Creation, wherein all the forces of Nature are integrated, the answer states, is the work, therefore, the proof, of this power's existence. And if that were not conclusive enough, it adds, further evidence has been provided by countless prophets who witnessed the divine existence through mysterious manifestations known as revelation. Whether this divinity is conceivable in images of the human male (as in Christianity's Trinity) or inconceivable, albeit still masculine (as in Judaism and Islam), his presence is constantly felt because he is always by our side, judging us, exhorting us to restrain from sinning, but persistently forgiving us.

However, for those who cannot achieve such a leap of faith – of whom I am one – these answers are not good enough. We 'doubters' see the phenomena of Creation as the evolutionary processes of cause and effect, as happenings that have incontestable – and sometimes predictable – scientific explanations. Even more analytically, we look upon revelation as the fiery visions of theopathy wherein the hyperactive imagination of the ascetic fuses with hysteria, emotional turbulence or delusion.

Moreover, for us 'doubters' yet another disturbing question arises. If we cannot accept the existence of a 'divine power' – 'higher and unseen' – why should we believe that this divinity has control of our destiny and is entitled to obedience, reverence and worship?

Well, many of us do not. Though it can be said that for most of us the belief in a divine power is inculcated so very early in our lives as to seem to be innate, we soon realize that the teaching that this divinity controls our destiny and that, therefore, he must be worshipped, has been imposed by the very institutions created around that divinity's persona. Anthropological studies have shown that in many polytheistic societies the relationship between people and their deities has been, in the main, fairly accommodating, sometimes like a practical business arrangement, at other times like an essential element of a person whereby he or she can establish a mystic, respectful, even if somewhat

bewildered, coexistence with the vagaries of the collective unconscious. But the moment this relationship is taken over by an inter-
mediary – a religious institution – the personal rapport between
the individual and his/her inner life becomes undermined.

The institution, claiming to base its authority either on its own
'profound understanding of the deity' or on the putative 'direct'
(and therefore sacrosanct) teachings received by that deity's
luminaries, elevates itself to the status of the deity's representative
on earth. Thenceforth, it is the institution which exacts obedience,
reverence and worship not only to the deity, but also, and particularly, to the institution itself and to its functionaries. Examples
of this obligation can be found in the Pauline doctrines; in the
total obeisance Shiite Islam commands for the clergy it has
designated as Allah's intermediaries; and in the similar self-
abnegation Orthodox Judaism expects from its adherents in the
execution of its laws, many of them archaic.

When institutions and their rulers take upon themselves the
control of humanity's destiny, they soon curtail notions of free
will – or worse, of evolving enlightenment. Not only can progressive developments not be accommodated, they are also
anathematized as heretical. Strategies of obedience, reverence
and worship, if they are to prove effective, must be structured in
such a way as to touch every person within their reach, to
take cognizance of their lives, aspirations and concerns. Such
structures need myriad tentacles; and each tentacle needs not
only to address the spatial and spiritual needs of the people,
but must also be seen to be vested with the authority of its
'higher, unseen' power – a power which can be nothing less than
omniscient and insuperable.

By their very nature, such structures cannot be created by any
one individual. Consequently, they have to be assembled as tenets
of an oligarchic institution. And such an institution endeavours to
establish itself not only as superior to secular and political bodies,
but also, and particularly, to other religious institutions. Even

more alarmingly, it seeks to elevate itself as a body that possesses 'the absolute truth' and, therefore, is untarnishable by revision. To achieve this objective, it is prepared to crush any dissension mercilessly, if need be with punishments which violate its original clement doctrines. An institution, in effect, which, stretching its ostensibly devotional aims to limits that are virtually limitless, seeks to evolve as a sole and inviolable monolith.

That is precisely how every religion has endeavoured to establish itself throughout history: as an omnipotent monolith. Even more irremissibly, as in the case of theocracies, they have sought to rule as the unchallengeable and unaccountable representatives of an indomitable god who is 'seen and is reachable' only by their sacerdotal order. (In our time, Iranian exiles who have fled the ayatollahs' rule have chilling stories about the period when dissenters and intellectuals were being systematically executed. On occasions when a particular intellectual was proven to be innocent of the charges against him, the presiding ayatollahs would often declare that if the accused were indeed innocent he would go straight to paradise and should therefore be grateful to the regime for ending his inconsequential earthly life ahead of its allocated time. History, of course, is full of similar crimes perpetrated by all religions.)

Though it is in the nature of ruthless individuals and institutions to wield power absolutely, this is not always an easy undertaking. Absolute power has always had one redoubtable adversary: humankind's ability to reason. Moreover, humankind is also blessed with an intrinsic essence of 'natural justice'. (Whole tracts can be written about natural justice. Suffice it to say here that the concept is universal, that in all probability we are born with an instinctive, if as yet unformulated, awareness of its truth. This awareness is essential to our development as moral individuals; and provided that indoctrination and fear of freedom have not distorted its core veracity, we carry its sense throughout our lives. (Some may dispute this contention, yet psychological studies of infants have shown that, unless impinged upon by their parents' insecurities, infants will develop this moral sense from within.) Natural justice is, in effect, our awareness of our 'ethical self', the 'self' that struggles against the injustices of limitless power. Indeed, it is the innate basic philosophy which, seeking a temperate way of life, produced the set of rules that became the foundations for morality, and imposed itself as commandments on most religions. In many countries, this sense of justice has led to procedural practice stipulating two primary rules: (*a*) to hear out the accused; (*b*) to be judged by an unbiased body of people.)

Thus, any institution that seeks power must devise strategies to defeat reason and refute this deeply personal sense of natural justice. Moreover, power is a Moloch; it needs constant feeding. And the more it is fed, the more insatiable it becomes. Consequently, the thrust for incontrovertible power, the corruption that invariably ensues, compels that institution to use any means to consolidate its existence. Thus whilst the institution may appear to uphold a benevolent morality – or at least speak in its language – it does so conditionally. And the condition is the imposition of total compliance to the particular religion's dogmas, hierarchies and, above all, to the God-given, therefore, immaculate, revelations it professes to possess.

In pursuit of this objective, it proceeds to promulgate strategies that, more often than not, amend or reinterpret the precepts originally inspired by natural justice. It creates doctrines that become all the more codified, all the more rigid, all the more blinkered, all the more authoritarian. As a last resort, it creates 'irrefutable' dogmas that subvert our sense of the ethical self. And, of course, by so doing, it soon loses its moral base.

One would be inclined to think that these strategies are subtly devious, the sort one would expect after serious deliberation. In fact, more often than not, they are quite simple: just crude doctrinaire 'truths' of 'divine authority' which exploit individuals' insecurities and destabilize their life-long struggle in search of a personal truth. For these strategists know, from schemes established over the centuries, that people's primordial fears over survival, confusions about the meaning of life and uncertainties about the existence of life after death, offer them the perfect vulnerable underbelly.

And thus they manipulate our cravings for the final resolution of these deeply personal conflicts as a vehicle to sustain their rule. Their guiding principles to secure eternal survival for our souls are invariably licences to intensify the codification of life and guarantee continuous and incontestable governance. Hence damnation becomes the weapon which threatens the dissident, with salvation and paradise the respite from the struggle for a personal life. Unquestioning submission is established as the ultimate resolution for the sense of a life that feels personal.

Consequently most religions – certainly the three monotheisms – teach us that our lives are of relative unimportance, that they are simply a test of merit for eternal salvation that will come with the Last Judgement. In effect they instruct us to worship death instead of life. The doctrine of an eternally exultant existence after death to which only the righteous will be entitled has poisoned our earthly life and promoted suffering as a fundamental goal, as the justification for being. Its most extreme policies have even condoned the extermination of so-called pagans and unbelievers so that in death they would attain salvation because their souls would be automatically purified. The Spanish Inquisition and the genocide of Amerindians in South America at the time of the Spanish Conquest are horrendous examples of such principles.

Today, there is a fast-growing faction among the Christian fundamentalists of the USA obsessed with impending salvation. These believers keep an eager eye on what they call 'The Rapture Index'. As reported by Jon Carroll in the *San Francisco Chronicle* of 23 February 2005 and accessible via the internet, this index 'based on 45 prophetic categories, things [sic] like drought, plague, floods, liberalism, beast government and mark of the beast' heralds the return of the Son of God and the advent of the Last of Days – 'The Rapture' – when the Index will exceed 145. At this time – predicted to be quite soon, since in March 2005 the Index stood at 153 and prompted the advice 'fasten your seat belts' (sic) – all true believers, meaning all those worthy of 'The Rapture', will be transported to heaven. They will sit by the right-hand side of God whilst the rest of humanity – Antichrists, every one of them – will be 'left behind', condemned to hell for eternity.

The concept of 'Those Left Behind' is one that all dogmatists have exploited throughout history in many tongues. It is a concept which leaves no room for mercy. It affirms endless bliss for the believer and eternal damnation for the rest.

Like all institutions, religions are in competition with each other. Their survival depends on the number – and power – of believers who embrace their doctrines. The larger their flock, the more assured they can be of maintaining authority by defeating the not inconsiderable challenge of rational thought. Consequently, proselytizing is one of their principal objectives. To this effect, they have developed yet another potent principle: exclusivity. Thus those who join them are 'guaranteed to be saved', those who do not join them will be 'left behind' and damned. The exception to seeking converts actively is Judaism; the adherents to that religion are 'saved' by the notion that they are the 'Chosen People'. Even if some of us would question what this 'favour' sanctions and what it has secured for the Jews, the belief is equally elitist. And since elitism is exclusivity by another name, Judaism offers a similar syndrome.

Exclusivity has two salient weapons: contempt and hatred.

As proof that their religion has been handed down to them by a supreme divinity – and by so doing refuting the humanist argument that all religions have evolved from our primal fears – religious institutions besmirch each other's dogmas as fantasy, delusion and falsehood. They strive to establish themselves as the purveyors of 'the true religion', the possessors of 'the ultimate truth', the visionaries who have recognized 'the real God' and have come to know Him as the legitimate 'King of the Universe'. Such contempt, pronounced as conclusive, holds great sway. It rids individuals of uncertainty and assuages their existential fears; it destabilizes reason even as reason struggles to discern a sense of personal truthfulness.

Should contempt fail, there is an even more toxic weapon: persistent hatred – hatred that is directed at other religions, nations, races, factions, identities; even hatred for the sexually different; hatred that transgresses one of the most important commandments in the Scriptures: 'love the stranger in thy midst' (strikingly, a commandment that failed to be listed among the ten that Moses brought down from Mount Sinai). This hatred is rooted in the most paranoid portions of our sacred texts – and not least in the minds of their exegetes. This hatred dehumanizes brothers and neighbours and creates the non-persons, the 'others', making them the culprit for all our grievances, past and present.

Permit me to refer to a talk I gave some years back in relation to the fatwa issued against Salman Rushdie by one of those 'good men of God', Ayatollah Khomeini. In it I referred to an unpublished article by the psychoanalyst Christopher Hering entitled 'The Problem of the Alien'.[1] This paper – analysing the science-fiction film *Alien* and its sequels – discoursed on a condition which Hering defined as 'emotional fascism'. Proposing that if a force can be mythified as life-threatening or, worse, as an arch-enemy that threatens all humanity, he postulated that psychotic fiction can masquerade as objective truth. Thereafter, he maintained, the most destructive impulses – impulses we would abhor at any other time – would be tolerated, even nurtured as a means of salvation. By the same token, all feelings of compassion, concern, doubt, proscription would be discarded.

1 Personal communication.

Thereafter the idea of annihilation would receive the sanction to develop into a justifiable objective, indeed, into a moral imperative.

Psychotic fiction as objective truth is precisely what religious institutions – and by their example, unscrupulous politicians – have often utilized. They have created a continuous narrative wherein other peoples and races are depicted as empty of soul, with no capacity for thought and with only one vision: the compulsion to destroy 'our values and way of life'. These people, therefore, they argue, must be subjugated – even exterminated – so that not only the followers of the particular religion, but also the very soul of humanity itself may be saved.

Undoubtedly my blanket condemnation of religious institutions will provoke strong protests. Many reading this thesis will argue that there have been numerous movements in every religion that have not only endeavoured to generate reforms, but also sought coexistence with other faiths. (For example: Pope John XXIII's convocation of the Second Vatican Council; the present-day US-Jewish organization Tikkun – meaning 'to heal' – which preaches, under Rabbi Lerner, a Universal Spirituality. And, of course, the Sufi teachings for total union with Allah that have defied Islamic fundamentalism for centuries.) Just as importantly, every religion has produced countless remarkable men and women who have toiled unselfishly – sometimes at the cost of their lives – to better the human condition.

I do not dispute these facts. There have indeed been people of religion who have put humanistic values above blind acceptance of dogma. But these people's eventual fates strengthen my argument, because, tragically, sooner or later, these good people and their reformist movements become marginalized by the conservative core of their establishment's oligarchic rulers. This core comprises individuals who, to use the old adage of the Soviet Politburo, have 'substantial tails' – subordinates in important or influential positions who either through ideological conviction or for personal gain have vowed allegiance to their patron. Though these 'tails' are neither homogeneous, nor, having their own internecine conflicts, stable, they nevertheless, in the main, subjugate their ambitions to preserve the status quo in order to ensure their own survival. Indeed, such is the power entrenched in these oligarchic structures that dissidents and innovators are either eventually compromised or find themselves forced to operate as singular voices with virtually no support. (Pope John XXIII's reforms have drained away like flash floods in a desert through the conservatism of his successors, including Pope John Paul II. No matter how valiant Tikkun's efforts are, its campaigns stand solitarily outside mainstream theologies. And fundamentalist Islam brutally persecutes the Sufi teachings of peaceful spirituality.)

Moreover, as entrants to religious institutions attempt movement and change with more radical aspirations, they are almost always neutralized by what the political philosopher Robert Michels long ago termed 'the iron law of oligarchy',[2] the state of mind whereby an organization becomes controlled by a small group who use it to further their own interests rather than the interests of the organization's members. Thus reformists, drawn at first into the institution's hierarchy as necessary innovators, are gradually rendered ineffective in the institution's bureaucratic quagmires. By the time they realize that their vitality has been utilized to strengthen the oligarchy's power and exclusivity, they have either lost their original élan or their credibility; thereafter, they either disappear quietly into oblivion or become what was once detestable to them, conformist strands of the establishment.

As for the heroes of religions – the martyrs and saints elevated to reverence – they are perhaps the most exploited by religious institutions. Much as they are depicted as paragons of righteous-

2 See various entries on the internet on 'the iron law of oligarchy'.

ness, they are used as armies utilize soldiers – expendable as long as their sacrifices keep their institutions in power. Moreover, the adulation bestowed on them has one principal objective: to endow the institution with fresh blood; to provide, by the example of their heroic sacrifices, the inspiration for martyrs that will be needed in the future. (Examples abound: the slain lay priests of the Liberation Theology Movement in Latin America, calumnied by their own churches during their lifetime, are now seen as Christ-like; the suicide bombers of Islam and Israel's ultra-Orthodox settlers in the West Bank are glorified as august defenders of their respective splintered faiths.)

Yet, the question remains: if we turn our backs on religion, where else would we find the anchor so needed by the human spirit?

Well, it is, of course, imperative that we have secular states that will kowtow to no religion. I say this knowing only too well that even secular states are prey to 'the iron law of oligarchy'. But at least secular states provide the individual with the freedom to reclaim his or her relationship with God as a deeply personal communion that has evolved from the ethical self.

If I may, I will go beyond that imperative and offer a wistful thought.

I am an ardent believer in the sexuality that binds together body and spirit. And as my last statement of this thesis, I must highlight the profound antagonism towards sexual desire, and most particularly towards women, promoted by almost every religion.

Women are the other 'other' of religions. They are excluded by the three monotheisms from virtually all human affairs. Among some factions they are considered unclean and untouchable, save for purposes of procreation – their only 'use' – undeserving of a place in the human family. The exceptions, exemplified by Lady Macbeth's desperation, are the 'unsexed' women who have become like men – such as the mythic Amazons who cut off their breasts in order to wield bow and arrow. This is, of course, the ultimate exclusivity for patriarchal society's vision of unalterable dominant norms.

Hence, my wistful prayer.

It is time, as my old gypsy friend in Istanbul declared, to feel God as a feminine force in us all. It is time to free ourselves from the poisoned teachings of patriarchal religions. It is time to seek a society where both the feminine and the masculine are represented as co-creators. It is time to worship life instead of death and go searching, as Fernando Pessoa writes in *The Book of Disquietude*, 'beyond God to surprise the Master's secret and the profound Good'. That 'secret and profound Good' can only be our femininity, chained and incarcerated.

Against 'Identity'

Philip Pullman

Is the proposed 'religious hatred' bill a bad idea? Of course it is. Of course it should be opposed. That's my instinctive reaction. But in trying to think about why I react like that, I've found myself wondering more and more about the question of 'identity', because that seems to be at the heart of the problem. Is our 'identity' a function of what we do, or what we are, or both?

It seems to me that:

1. What we are is not in our control, but what we do is.

2. On the other hand, and simultaneously, what we do depends on what we are (on what we have to do it with), and what we are can be modified by what we do.

3. What we do is morally significant. What we are is not.

4. With respect to the past: it's important to some of us to know that our ancestors came from this or that part of the world, to know a little of the history of our family, to feel a connection with a landscape, or a language, or a climate, or an artistic form of expression, or a religion that our ancestors knew as theirs.

5. With respect to the present: it's important for each of us to feel that we belong somewhere or with some group that is like ourselves in some way. We need to be free to live in a place and among people where we feel at home, and not in exile, or under threat.

6. Praise or blame, virtue or guilt, apply to our actions, not to our ancestry or to our membership of this group or that.

7. Belief or faith is partly the result of temperament. I may be temperamentally inclined to scepticism, you to belief in supernatural forces. As far as the temperamental component of our beliefs is concerned, I am not to be praised or blamed for my scepticism, nor you for your faith.

8. It's when we act on a belief that praise or blame comes in. That is where the temperamental component of religion ends and the moral component begins.

Britain is still officially a Christian country. The Christian Church, or to be more accurate the Anglican part of it, is closely involved in the great rituals of public life, such as coronations and state funerals; prayers are said before parliamentary sessions; bishops of the Church of England sit by right in the House of Lords; there is a blasphemy law that protects the Christian religion; the heir to the throne is not allowed to marry a Catholic.

For a long time now, the kind of religion the Church of England (or of Scotland, or in Wales, or of Ireland) embodies has been a mild, tolerant, broad-minded sort. There have been zealots, but they have tended to leave and form their own sects, not to occupy the parish pulpits or episcopal thrones. The tendency of the established religion has been liberal, worldly, inclusive. But this involved a certain amount of not-speaking-about-things. For example, there have always been clergy who had homosexual feelings, but while these remained unspoken about ('don't ask, don't tell') it never became an issue of public discussion, denunciation, exposure, justification, confession, condemnation, punishment, and so on.

That particular matter has become painfully inflamed in recent years, and now looks as if it might split the Anglican communion in two. The zealous faction has been feeling its power, and is beginning to exercise it, and it's partly over this 'identity' business: the stress on being, rather than on doing. Canon Jeffrey John was recently prevented from becoming Bishop of Reading because although he lived a celibate life it was what he was that mattered, not what he did. If you 'are' homosexual, then even if you live an entirely celibate life, you will still be tainted and abominable and unfit to belong to the clergy. In the concise and unambiguous words of a poster brandished by an American preacher in a recent photograph, 'God hates fags.'

In some ways this attitude is a development of the Reformation emphasis on justification by faith. It didn't matter what good works you did: it was only when you made the commitment of faith that you were able to receive the divine grace of forgiveness and healing that made you righteous, and then you were utterly changed. Hence the modern American phenomenon of being born again: to be born again is not just to change your behaviour. It's to have a new 'identity', to leave the old sinful one behind, to be someone different.

But the emphasis on the inwardness of 'identity' has deep roots. The *conversos* or Spanish Jews who had been forcibly converted to Christianity during the fifteenth century and afterwards 'remained a perennial object of worry, to be scrutinized for doubtful loyalty in any time of heightened tension . . . [The Inquisition] reinforced an existing tendency in Spanish society to regard heresy and deviation as hereditary: so it became increasingly necessary for loyal Spanish Catholics to prove their *limpieza de sangre* (purity of blood), free of all *mudéjar* or Jewish taint.' (Diarmaid McCulloch, *Reformation*, 2003.)

That attitude took a new and 'scientific' turn in the late nineteenth century, based on a notion of 'race' that was modern and exciting. According to this, Shylock's descendants could eat pork and go to Mass as much as they liked, but they would still be Jews, because Jewishness was a matter of genetics and not of behaviour. What you were was more important than what you did. And out of this terrible nonsense came Hitler and the Final Solution.

The issue of paedophilia is another example. The wickedness the public are invited to hate, by the tabloid press that feeds off their hatred, consists of 'being' something: of being a paedophile. That's the way they put it; that's what led to the ludicrously horrific occasion when a hysterical mob attacked a . . . paediatrician.

At its extreme, this attitude can lead to a sort of cognitive dissonance, when people claim an inner 'identity' that has nothing to do with their actions: 'Yes, I murdered my wife and children, but I'm a good person.' The lawyer of a Texas boy scout leader recently found guilty on a child pornography charge was quoted in the *New York Times* as saying, 'I've got to tell you, this is a good man.'

So 'being', in the eyes of many people, apparently has its own moral quality, which may be good or bad, but which is resistant to any form of change except the miraculous (being born again). 'Being' trumps 'doing'.

It's hard to convey the sheer bafflement and distaste I feel for this attitude towards 'identity'. I feel with some passion that what we truly are is private, and almost infinitely complex, and ambiguous, and both external and internal, and double- or triple- or multiply-natured, and largely mysterious even to ourselves; and furthermore that what we are is only part of us, because identity, unlike 'identity', must include what we do. And I think that to find oneself and every aspect of this complexity reduced in the public mind to one property that apparently subsumes all the rest ('gay', 'black', 'Muslim', whatever) is to be the victim of a piece of extraordinary intellectual vulgarity. Literally vulgar: from *vulgus*. It's crowd-thought.

Of course, someone might choose to wear a single kind of 'identity' as a badge – perhaps a badge of difference, perhaps one of solidarity. If you're being discriminated against for one of the multifarious aspects of your complex entirety, then it makes every kind of sense to join with others in the same position, and deliberately and publicly adopt that 'identity' ('gay', 'black', 'Muslim', whatever). But 'identity'-claims are not free of consequences. They narrow as well as strengthen.

For myself, I like it best when I have no such simple and public 'identity'. I don't know what I 'am', and I don't especially want to. But I know full well that I am free to feel anonymous and invisible, which I like feeling, even if deludedly, only because I am white and male and reasonably affluent. I look like the people who have the power; I don't stand out in a crowd; I have never been stopped by the police. Other people have less of that sort of freedom than I do.

Now: what does it mean to say 'I am a Muslim'? Is it the same sort of thing as saying 'I am a Jew' or 'I am a Sikh'? Not quite, because being a Jew or a Sikh is a matter of race as well as of belief, according to the law as it stands.

Is it the same sort of thing as saying 'I am a Catholic'? It might be more like that, because saying you are Muslim or Catholic says nothing about your ethnic origin. But it isn't quite like that, because you can choose to leave the Catholic Church without facing a penalty on earth, though you might go to hell when you die. If you choose to stop being a Muslim, you are an apostate and, depending on where you live, liable to severe punishment, which might include the death penalty. So being a Muslim is partly a matter of choice and partly one of coercion. If you are born into a Muslim family and brought up in that faith, you will not be able to leave it as easily as a child born into a Catholic family can leave the Church.

However, the latter child is likely to retain Catholic habits of thought long after they cease to believe in God, especially if the Jesuits had charge of their first seven years.

So it's all very complicated.

Then there's another kind of complication. Apparently more and more British people of Asian descent are choosing nowadays to identify themselves by their faith rather than by their ethnic or geographical origin. I can see why they do – (5), above. But is saying 'I am a Muslim' or 'I am a Hindu' the same sort of thing as saying 'I am British'? Is it the same sort of thing as saying 'I am Asian' or 'I am black'? Is it saying 'This is what I do', or 'This is what I am'?

Because one of the consequences of this is that if someone's primary 'identity', according to their own definition, consists of what their religion is, then Fiona Mactaggart's claim about the religious hatred bill doesn't hold up. She has said that the proposed law won't prevent the criticism of religion, because it's merely designed to stop us inciting others to hate particular people.

But to criticize the religion of someone who makes that religion the primary marker of their identity will be, specifically, to criticize them. It will be criticizing what they are, not what they do. And if it comes to the courts, will the law be capable of distinguishing between a rational analysis of theology and an incitement to brutal violence? Home Office Minister Hazel Blears doesn't think it will: she has said that she can't predict how the courts will act. Better safe than sorry, is the implication.

The inevitable consequence for literature – as many others have pointed out – will be that publishing decisions will increasingly be made not by editors, as they used to be; nor by accountants, as they now are; but by lawyers. And my learned friends will be throwing the pall of their caution over the theatre as well, to the impoverishment of all of us.

I'd better say why I would like to be free to criticize religion, and think about its effects on society, without fear of prosecution. Religion is something that human beings do. Like art, it's a phenomenon that has characterized every society we know about. Thanks partly to the Enlightenment, it's been possible in the past couple of hundred years or so to consider religions dispassionately, to look at their historical development, to examine their social effects, to appreciate the art they inspire, to question the philosophical implications of their claims to truth, and so on.

It's easier for someone who is not a zealous believer to do this. Those who are passionate adherents of their faith, who are willing to kill and die for it, are less likely to take a wide and considered view of the subject. And the fact that religion makes people willing to do these extreme things is one of the reasons we need to examine it. Something in the nature of religious conviction gives believers the chance to experience sharp and intoxicating tastes; those inclined to it can become addicted to the gamy tang of the absolute, the pungency of righteousness, the furtive sexiness of intolerance. Religion grants us these malign sensations more strongly and more deeply than any other human phenomenon.

And it's religion that allows otherwise intelligent people to discard the fundamental methods of science and to teach 'creationism' to schoolchildren. It's in the name of religious law that vile and grotesque punishments (mutilations and stonings) are carried out in parts of Africa and the Middle East today, as they were in Europe (torture, burning at the stake) only a few hundred years ago. And in the USA especially, it's religion that's called in to justify the rapacity of the giant corporations that despoil the environment, by saying that there is no shortage of resources in God's earth, and in any case it doesn't matter if the earth is ravaged beyond repair, because all the good people are going to be whisked up to heaven in the Rapture. That sort of religion is aesthetically nauseating, intellectually toxic, and ethically squalid, and I can think of few activities more valuable than saying so loudly and clearly.

Fiona Mactaggart claims that nothing in the Bill would prevent us from doing that. I think she's wrong, because the tide of religion is coming in again. This Government, led by a weak man who is attracted to power, has sensed a gathering strength in the religious lobby, and is anxious to appease it. The way they use the word 'faith' is interesting, and typical of this mood: it used to be a noun. Now it's an adjective ('faith schools', 'faith communities') and it carries the implication 'good, admirable, worthy of approval'. Everything in the temper of the times suggests that religion is getting stronger and more influential, and that those who are most zealous about it will want more and more privileges, and that this Government will give in to them.

Well, I think we should resist this tendency stoutly. I think that to make things fair and level we should begin by abolishing the special protection the blasphemy law now gives to the Church of England – and I don't mean extending it to other religions: I mean abolishing it altogether. We might usefully continue with disestablishment, even if this deprives our future King Charles of the title 'Defender of the Faith'; but since he's said that in any case he would rather be known as 'Defender of faith', he would be free to call himself that, though he'd have to do it as a private individual rather than as Head of State. We might go on to consider the place of religion in the House of Lords. I'm not against giving some sort of representation to special interest groups, but if the Christians are going to be there, so should the Jews and Sikhs and Hindus and Muslims and Buddhists and Zoroastrians and pagans and humanists. And as for education, there should be no more 'faith' schools; and we should certainly not allow rich individuals with a religious agenda to buy their way into the school curriculum by means of setting up a so-called 'academy' and diverting public money to the service of their private beliefs.

But I think there must be something genuine behind this idea of identity, even if 'identity' is a coarse and inaccurate parody encumbered with half-examined baggage, and with misunder-standing, resentment, and hostility trailing behind it.

True identity is surely a matter both of what we are and of what we do. It must include everything we inherit from our remotest ancestors in the way of our physical body and our animal instincts: the ones we know about and the ones that operate too deeply for us to be conscious of. It must include our physical appearance, the colour of our skin, the shape of our eyes, and so on. It must include everything we know about the history of our family and our nation, though I don't see how it can include the things of this sort that we're not aware of. It must include the language we speak and our consciousness of belonging to a group that speaks the same language, and the same variety of that language, and if we can use more than one variety (standard English as well as a regional dialect) then it must include that fact as well. It must include our own edu-cational history, and our place in the economic life of the com-munity around us; it must take account of the amount of choice we have in the matter of spending money. Can we afford a bowl of rice? Can we afford a new car? They are matters of identity. Unless we use cash, we can't buy anything without proving who we are. Our tastes in food, and entertainment, and fashion are matters of identity too; so are our talents and our interests and our opinions on politics.

Furthermore, to some extent we can shape our identity by the way we behave. Trustworthiness, kindness, industriousness, and the like are acquired characteristics: we can make ourselves trustworthy, kindly, and hard-working by being so. It takes time and effort, of course, not a miracle. But identity is what we do as well as what we are.

And identity, as opposed to 'identity', will of course include religion. But a religious identity will be a matter of almost infinite subtlety – a matter of different degrees of belief in different aspects of a creed; or believing something passionately when young, but less urgently when old – or the opposite; or assenting to the moral teaching while withholding full credence in the supernatural – or cleaving to both; or responding with delight and warmth to the aesthetic elements of religious ritual while being ignorant of the theological, or being indifferent to the aesthetic and fiercely doctrinaire about the theological – or neither; or finding more comfort in the memory of childhood worship than in the prospect of a life after death, or vice versa; or being more conscious of the threat of hell than of the promise of heaven, or being more concerned with doing good on earth than either; and so on, in a dynamic complexity of influence and inclination, of knowledge and emotion that would be impossible to describe in full, and that is constantly changing and evolving – because of what we do as well as what we are.

That is more like what I think a religious identity might be, and it would still be only part of the whole. The pity of religious identity-claims, like any other, is that they mutilate this wholeness so brutally. A French Muslim girl was quoted recently in the *Guardian*, on the subject of the headscarf ban in French schools, as saying: 'The new law broke my heart. I was being asked to choose between my religion and my studies, between being myself and having a future.'

Whoever had told her that if she removed her headscarf she wouldn't be herself any more had done her a disservice: she was a great deal more than that. As it happens, I think the headscarf ban is a law almost exactly as stupid as the one we're talking about here. Each of them seeks to reduce an intricate and dynamic complexity to a fixed and vulgar simplicity.

So I think we should be free to examine the matter of religion, and criticize it, in both senses of 'criticize' – to examine it as a literary critic examines a book, evaluating its merits and strengths as well as its weaknesses, tracing influences, seeing patterns of imagery and rhetoric; and to condemn its propensity for liberating, empowering, and justifying the worst qualities of human nature.

In the course of doing that we need to distinguish between (7) and (8) above, and we need to remind those who claim that their 'identity' is primarily religious that no identity-claim comes free of consequences. The consequence of this one for those who make it of themselves is that they must put up with the criticism of religion.

Respecting Authority, Taking Offence

Hari Kunzru

Remember the Death of God? A twentieth-century idea which now seems rather 'old Europe', a topic for superannuated *Kaffeehausliteraten* to debate over espresso and cigarettes. These days in identical smoke-free Starbucks across the world, customers scanning the news on their laptops are faced with jpegs of a resurrection. It's bad B-movie stuff, crass and gory, God-the-undead stumbling across the social terrain, flattening everything in His path. Religious war, martyrdom, eschatology, even apocalyptic natural disasters – they're all back, just in time to catch the new millennium.

Globalization has forced secular Western liberals to open their study doors and confront the uncomfortable fact that for most of the world God never died at all. The whiggish tone of much post-war academic writing about religion and society, with its assumption that faith had been rendered obsolete by reason, now seems both short-sighted and complacent. Perhaps the perception that the battle was won explains why the intellectual response to God's post-9/11 revival has, by and large, been so supine. The humanities, ever susceptible to volatility in the intellectual markets, are pragmatically realigning themselves. Various cultural concepts which had acquired inverted commas are hurriedly shrugging them off again. Irony, once the hippest trope in the seminar room, is treated like an embarrassing aunt.

Much of this was inevitable. The world of contemporary belief, with its binary logic and tone of righteous anger, is certainly not a playful (let alone *jouissant*) place, nor one which has much time for nuances of interpretation. Whatever dregs of postmodern amusement can be derived, say, from the spectacle of tea-and-biscuits Anglicanism being bitten on the arse by the fruits of its colonial missionary work in Africa ('Yes we *know* we told you it was literally true, but we've been reading some phenomenology . . .') are woefully outweighed by the horrors which fringe religious organizations like Al-Qaeda and the US Defense Department are offering up on a weekly basis. But if all that bracketing, all those erasures and floatings-free currently appear whimsical, self-indulgent or myopically scholastic, the politics, and (whisper it!) the *ethics* which informed the project of chipping away at the grand monoliths of religion, race, science and culture are sorely missed in public debate.

In Britain, the political class has been shoving its secular clothes to the back of the wardrobe and trying on something more appropriate for the New Age of Faith. The recent proposal to grant religious belief a similar legal status to race, gender and sexual orientation was presented as a pragmatic move, a way to deal with loopholes and inconsistencies in current legislation. The small print identified it as an election-year sop to alienated British Muslims, a sign that their faith was recognized, albeit not actively *liked*, at Number Ten, and if only they could find a way to ignore Iraq, Afghanistan, Belmarsh and Guantanamo, they'd realize they were better off under Labour. The proposal suggests an interesting cultural party game: Who would go down? During the parliamentary debate one had the impression that even if the Home Secretary was unwilling to throw Salman Rushdie to the Bradford Council of Mosques, he would quite like to have given them Bernard Manning, which would have had the added bonus of playing well in Islington.

Throughout, we have been assured that freedom of expression is under no threat, though the soothing tone in which these assurances are delivered will grate with anyone who has spotted how discomforted Her Majesty's Government is by over-use of the word 'freedom', or indeed any reminder at all of our inconvenient tradition of civil liberties. The inference is that any such new law wouldn't get used much, and then only against people who deserve it, shaven-headed racists in smoky rooms who employ 'Muslim' as a sneaky substitute for 'Paki' in their rabble-rousing. We're directed to make comparisons with the inert blasphemy laws, last *successfully* invoked in 1922 to dish out nine months' hard labour to a man who compared Jesus to a circus clown. No one seriously expects Stewart Lee to be breaking rocks, or even picking up litter, to atone for *Jerry Springer – The Opera*. At least not until there are more votes in it.

Leaving aside the folly of passing a law only intended for recreational use, the most insidious aspect of the move to grant legal protection to religion is the invocation of human rights and multiculturalism to justify it. In Britain it sometimes feels as if this language, which seemed so vital and necessary as it emerged from the ashes of the Second World War, has become a kind of Newspeak, used to justify violence abroad and authoritarianism at home. An 'ethical foreign policy' turns out to mean humanitarian invasion. 'Community' usually book-ends compound phrases ending in 'order', while 'diversity' boils down to a kind of Mexican stand-off in which social conservatives of various ethnicities get to point six-guns at each other while snarling about respect.

As public policy, multiculturalism has been gradually hollowed out, functioning now as a substitute for the progressive politics it once embodied. Peculiarly, given its subsequent history, it first emerged in Canada as a response to tensions between its English- and French-speaking populations. Enshrined in the Canadian Multiculturalism Act of 1971,[1] it was quickly implemented elsewhere, and initially acted as a powerful ideological corrective to the injustices of state nationalism, which insists (often against

1 The full text of the act is available at http://www.canadianheritage.gc.ca/progs/multi/policy/act_e.cfm

evidence) on the existence of unitary national cultures, demanding absolute assimilation and the erasure of difference as the price immigrants must pay to gain admission. Current Canadian legislation aims to 'ensure that all individuals receive equal treatment and equal protection under the law, while respecting and valuing their diversity'.[2] The Canadian Government runs a multiculturalism website, which lists the benefits as follows:

Multiculturalism ensures that all citizens can keep their identities, can take pride in their ancestry and have a sense of belonging. Acceptance gives Canadians a feeling of security and self-confidence, making them more open to, and accepting of, diverse cultures. The Canadian experience has shown that multiculturalism encourages racial and ethnic harmony and cross-cultural understanding, and discourages ghettoization, hatred, discrimination and violence.[3]

Multicultural politics have certainly been useful in reconfiguring the public discourse of former colonial powers[4] as they adapt to mass immigration. 'Chicken Tikka Masala' is a genuine step

2 Ibid.

3 http://www.canadianheritage.gc.ca/progs/multi/what-multi_e.cfm

4 In this category I would include various European countries as well as white-dominated former colonies such as Australia and New Zealand, where multicultural politics have played a role in negotiating relations between immigrant and indigenous groups. Multiculturalism has never much found favour in American public policy at the federal level. The preferred US model is that of the 'melting pot', which sustains the fiction of a blank land in which all immigrants arrive as equals and are transmuted into citizens by the shared experience of freedom and other 'American values'. Multiculturalism's implicit dynamic of dominant and subjugated cultural groups fits badly with this, as does the notion of merely partial acceptance of host country values. Multiculturalism tends to be criticized from the Right in the US as an attempt to deny the possibility of value judgements, as in this definition from Christian think-tank Probe: 'Multiculturalism is a politically correct attempt to over-correct cultural bias by elevating all subcultures to equal status' (www.probe.org).

forward from 'no blacks, no dogs, no Irish'. However, 'respecting and valuing diversity' (a quintessentially information-age activity, performed largely through the production and consumption of various kinds of media, from street festivals to television advertisements) is gradually replacing genuine action to redress social and economic inequality. As such, contemporary British multiculturalism is a pessimistic affair. Lacking belief in the power of their politics to produce fairness, our politicians are offering up the pageantry of respect as a consolation prize. So Islam will be valued in law, on government websites and in glossy brochures as part of the tapestry of British diversity, but individual Muslims will remain poor and marginalized.

Economic liberals will always suspect that 'equality' is code for 'economic redistribution', but regardless of one's position in that debate, there is reason to worry about the current state of multiculturalism as public discourse. The demand for respect and the 'security and self-confidence' which goes with it is being co-opted by a new form of authoritarianism. American university speech codes provide a salutary study of the way once-emancipatory anti-sexist and anti-racist impulses can be harnessed to enforce norms of behaviour and stifle dissent. After the protests of the 1960s, when institutions appeared to have thrown off the old *in loco parentis* model of governance, top-down control of students and faculty was wrested back through a variety of means, including strict enforcement of charters such as the one passed by the University of Michigan in 1987 prohibiting 'any behaviour, verbal or physical, that stigmatizes or victimizes an individual on the basis of race, ethnicity, religion, sex, sexual orientation, creed, national origin, ancestry, age, marital status, handicap or Vietnam-era veteran status'. By the early nineties, similarly wide-ranging codes were in force everywhere, and an atmosphere prevailed in which the possibility of offence was justification enough to censor speech and writing, marginalize those whose views did not accord with the prevailing consensus and, ironically (given that many of the enforcers were veterans of the sixties student revolt), prevent many kinds of campus protest.

Several speech codes fell foul of constitutional challenges, but these university experiments paved the way for the general culture of offence which now dominates America. Tight behavioural regulation is ensured by the need to pre-empt expensive litigation. Precedent has established that in politically sensitive contexts the right to free speech can sometimes be restricted to corralled 'first amendment areas',[5] designated protest zones which effectively marginalize dissent, a property which makes them a popular feature at national political conventions. As Christian fundamentalism has gained strength in American life, so 'political correctness' has merged seamlessly with the religious instinct to police reproduction and sexuality, culminating in the degraded spectacle of wartime America howling in protest at the two-second televisation of a female nipple, while behind the scenes its interrogators were sexually abusing detainees in offshore prisons.

British social democracy has its own locally produced obscenities, and here too the joke seems to be on the cultural-studies brigade. The migration of progressive politics into issues of language and vision, of 'hate speech', 'presence' and 'visibility', was initially welcome in a country which looked to multiculturalism to provide a ray of hope in the post-imperial twilight. As policy it has had its successes, not least in providing a lever to open up public institutions like the police and social services.

---

5 The first amendment reads 'Congress shall make no law respecting an establishment of religion, or prohibiting the free exercise thereof; or abridging the freedom of speech, or of the press; or the right of the people peaceably to assemble, and to petition the Government for a redress of grievances' (http://www.archives.gov/national_archives_experience/charters/bill_of_rights_transcript.html). An introduction to issues relating to the first amendment can be found at www.firstamendmentcenter.org

However, the dominance of identity politics has bequeathed us a peculiarly two-faced nation. In one Britain, ministers wear beanie hats at the Notting Hill Carnival and prison officers attend diversity-awareness seminars, scrupulously discussing who exactly is allowed to use the phrase 'my nigga'. In the second, everyone in public life competes to deport as many immigrants as possible in the time permitted, the one with the highest score earning the fleeting approval of Worcester Woman or Norwich Boy and the chance to play for Europe.

The failure to acknowledge the coexistence of these two Britains – the one which talks of inclusiveness and the other which operates a ruthless (and popular) policy of exclusion – has reduced multiculturalism to a screen for those aspects of the post-9/11 security state which British people are as yet unwilling to contemplate directly. As its atrophy accelerates, we see multi-culturalism rapidly retreating from any coherent commitment to hybridity or the formation of new identities and becoming an ideology that puts power into the hands of cultural conservatives, who can use it to shut down debate and enforce their dominance within their own communities. Preservation, rather than growth. Respect, rather than engagement. Everyone stands in their corner with their own little pile of books (scripture, language, costume, recipes) and growls.

Against this backdrop we find the hapless management of the Birmingham Repertory Theatre contacting Sikh religious leaders about a potentially controversial play and getting burned when the Sikhs mistake a bit of Arts Council diversity-policy box-ticking for an invitation to enter into dialogue about the play's content. In India, taking offence on behalf of God comes second only to the cinema as a national pastime, so it didn't take long for the Khalsa to swing into action. The protests turned violent. The play was shut down. In response, ministers were shockingly equivocal, one coming close to saying that the Birmingham Rep should be grateful to the Sikh community for taking their art so seriously. It was a situation which pitted two liberal impulses against one another – the assertion of freedom versus the wish for inclusiveness. It's also the point (reached, and never satisfactorily resolved, during the *Satanic Verses* furore) where in order to proceed liberals have to identify the limits of their tolerance. Socially conservative state multiculturalism is designed to fudge precisely this issue. It's only a temporary fix. Sooner or later respect will have to give way to debate. Or else debate will have to give way. And what then?

Anyone asserting freedom of speech in multicultural Britain has to contend with the existence of communities in which shame and honour govern social life, and in which plurality of belief, let alone the right to mock religious dogma, is far from universally tolerated. In this context, offending against religion is viewed as a kind of public violence against the believer. The possibility of legal recourse, offered as a cheap bit of toadying by an election-year Government, will be eagerly taken up as a legitimate, honourable and non-violent way of saving face. If attempts under such a law to prosecute popular targets like Rushdie fail, as they surely will if it is applied as we are told, further disaffection will result and pressure will grow for more substantial powers. The principle that offence against religious belief is actionable will already have been conceded. The proverbial slippery slope will present itself.

While beating ourselves up, it's worth remembering that elsewhere in Europe the heirs of the Enlightenment are making their own hash of things. The French Government's aggressive promotion of secularism is predicated on a refusal to make a distinction between religious symbol and cultural practice. A style of dress, while inflected by religious belief, is not straightforwardly or two-dimensionally 'symbolic', and the expectation that large numbers of women will alter their standards of modesty overnight must at best be considered naïve and at worst flagrantly provocative. An analogy for the average secular Frenchwoman might be like moving to some former part of *France d'outre-mer* in West Africa, and having to go bare-breasted to the council offices because of the local government policy of Afro-centrism. The major targets of the French legislation are, of course, North African Muslims, who find themselves in an impossible position: the price of access to public institutional spaces becoming the erasure of their identity; all this in a country where they are already at the bottom of the social and economic heap. If the secular state is indeed the best guarantee of religious freedom, this is only true if secularism doesn't itself take on the self-righteous tone of religious absolutism. The absurdity of a law which requires the definition of a 'religious beard' should require no further comment.

The British and French situations represent the polar dangers of the current international confusion about religion, tradition and identity. French state secularism and British religious protec-tionism both turn identity politics to authoritarian ends, as does the unholy alliance between culture-warriors and conservatives in the US. The stakes become even higher when we remember that the terrain of contemporary racism has moved away from biology. The idea that culture dictates identity can be used to justify much of the same bigotry which, a generation ago, used to rest on the sandy foundations of biological determinism. Even the British National Party is aware of the opportunities presented by the contemporary neurosis about offence, complaining to Ofcom about a Channel 4 documentary (Kenan Malik's *Let 'Em All In*, 7 March 2005) in an impeccably multicultural idiom:

This use of the music from the soundtrack from the film deliverance [sic] was designed to portray the White Anglo-Saxon people those comments [sic] during the interview as being idiotic, redneck, inbred yokels as per the film 'Deliverance'. This was both racist and highly offensive to the individuals filmed and the White Anglo-Saxon com-munity itself.

(www.bnp.org.uk)

All this suggests that freedom of speech exercised in the interrogation of religion, culture, sexual mores and established beliefs of other kinds is more than 'permissiveness' – it's a political imperative. Back in the happy nineties, great play was made of the role of the internet both in lowering the global moral tone and promoting freedom of speech. The net is, like, a distributed system, right? Built to withstand a nuclear attack? So when it encounters censorship IT ROUTES ROUND IT! As we grappled with the new possibilities of the network form, this was an intriguing story. What if cyberspace was some kind of autonomous trans-national territory, a testing ground for libertarian notions of self-regulation and bottom-up control?

In the decade since those romantic arguments first gained currency, we have been brought up sharply against their limits. For although the internet has proved to be a highly robust and reliable way for people to share information other people don't want them to share (so far, mostly MP3s and pictures of Paris Hilton), and peer-to-peer software has made centralized control, if anything, even more difficult to exert, the internet is nevertheless still a physical thing, made up of computers and other hardware located in particular countries with particular police forces who can break down your particular door and take your server if they feel that is the right and proper thing to do.

In Britain, using the twin issues of terrorism and paedophilia (the shock troops of offence culture) to win popular support, the Government has asserted considerable control over the internet. Under the Regulation of Investigatory Powers Act, internet service providers are required to track all data traffic passing through their computers and route it to the National Technical Assistance Centre at Thames House, Millbank. It was announced that 'Black Box' devices were to be placed in every ISP and telecoms company for the purpose, but there are reportedly disputes with the industry over who pays, and how to handle the immense amounts of data all that snooping will generate. One of the most blatant violations of British freedom of speech in recent years was the under-reported October 2004 seizure of servers in London belonging to the UK Independent Media Centre. The FBI later confirmed they had ordered the seizure 'at the request of Italian and Swiss authorities'. The British Government refused to respond to questions tabled by MPs on the grounds that 'no UK law-enforcement agencies were involved' in the raid. The Home Office's apparent lack of interest in court orders from non-UK jurisdictions being enforced on UK soil without their involvement is either highly disingenuous or breathtakingly complacent.

The trans-national internet seems to have spawned friction-free trans-national systems of control. However pressing the security needs which brought about the Indymedia seizure (and with no information in the public domain that is impossible to judge), the effect was to close down an important international news organization. That this could happen in London without the British Government feeling the need to comment, let alone justify the raid, is at the very least an indication of a terrible casualness about freedom of expression, the blasé attitude of an instinctively authoritarian administration operating in a political climate in which any appeal to national security, however flimsy, trumps civil liberty concerns every time. This is the climate in which (and the Government by whom) we are being asked to contemplate further 'pragmatic' limitations to freedom of expression in order to buff up the tarnished bodywork of British multiculturalism. Who would we be doing it for? British Muslims? The International Olympic Committee? Personally, I'm not feeling particularly pragmatic just now.

Respect and the Rules of the Road

Michael Ignatieff

If freedom of expression were the only issue at stake in the debate over whether anti-religious speech should be penalized, there wouldn't be much to argue about. Writers who criticize Islam's history and traditions should not be driven into hiding by a fatwa; film-makers whose films denounce Islamic treatment of women should not be gunned down in the street; a theatre performing a play critical of Sikhs should not be forced to stop performing. It is a mistake to criminalize expressions of contempt, dislike or even hatred of religion, because this blurs necessary distinctions between critical speech acts and acts of incitement. Since British law already provides penalties for disturbing the peace and for inciting violence against religious and racial minorities, new laws penalizing anti-religious speech will violate important rights of free expression by chilling critical speech acts that do not incite violence.

The proposed legislation is a political gesture designed to reach out to religious minorities who are angry at the apparent freedom with which their religious traditions can be insulted on television, on stage and in print. This anger is real enough, even if it may be stirred up by minorities within the minorities. To say it is real is not to say that the violence it can generate is justified. Violent threats against a writer or attacks on a playhouse cannot be justified under any circumstances whatever. Again, all this is easy to say. The lines between criticism and incitement and between violent dislike and overt threat are clear. In principle, we know how to reconcile freedom of expression and public order. When freedom of expression becomes a direct threat to life and limb, we ban or restrict or punish such expression, and we are right to do so. Expression is not sacred, and public order is not sacred. We draw the line and the line is incitement to violence.

Again, all this is not the hard part. The hard part is how to reconcile freedom of expression with respect. The issue here is not a legal one, but a moral one. The British Government wants to use law to reassure religious minorities that the content and practices of religious faith are entitled to legal protection when they are exposed to defamation, hatred, contempt and abuse. But this blurs the line between hatred and incitement, and unless that line is maintained, freedom of expression, which benefits minorities and majorities alike, will be harmed. What follows from this is that the law cannot enforce inter-cultural, inter-religious respect.

If the law cannot enforce respect, how do we protect and encourage respect as a social and moral practice? That is, if the law should not penalize remarks hostile to religious doctrine, practices and faith communities in general, what marks of respect can a religious minority lay claim to from the majority community? The mutual indifference sometimes called tolerance? Chilled political correctness?

Religious minorities may feel that while the law can protect them against violence, just as it will punish those in their midst who feel tempted to riposte to insult with violence, the majority society will be left free to express its sarcasm, contempt, hostility and hatred. No one defending free expression can be happy with a cultural climate in which freedom exposes religious minorities to the daily drizzle of cheap jokes on television, ignorant remarks in the supermarket and the public house, and the occasional taunt and epithet on the way to the mosque or temple.

One argument made by defenders of free expression makes the problem worse by appearing to misunderstand what religion is. It is difficult to generate respect for religion if it is regarded as a set of beliefs or opinions like any other, since we do not accord respect to opinion by itself. The crux of the liberal case against the Government's proposed legislation rests on this assumption – that religion is simply a set of opinions, and that no set of opinions should receive the legal privilege of immunity from insult. This equation of religion with opinion emerges when defenders of free expression contrast it with race. It is commonly believed that it is unacceptable to insult someone's race, but acceptable to criticize their religion, since race is an attribute that an individual can do nothing to change and is irrelevant to their moral conduct, while religion is a set of beliefs that an individual is free to change and which does dictate moral conduct. But this seems to misunderstand that for billions of people religion is as integral to identity as race is and as little chosen. People are born Muslim or Jews, the way they are born white or black. To be sure, a person can renounce or alter religious beliefs inherited from their parents, as they cannot do with their race, but this does not change the fact that religion is just as constitutive of identity as race or any other collective physical characteristic or marker. Indeed, to the degree that belief is chosen, it becomes, by that very act, all the more central to moral and spiritual identity. How else can we explain the particularly intense devotion of recent converts?

Religion is not just any set of opinions, but a particular kind that provides central elements of moral and metaphysical identity for particular communities of people. Since many millions of people identify themselves by their religious faith, it is as wrong to insult a person for their religion, as it is to insult them for their race.

Two types of insult towards religion need to be distinguished: insulting particular religious tenets or practices; and insulting a religion in general or religions in general. The first would be to criticize a particular doctrine or belief: virgin birth; dietary laws; rules regarding the treatment of women. While criticism of this sort, especially coming from someone outside a faith, might be regarded as insulting, it seems legitimate. What seems less legitimate – i.e. actively disrespectful – is to dismiss a religion en bloc or to dismiss religious belief as a whole.

Not all liberal defenders of the absolute priority of free speech go this far, but some do. They characterize all religious opinion as a stubborn or irrational prejudice that any reasonable person would change if they allowed reason to influence their opinions in religious matters. It is a vulgar form of disrespect by secular rationalist liberals – and I count myself as one, by the way – to treat religion in this way. While specific religious doctrine or practice is not entitled to any legal immunity, and anyone should be free to dismiss a religion or religions in general, it seems actively disrespectful to engage with religious people as if they were in the grip of a deluded prejudice.

The disrespect takes the form of an unjustified and – in my view – unjustifiable assumption of the superiority of secular forms of reason. Most secular liberals believe that religious claims cannot survive the inquisition of reason, but this may simply be a form of arrogance. A more respectful attitude towards religion might start from a humbler claim on behalf of reason itself, namely that since human reason is human, there is bound to be a lot we do not know, including whether God does or does not exist. Anyone who wants to make a stronger claim – namely that God is unthinkable, inconsistent with what reason empirically discovers – ought to be free to say so, but it would be carrying the claims of reason much too far to give such a claim the right to disrespect those who believe otherwise. In other words, if respect correlates with tolerance, tolerance in turn correlates with humility, with an awareness of the limits of secular reason itself. Respect towards religious groups depends on humility, since it is humility that might generate curiosity towards religious practice itself. In place of curiosity, liberal secularists mostly have contempt or indifference. It's hard to generate respect without a willingness to learn.

Humility needs to be distinguished from deference. To defer to religious doctrine or argument is to suspend rational disbelief, and humility need not entail the suspension of rational disbelief. We have solid ground to put our faith in reason, as far as it goes, and to the degree that we find religious claims unfounded, a rational person should say so. But a rational person might also say: there is a lot more in heaven and earth than is imagined in our philosophy.

Humility makes empathy possible, and empathy is crucial to a practice of respect. Here I mean political empathy, the capacity to see the world of modern multicultural societies as religious minorities experience them. The plain fact is that untrammelled free expression is a solidly majoritarian preference in most secular democratic societies, and religious minorities may experience this preference as explicitly disrespectful of their creedal commitments. A defence of free expression by the majority – accompanied by rationalist contempt for religion on the part of respected intellectuals and writers – is bound to be seen, by minorities, as simply a form of majoritarian tyranny enforced by *bien-pensant* metropolitan liberals.

A less oppressively majoritarian defence of free expression is possible, one that makes it plain that free expression defends minority rights as much as it does majority preferences, and makes it clear that religious faith belongs in both the public and private sphere of a liberal democracy. Liberals will simply have to choose whether they want a politics of empathy and inclusion on religious matters or whether they want to pursue a Voltairian agenda of combating religious dogma under the banner of free speech.

We must not mistake the times we live in. In Voltaire's time, religious authority was a genuine tyranny. In contemporary liberal democratic societies, religious communities are either declining enclaves within the majority community or else immigrant communities struggling to find a foothold in their countries of adoption. For these immigrants, it is impossible to disaggregate the disadvantages they encounter by virtue of their race, faith, income and language. If they act out their outrage at a play or a book that appears to them to defame their faith, who is to say that their feelings of exclusion – on grounds of race, income and language – are not also playing a driving role. Again, *nothing* justifies attacks on free expression, but a politics of empathy would take care to situate the problem of anger where it actually lies, in the real oppression that religious minorities sometimes feel in our supposedly free, open and democratic societies.

Across Europe and North America, the anger of immigrant religious minorities is then exploited by global fundamentalist movements who seek to turn them against the secular and liberal premises of their host societies, mainly by pointing out the degree to which these societies do not practise what they preach. But this challenge cannot be met by pronouncing liberal anathemas on religious fundamentalism. It can only be met by making sure our societies keep the promises we are supposed to keep: genuine equality before the law, equality of opportunity, protection from violent attack, and obvious practices of respect: the participation of religious minorities in national ceremonies of commemoration and remembrance, the inclusion of minority faiths in ecumenical services, the representation of religious minorities on boards, commissions, assemblies and all forms of public life.

Respect, of course, is a two-way street. Indeed, respect cannot be respect unless it is mutual. That entails compromise on both sides. A liberal democratic society is entirely entitled to define the rules of the road for immigrants. For example, if equality before the law is a condition of respect for minorities, equality entails privileging the individual rights of women over claims of obedience grounded in religious faith and paternal authority. If a young woman wishing to study at university is opposed by a father who wishes her to stay home, and she seeks legal assistance to prevail, a liberal society will side with her against her father's wishes. If a woman wishes to choose her marriage partner, and paternal and religious authority align against her, a liberal society's institutions should defend her freedom. To the extent that women wish to remain obedient to the religious and family values of their culture of origin, they should remain free to do so. But if they choose to exit, a liberal society is duty bound to defend their right to do so.

Liberal democratic societies are not all the same. How France decides to balance the religious rights of minorities against majority interests will not be the same as Britain or the United States. To the degree that we want to evaluate and compare these practices, it seems hard – at least to me – to justify the banning of ostensible religious symbols in public education, as they do in France. I appreciate that building a common experience of public citizenship, through the national education system, is important to national cohesion, but it seems a mistake to enforce common citizenship by restricting individual religious freedom. But national traditions matter here, and so do the particular immigrant demographics of societies. One size will not fit all, and what matters most, in each society, is a transparent, public process of discussion in which a balance between majoritarian interest and private religious freedom is worked out.

All of this is difficult for religious minorities and highlights the price they may have to pay in maintaining religious authority within a liberal democracy. But this price seems intrinsic to the act of immigration. To the extent that immigration is a free choice, it entails accepting the rules of the road of the society which immigrants enter, provided that these rules are consistent with international rights norms. These norms do privilege individual freedom over group allegiance. We cannot generate a practice of respect unless minorities and the majority understand this. Liberal society ought to observe a duty of non-interference towards the religious practices and domestic customs of religious minorities, just as it bears a duty of non-interference towards other groups. But when individuals within that group actively seek protection against unjust religious or family authority, liberal society should seek to protect individual rights.

Free expression in a liberal society does not mean banning religious speech from politics, political deliberation and the public sphere. It simply means refusing to privilege religious speech as true, just as free expression refuses to privilege secular speech as true.

The claim here is that free expression simply mandates that no one in a democratic process holds trump cards, by virtue of the religious or secular character of the arguments they make. Were one type of argument to be privileged, democracy could not function. So on moral matters sensitive to religious groups, they have as much right to make their case as anyone else. Secular groups may object to the type of claims that are made, for example, that some contemporary moral dilemma can be solved, definitively, by parsing an ancient text written millennia before, but such religious arguments from spiritual authority should have as much standing in democratic fora as any other. Which argument will prevail should not depend on its formal character, i.e. on whether it is secular or religious, but on whether it succeeds in persuading a freely consenting and uncoerced majority. What is tyrannous is the claim of epistemological or metaphysical privilege in democratic argument. Respect thus entails listening to arguments whose claims and forms one does not agree with and granting that the persons who make them have as much right to participate in the decision as you do.

We will all have to live and learn here. Respect might mean that religious minorities simply have to live with the fact that the dominant myths and rituals of the majority – national narratives and histories, majority religious festivals – prevail in the public sphere, in public instruction and in national festivals of commem-oration. Equally, however, majority communities will have to learn to accept – and hopefully welcome – the participation of religious minorities in these public moments of national affirmation. This may mean, for all concerned, that liberal democratic societies find more of a place in public life for religious ritual and ceremony representing the faith communities who make up the national community. If that means dyed-in-the-wool agnostics and secularists, like myself, have to grin and bear it while the prayers are read, the incense is waved and the incantations are intoned in the public square, if we are told our arguments in politics will lead us straight to damnation, so be it. It might even do our souls some good.

Final Cut

Ian Buruma

'It's the South Bronx,' my friend Max Pam said as he drove me to his old neighbourhood, the Overtoomse Veld, in west Amsterdam. Whatever it was, it wasn't the South Bronx. Dreary rather than menacing, more shabby than poor, the neighbourhood of grey concrete 1950s tenements had changed drastically in one respect since Max lived there as a child. Once a suburb for young Dutch families, the Overtoomse Veld is now inhabited almost entirely by immigrants, mainly people of Moroccan or Turkish origin. Areas like this, to the west, east, and north of Amsterdam, are often called 'dish cities', because of the many satellite dishes picking up TV stations in North Africa and the Middle East.

The men came first, as migrant workers in the late 1960s, to do jobs that the Dutch no longer wished to do: hard and dirty jobs in industry, or cleaning buildings and streets. Women followed about a decade later, often as brides, usually illiterate, dispatched straight from their villages to strange men in an even stranger land. Most of the workers are now worn out, unemployed, living on welfare. Their wives still inhabit a strange country, whose language and customs they never mastered.

There are roughly a million and a half first-generation immigrants in the Netherlands (ten per cent of the population), among them Turks and Surinamese, along with refugees from all over Africa and Asia. The Surinamese, mostly of Indian or African descent, already spoke Dutch in their native country, a former Dutch colony, and are relatively well integrated. The Turkish immigrants live mainly quiet and increasingly prosperous lives. The most problematic minority, in terms of street crime and other forms of maladjustment, is the Moroccans – many of them Moroccan Berbers originally from remote villages in the Rif Mountains.

The streets of Max's old neighbourhood were remarkably empty, except for some veiled women and old men in djellabas, frequenting halal butchers and stores that offer cheap telephone connections to North Africa. Young men with little to do – *hangjongeren*, or 'hangabouts' – loitered around August Allebe Square, where petty crime is common. Max pointed out the broken windows in his old school, now a so-called black school, where most of the children are from Muslim families.

Max is a successful writer and newspaper columnist, a figure on the Amsterdam literary scene, and a close friend of the film-maker Theo van Gogh, who was murdered on 2 November 2004. Van Gogh was riding his bicycle to work when a bearded young man, dressed in a long Middle Eastern-style shirt, shot him several times. Van Gogh begged for mercy, and reportedly said, in a peculiarly Dutch phrase, 'Surely we can talk about this.' The young man then pulled out a knife, slit van Gogh's throat from ear to ear, kicked the dying body, and walked away. He had apparently hoped to die himself, as a martyr in his holy war, but was arrested a short time after the murder. Van Gogh, meanwhile, lay on the street with a letter pinned to his stomach by the killer's knife.

Mohammed Bouyeri – or Mohammed B, as he is called in the Dutch press – is not a great stylist, but his letter is written in the clear prose of an educated Dutchman. It contains a farewell poem that begins, 'This is my last word, riddled with bullets, baptized in blood, as I had hoped.' The poem is followed by jihadist slogans, and a letter to the Somalian-born Dutch politician Ayaan Hirsi Ali, who wrote the script for Theo van Gogh's last film, *Submission*. She is called an 'unbelieving fundamentalist' and a heretic in the service of her lying 'Jewish masters', 'products of the Talmud' who 'dominate Dutch politics'. Hirsi Ali would be smashed against the hard diamond of Islam. The United States, Europe, Holland – all were doomed.

Mohammed Bouyeri, twenty-six at the time of the murder, was born in Amsterdam and grew up in Max Pam's old neighbourhood. His family background is fairly typical for a second-generation Moroccan immigrant. His father speaks halting Dutch, and has been crippled by years of menial labour. No longer able to kneel, he has to pray sitting in a chair. Mohammed has three sisters and one brother. His mother died of cancer in 2002.

Mohammed was never a hangabout. On the contrary, he had a good high-school education, and was known to his teachers as a promising young man. He was, as they say in the neighbourhood, a *positivo*, who would surely make it in Dutch society. Not just ambitious for himself, Mohammed was always helping out troubled Moroccan kids, making plans for a youth programme at his old school, and writing uplifting articles for a neighbourhood bulletin. He was someone who could talk to city councillors and social workers. He knew his way around the intricate byways of Holland's generous welfare system, where applying for subsidies is an essential skill.

Things didn't quite work out as Mohammed had hoped, however. A subsidy for a community centre he'd been lobbying for was turned down. A promised renovation scheme for public housing never materialized. His mother's death came as a shock. That year, Mohammed abandoned his studies in social work, went on welfare, and behaved in ways that were increasingly odd. In a meeting with community officials, he loudly proclaimed that Allah was the only God. He gave up alcohol, prayed all the time, refused to shake hands with women, and drifted to a fundamentalist mosque, El Tawheed. There he met Syrians and Algerians who had been coming to Holland since September 11th, usually from France and Germany, to give religious instruction. Messages appeared on a website called Marokko.nl, allegedly written by Mohammed, promoting fundamentalist views on such subjects as the proper place of women.

Perhaps it was his mother's death, or perhaps it was the series of setbacks and disappointments he encountered; in any event, Mohammed became unhinged. In his tiny apartment, he held meetings with an extremist group based in The Hague. A Syrian cleric spoke to the group about holy war. Two of his new friends were Western converts – one the son of an American – who made plans to blow up the Dutch Parliament. Once a model pupil, apparently well adjusted to Dutch society, Mohammed Bouyeri became a holy warrior.

Theo van Gogh – fat, blond, absurdly generous towards his friends and madly vindictive towards his enemies, a worshipper of Roman Polanski, a talented film-maker who never had enough patience to produce a masterpiece, a heavy smoker and consumer of cocaine and fine wines, a columnist of some style and shocking vulgarity, a doting father, a disgusting slob adored by many women, a provocateur, and a man of principle – had embarked on a very different kind of war: a war against what he regarded as hypocrisy and cant. We were slight acquaintances, and I always enjoyed his company. Not being part of the Amsterdam scene, I never felt the sting of his enmity.

Like most people of his and my post-war generation in Holland, Theo van Gogh was marked by stories of the Second World War, when the majority of Dutch people minded their own business while a minority (about 100,000 Jews, out of an estimated 140,000) were taken away to be murdered. Van Gogh's family, descended from Vincent's brother Theo, was exceptional. His father fought in the Resistance, as did his uncle, who was executed by the Germans. Van Gogh often referred to the war in his writings. 'The jackboots are on the march again,' he wrote of the

Islamists in Holland, 'but this time they wear kaftans and hide behind their beards.' The Dutch officials, social workers, and politicians who appeased them were, in van Gogh's eyes, akin to collaborators. A frequent target of his abuse was Amsterdam's mayor, Job Cohen, who has tried to preserve civic harmony by making a show of treating Muslims with respect and understanding. 'If anyone has not learned from '40–'45 how unwise it is to want to live with marching jackboots who demand "respect", it's the mayor,' van Gogh wrote. Cohen, as it happens, was among the 'Jewish masters' whom Mohammed Bouyeri singled out as enemies of Islam.

For van Gogh, the worst crime was to look away. One of his bugbears was the long-standing refusal (since abandoned) of the Dutch press to identify the ethnic origin of criminals, so as not to inflame prejudice. He saw this as a sign of abject cowardice. To show respect for Islam without mentioning the Islamic oppression of women and homosexuals was an act of disgusting hypocrisy. In a free society, he believed, everything should be said openly, and not just said but shouted, as loudly and offensively as possible, until people got the point. It was not enough to call attention to illiberal Muslims; they were to be identified as 'goat-fuckers'.

Van Gogh often expressed his admiration for the late Pim Fortuyn, the populist politician, who regularly proclaimed that there was no room for a bigoted religious minority in a liberal society, and that 'Holland was full.' Van Gogh called Fortuyn, who was assassinated in 2002 by a deranged animal-rights activist, 'the divine baldie', partly to annoy the *bien-pensant* liberals, who were quick to denounce any criticism of minorities as racism. His friend Max Pam thinks that van Gogh's attitude was mixed with professional rage; like Mohammed Bouyeri, van Gogh had trouble getting state subsidies, not for community centres but for his films. Yet there is no getting around van Gogh's nasty streak. When the novelist and film-maker Leon de Winter, whose work often revolves around his Jewish family background, managed to get public money for his projects, van Gogh detected cynical manipulation and sentimental cant. 'Hey, it smells like caramel today – well then, they must be burning the diabetic Jews,' he wrote, mocking what he saw as a Jewish cult of victimhood. He described the Jewish historian Evelien Gans as 'having wet dreams' about the Auschwitz doctor Josef Mengele. In the guilt-ridden land of Anne Frank, there is a certain amount of strained piety about such topics, but van Gogh's response had all the subtlety of the Dutch football hooligans who find it amusing to abuse an Amsterdam soccer club known as 'the Jews' club' by mimicking the sound of escaping gas. Van Gogh seemed to regard delicacy as a sign of fraudulence, and in this he spared no one; Jesus, in his book, was 'that rotting fish in Nazareth'.

For all his seeming intolerance, though, van Gogh was one of the few Dutch film-makers to take a real interest in actors with a Moroccan background. *Najib en Julia*, a series made for television, is a highly sympathetic story about the love between a Dutch girl and a Moroccan boy. And personal attacks, though seldom as virulent as van Gogh's, are a common feature of Dutch literary politics, where everyone knows everyone else. It is the violent rhetoric of a place where words are normally without serious consequences.

This is not the kind of place that Mohammed Bouyeri yearned for, and it was not the kind of place that Ayaan Hirsi Ali came from. They take things more seriously in Somalia, where she was born, and in Saudi Arabia, where she partly grew up. Suffering genital mutilation as a child was serious, as was a horrific beating she told of having received from a Muslim teacher in Kenya, when she no longer wished to attend his lessons. When her father, a dissident Somali politician, promised her in marriage to a distant cousin, his word of honour was absolute. And so was her resolve to defy the culture whose strictures she could no longer endure.

She escaped to Holland in 1992, learned to speak perfect Dutch, studied political science, worked with abused Muslim women, and became a politician, first in the social-democratic Labour Party and then in the more conservative Liberal Party. Hers is a politics of rage. Pim Fortuyn was right, she said, to call Islam a 'backward religion'. Muslim schools should be abolished, and men who beat their wives and daughters should be punished by law. There is no doubt about the seriousness of her aims, and there is no doubt about the seriousness of the Muslims who regard her as an apostate and have called for her death.

Since September 11th, her views have had a receptive audience, but the collaboration with Theo van Gogh – the combination of her rage and his desire to offend – was bound to be particularly explosive. The subject of the eleven-minute film they made, *Submission*, is the abuse of women in the name of Allah. A young narrator tells the story of Muslim women in a quiet voice: flogged for a youthful love affair, raped by an uncle, forced into a repulsive marriage. All the while, words from the Koran appear, written on naked female bodies. Friends advised Hirsi Ali against making the film. It would lead to violence, they said. Muslims, distracted by the form, would not be receptive to the message. Her answer was that shock was the best route to awareness, and she is planning a sequel.

Many things happened as a result of Theo van Gogh's murder, some violent, some merely bizarre. The rash of arson attacks on mosques and Muslim schools was perhaps to be expected, as were racist messages on websites and walls, and even on some of the floral tributes to van Gogh. 'R. I. P. Theo!' was the message of one of the arsonists. Almost as predictable were some of the defensive reactions by young men of Moroccan origin, who cheered as they passed the spot of the film-maker's death.

In the week following the murder, politicians showed signs of panic. The Justice Minister, Piet Hein Donner, who is a Calvinist of the old school, suggested that a rather archaic law against blasphemy should be applied, something that had not been done since 1966, when the novelist Gerard van het Reve was prosecuted for comparing his conversion to the Catholic faith to making tender love to a donkey. Donner's suggestion was not followed. Another politician, Geert Wilders, started a party of his own, the Groep Wilders, with a platform of barring all non-Western immigrants for five years and arresting Islamists, even when, as he put it to me, they are only 'prepared' to break the law. Although, like Hirsi Ali, he has to hide from people who wish him dead, this hitherto obscure parliamentarian has soared in the opinion polls, and has positioned himself as the next Pim Fortuyn. In some estimates, his party would capture almost twenty per cent of the Dutch house of representatives if there were to be an election today. (In another poll, asking who the greatest figure in Dutch history was, Pim Fortuyn came second only to William the Silent.)

In the midst of all this zaniness, the commentators talked and talked: 'Holland has lost its innocence'; 'the end of multi-culturalism'; 'tolerance has its limits'. The general trend was rightwards, and towards an atmosphere of perhaps exaggerated anxiety. Max Pam was not the only person I spoke to who believed that if the authorities didn't tackle the Islamist problem now Holland would eventually have a civil war on its hands. Conservatives, who had warned for many years that Muslim immigration would cause problems, found new allies among former leftists. And liberals, such as Job Cohen, who had promoted tolerance and multiculturalism, were denounced as irresponsible softies.

A key text in this national discussion was by Paul Scheffer, a social critic and an influential thinker in the Labour Party. In *NRC Handelsblad*, the most important national broadsheet, he wrote:

Segregation in the big cities is growing, and this is very bad news. That is why the soothing talk of diversity and dialogue, of respect and reason, no longer works. Tolerance can survive only within clear limits. Without shared norms about the rule of law, we cannot productively have differences of opinion . . . The self-declared impotence of our Government to guarantee public order is the biggest threat to tolerance.

To be sure, Scheffer had been saying this kind of thing for some time, but when old lefties cry out for law and order you know something has shifted in the political climate; it is now a common perception that the integration of Muslims in Holland has failed.

The Pieter Nieuwland College, situated in eastern Amsterdam near the spot where van Gogh was murdered, is a so-called confessional school, of Protestant denomination. Around sixty per cent of the pupils are from ethnic minorities – not an unusual number for schools in Amsterdam, Rotterdam, and The Hague. Most Dutch educational establishments have a religious affiliation, as is true of some broadcasting companies, newspapers, and several political parties. These so-called pillars of Dutch civil society were developed in the late nineteenth century to pacify tensions and conflicts between the different religious communities. Most have been drained of their religious content by now, but the forms remain, and the State continues to subsidize confessional schools, including Muslim ones. What once worked to keep the peace among Protestants and Catholics, some people argue, now encourages illiberal religious prejudices, imported from the Middle East by people who don't even speak Dutch.

I asked the principal of Pieter Nieuwland, W. J. M. Raeven, about the reaction in his school to the murder. He replied that there had been more tensions among the teachers than among the pupils. Adults, he said, 'have this "us and them" feeling that pupils don't really share'. Still, he continued, there had been serious discussions in the classrooms, and these were encouraged, as long as they were carried out politely and in Dutch. (Only standard Dutch may be spoken in school.)

When our conversation turned to Mohammed Bouyeri, Raeven said that teachers had learned a lesson in recent years. It was wrong, he concluded, to put too much pressure on minority children. 'We used to encourage them to work harder than other children, to go that extra length,' he said. 'And many of them did, especially the girls, because education is one way of gaining independence from their fathers. But we put too much pressure on them. Even when they have done everything we asked of them, they will have disappointments. It is often harder for Muslim children to find jobs, for example. And when that happens they can get very angry indeed.'

A social-studies class I visited included Africans, Indians, Turks, Moroccans, an Egyptian, and a few whites. We had a discussion about van Gogh and Hirsi Ali, and the only girl in class who wore a veil spoke more often and more passionately than the others. The girl, who was born in Amsterdam to Moroccan parents, didn't condone the murder but could 'understand why Mohammed B. had sought comfort in Islam'. She said that people had insulted her in the streets after the murder, spitting at her feet or telling her to take off her veil. 'When I hear people talk about "those fucking Moroccans", I feel defensive and really want to be Moroccan, but when I visit Morocco I know I don't belong there, either.' A Moroccan-born boy said that it was because of her Dutch accent.

I noticed that some of the Muslim boys, who were described to me later as 'quite fundamentalist', snickered every time the veiled girl spoke, even when she argued, to loud protests from the other girls, that Muslim women were not oppressed. 'Hirsi Ali is a dork,' she said. 'She doesn't look beyond her own experience.'

The whites in the class remained silent, as though afraid to enter this treacherous terrain. One of the black students made fun of the Muslims' preoccupation with 'identity' and said, 'Moroccan, Egyptian, Algerian – who the fuck cares. They're all thieves.' The others laughed, even some of the Muslims.

A dark-skinned girl with Indian features suddenly spoke: 'I think Hirsi Ali is really brave. She is saying things no one else has the guts to talk about.' A Turkish boy who had tried to see both sides of the question said that maybe Hirsi Ali's film had not been the best way to convince moderate Muslims.

One thing that angered both the Turkish and the Moroccan pupils in the Pieter Nieuwland College class was the tendency to lay the blame for terrorism indiscriminately on all Muslims. 'Everything they hear about the culture of their parents is negative,' Raeven told me. One response to this is to view Mohammed Bouyeri simply as a madman. This is what Ahmed Larouz, a Moroccan who came to Holland as a teenager in the late 1980s, thinks: 'I can't explain what he did. If 280 others had done the same thing, you could perhaps find an answer, but what he did was crazy. Maybe Islam made him even crazier. Then again, he knew nothing about Islam. I grew up in Muslim schools. Mohammed B. just cobbled his religion together in two years.'

Larouz sees himself as a Dutch–Moroccan role model. In 1997, together with four other Moroccan students, he set up TANS (Towards a New Start), an organization that aimed at giving Muslims a more positive role in society. Today, Larouz works in an ultra-modern office, wears snappy pin-striped suits, is attended to by secretaries in miniskirts, and talks like an old-fashioned American booster, full of pep and vigour and lines from rappers such as Tupac Shakur. English is only one of the many languages he speaks. 'Cultural management', in the private and public sectors, is his business.

Naturally, it is Bouyeri, not Larouz, whom Frits Bolkestein, the former leader of the Dutch Liberal Party and, until last

November, a European Union commissioner, had in mind when, in the early nineties, he began to warn about the possible consequences of an uncontrolled influx of Muslims. The foreign-born population of Amsterdam was growing at one per cent a year. At that rate, he said, the main Dutch cities would have Muslim majorities in a decade or two. The Government policy at the time was 'integration while maintaining identity'. In practice, the idea was to deal with Muslims much as previous Dutch Governments had dealt with Protestants and Catholics, by creating another 'pillar'. Bolkestein disagreed, and wanted to have a debate.

Sitting with Bolkestein in his new office in the centre of Amsterdam, I asked him to recall the days when he spoke out against the Government's policy. 'The policy was complete nonsense, of course,' he says. 'I wrote a piece in 1991 saying that integration would not work if our fundamental values clashed with those of the immigrants: separation of Church and State, for instance, or the equality of men and women. Those things could not be negotiated, not even a little bit.'

What happened? 'Well, half the world came down on me,' he says. 'I was called racist, a hater of Islam. At one point, I feared for my personal safety.' None of the mainstream political parties wished to engage in a serious debate on these issues. 'Blinded by ideology, people could not see what was going on,' he says, 'but I was enough of a politician to sense what ordinary people in "church and bar" were feeling, and I decided to tap into that.' This might sound like the typical talk of a right-wing populist, but many liberals, including Paul Scheffer, now regard Bolkestein as a hero, someone who had the courage to speak the truth when others were dodging the issue. Certainly, Bolkestein is a sophisticated thinker, and the refusal to take his arguments seriously had the unfortunate result that church and bar – *kerk en kroeg*, as the Dutch say – fell into the hands of demagogic politicians such as Pim Fortuyn. A flashy dresser and an openly gay man, Fortuyn was an unlikely hero in this ultra-bourgeois country, but his message that foreign intolerance could no longer be tolerated, and that it was time to restore bourgeois order by kicking out those foreigners, made him wildly popular. It was as though the Dutch, having looked the other way for so long, had woken up to a problem and were now demanding a radical solution.

Geert Wilders, the current promoter of anti-immigrant populism, has none of Fortuyn's flamboyant appeal, although his extraordinary hairdo, a kind of lacquered blond bouffant, draped around a pink baby face, could be seen as a brave attempt at it. A former deputy and speechwriter for Bolkestein, he left the Liberal Party in September 2004 because he felt it was pulling too much toward the centre, while he wanted to go further to the right. Wilders has become an important figure on the post-van Gogh scene, though his efforts to organize a new party are somewhat hampered by the fact that he needs twenty-four-hour protection and has to stay in safe houses.

I saw him in his well-guarded office at Parliament, in The Hague. Wilders is a man obsessed with one idea: Holland's failure to confront the Islamist threat. Nervously shuffling the few items on his desk, he spoke fast, as if there were no more time to lose: 'It's no coincidence that the first ritual slaughter happened here. We just let everybody in. There is no sense of urgency. The French intelligence people can't believe how sloppy we are.' He reeled off names of people and organizations that, he said, have been operating in the Netherlands with impunity. 'I'm furious that the Dutch Government is incapable of taking hard measures. That would be better for the moderate Muslims, too. We must crack down. In this country, politicians have always tried to pacify minorities by mollycoddling them. All that holding of hands. It makes me sick.'

If fear has been stoked among the white population of the Netherlands, it is perhaps even more acute among the Muslim minorities. One afternoon, I took the ferry to a district called Amsterdam-North, built for dockworkers in the 1910s and 20s. It is now the poorest Moroccan area of the city. Paul Scheerder, a former newspaperman, opened a home there for abused women and children. He married a Moroccan and converted to Islam. We drank mint tea in his office, and he told me about three girls staying in his shelter whose father stabbed his wife to death two years ago. We were joined by the neighbourhood cop.

I asked them both how van Gogh's murder had affected the streets of Amsterdam-North. 'Fear,' the policeman said, while Scheerder nodded. 'People were afraid of going out, frightened that they would be attacked for being Muslims. We put some extra security around the mosque, and people were very grateful for that.'

Things have calmed down since the first weeks after the killing, but Scheerder is still worried. He doesn't like the idea of a new mosque being built in the area. It might be seen as a provocation. 'We don't want another murder, because then all hell could break loose,' he says. Scheerder tells me that he has seen boys like Mohammed Bouyeri, who seem all right one day and then suddenly go berserk. 'People watch Moroccan and other Arab television stations,' he said, 'and they see the Americans as the greatest criminals in history.' In a news segment about Theo van Gogh on Moroccan TV, a Moroccan immigrant in Amsterdam had said that 'his death was just, and he was punished by God'.

This is the problem. Although Theo van Gogh was Dutch and was killed by a Dutch citizen, in the end this is not just a Dutch story but a Middle-Eastern one imported to the heart of Europe. Mohammed Bouyeri, and hundreds like him, have plugged into a wider world of violent web-based rhetoric and terrorist cells. The integration of Muslims in the Netherlands has not been a greater failure than anywhere else. But the country may have been less prepared for the holy war.

When the world comes to an end, Heinrich Heine is supposed

to have said, one should go to Holland, for everything there happens fifty years later. This has not been true for quite a long time, but the attitude, bred by centuries of peace and prosperity, has lingered. The First World War passed by the Netherlands, which remained happily neutral. The Second World War did not, which is why the German Occupation, though much less brutal than it was, say, in Poland, was so traumatic.

After the war, and especially since the 1960s, the Dutch prided themselves on having built an oasis of tolerance, a kind of Berkeley writ large, where people were free to do their own thing. Liberated, at last, from the strictures of religion and social conformity, the Dutch, especially in Amsterdam, frolicked in the expectation that the wider world would not disturb their perfect democracy in the polders. Now the turbulent world has come to Holland at last, crashing into an idyll that astonished the citizens of less favoured nations. It's a shame that this had to happen, but naïveté is the wrong state of mind for defending one of the oldest and most liberal democracies against those who wish to destroy it.

Loose Tongues

Hanif Kureishi

That exemplary dissident Oscar Wilde, whose punishment failed to erase his words but taught us something about where a loose tongue might get you, wrote, at the end of the nineteenth century, 'When people talk to us about others they are usually dull. When they talk to us about themselves they are nearly always interesting.'

This essay concerns something we are and take for granted: the fact we are speaking animals, full of words which have a profound effect on others, words that are sometimes welcomed, and sometimes not. I want to say something about words which seem possible and others that seem impossible.

It is no coincidence that the political and social systems which have dominated our era – communism, global capitalism, fascism, imperialism, the nuclear family, different varieties of fundamentalist religion, to name but a few – are marked by a notable factor. There are circumstances in which they don't want people talking about their lives. Tyrants are involved with silence as a form of control. Who says what to whom, and about what, is of compelling interest to authorities, to dictators, fathers, teachers, and officials of whichever type.

As Milan Kundera pointed out in his great novel *The Joke*, there are times when the need to be funny is so subversive that it can land you in jail. Isaac Babel, who was murdered in prison, and called a book 'the world seen through an individual', was himself not unaware of the ironies here, and said, 'Whenever an educated person is arrested in the Soviet Union and finds himself in a prison cell, he is given a pencil and paper and told "write!" '

What his interrogators wanted were words. But of course the meaning of 'corrupt' is to falsify, adulterate, or debase, in this case the language – that which links us to others.

In his short fiction 'In The Penal Colony', Kafka describes an ingenious machine for torturing to death a man condemned for disobedience. The device is equipped with ink-jets which inscribe the name of the crime on the victim's body, even as he bleeds to death. '"This condemned man, for instance" – the officer indicated the man – "will have written on his body: 'Honour thy superiors.'"'

The whole process of writing as killing takes twelve hours. This calligraphy of colonialism might be called 'being killed by description', as the body is ripped to shreds by those who hold the pen. There is no question here of the victim having his own pen; he doesn't speak. His version of events, his story, will not be considered. Even his own body carries the inscription of the other.

Collective or shared stories, linked by implicit agreement about how the future should be, or about the sort of people who are preferred – heroes, leaders and the morally good on one side, devils, villains, the ignored and the bad on the other – can also be called ideologies, traditions, beliefs, ways of life or forms of power. After they've been told for a while, stories can turn into politics, into our institutions, and it is important that they seem to be just the way things are, and the way they have to go on being. It is always illuminating to think of those groups and individuals who are denied the privilege of speaking and of being listened to, whether they be immigrants, asylum seekers, women, the mad, children, the elderly, or workers in the Third World.

It is where the words end, or can't go, that abuse takes place, whether it's racial harassment, bullying, neglect, or sexual violence. Silence, then, like darkness, carries something important about whom the authorities want others to be, something important about the nature of authority itself, and the way it wants to dehumanize others in the silence.

Of course different systems use different methods to ensure silence. From the cutting off of tongues to the burning of books, or the use of sexual morality as well as covert prohibition – like ignoring people, for instance – all are different ways of ensuring a dictatorship of voices, or of maintaining the single voice. If one person tells another who they really are, while denying them the right to self-description, certain kinds of self-doubt or inner disintegration will follow. People can be formed and also deranged by the stories others tell about them. When Jean Genet was told he was a thief, it was an idea it took him most of his life to escape.

The necessity of a certain interpretation of reality, and the imperative that this idea be maintained, couldn't be clearer than in families. Children are soon made aware of the force of a particular description, and of its authority. While most parents are aware that children develop when they are listened to, they don't always want to hear them.

On their side, of course, children are fascinated by language, especially when they discover that there are words which make the adults crazy or frightened, which make the adults want to slap them, or shut them up. Children can become compelled by any discourse which provokes terror in adults. Therefore children learn about the language community by discovering what cannot or should not be said. They learn about prohibition and limits, about punishment, about hiding and secrets, and about privacy. When they discover what cannot be said, they have to learn to lie or conceal their words, often from themselves. If they are lucky they become creative and use metaphor. If they are unlucky they go mad.

Depression, for instance, might be called a kind of slowness. It could be seen as a subversive refusal to move at the speed of the others, as the rejection of a banal, alienating consumerist world in favour of an authentic inner puzzlement. But, more commonly, without such an idealization, it is a slowness which usually takes place in silence, beyond or outside language and symbolization. The depressed, therefore, do not believe in language as the carrier of meaning. The dead cannot make friends. The depressed person, self-silenced you might say, feels far removed from the source of her words, which may well multiply on their own, and can seem to circulate wildly and without meaning, like birds trapped in an empty room.

The deliberately silent are at least making a point – to themselves – when they suppress or break up their own stories. The involuntarily silent, on the other hand, might feel as though they've had their words fruitlessly stolen from them. But this enforced silence on behalf of the powerful is not for nothing. The mythologizing of those not heard is the opportunity for difficult and busy work. The silent other has to be called, for instance, a stranger, foreigner, immigrant or asylum seeker. She might be an exile, an interloper, the one who does not fit or belong, the one who is not at home, the one whose words do not count.

This range of denotions at least makes it clear that we can never stop wondering about our own alien, awkward or foreign parts, the elements which cannot speak except through the use of others. Racism might at least teach us that we are always strange – or other, or unwelcome – to ourselves, particularly when it comes to our need. We might even be aware that there is an odd but intriguing silent reversal here. The sort of capitalism we have has always depended on colonialism, and has always required both labour in the Third World and labour from the Third World – the immigrant, in other words. And yet our own need has only ever been represented in terms of their need, as their dependence on us. This is frequently manifested as an image of desperate people climbing over barbed-wire fences, eager to come over here and strip us of all we have.

The subject chosen to be strange has an important place. He or she has to be kept constantly in mind; worked over and worked on. It is a passion, this attitude to the threatening foreigner, the outsider, the one who doesn't know our language. Someone has to be kept in their place in order that the other can exist in a particular relation to them, so that hatred can flourish. I call this a passion rather than an opinion because these fictions have to be constantly reiterated. They cannot be stated once and for all, since the victim seems always about to escape his description. Unless he's constantly buried and reburied beneath a deluge of words – and, of course, the actions which words entail – he might turn into someone like us.

If a plausible version of the twentieth century can be told in terms of silence and its uses, there is reason for optimism too. That period was also about people insisting on their own words and histories, speaking for themselves. The 1970s, as I recall, were about the formally colonized, gays, women, the mad, children, putting their side of the story, telling it in their own words and being heard. As a result, in some places, there were significant social advances. It has been said that when Pinochet was arrested in Britain, things changed in Chile. The dictator wasn't sacrosanct; people began to speak; his mystique was penetrated at last.

Clearly, though, this description is simplified; there is an absence here. I have implied that on one side the words are there, ready and waiting to go, while on the other they are unwelcome or prohibited, that the only problem with the words is that the authorities don't want to hear them.

However, at the centre of this is something else: the person who doesn't want to hear their own words. This is the person who owns them, who has made them inside his own body, but who both does, and does not, have access to them, who is prisoner, prison and the law. Real dictators in the world are a picture, too, of dictators within individuals, of certain kinds of minds.

If we wanted to create an authoritarian system which was complete, in which there were no loose tongues – or, within an individual, no significant inner life – it would have to be one in which dreams were controlled. Even in prison, under the strictest supervision and observation, a human being can at least dream. Here he might, at least, represent or symbolize that which cannot, or must not, be said. But how would these dreams be understood? Who would be there to receive the scrambled communications which might be his only hope?

In 1906 an English surgeon, talking to Ernest Jones, mentioned, with some astonishment, a strange doctor in Vienna 'who actually listened with attention to every word his patients said to him'.

What Freud realized was that because there are forms of speaking which are radically dangerous and unsettling, which change lives and societies, people don't want to know what those words are. But, he adds, in another sense they do really want to know, because they are made to be aware, by suffering, of a lack; they at least know that they will not be complete without certain forms of self-knowledge, and that this will be liberating, even though the consequences of any liberation could also be catastrophic.

Human beings leak the truth of their desire whether they like it or not: in their dreams, fantasies and drunkenness, in their jokes and mistakes, as well as in delirium, religious ecstasy, in babble and in saying the opposite of what they mean. It takes a rationalist, then, to see that rationalism can only fail, that what we need is more, not less, madness in our speaking. Otherwise our bodies take up the cause on our behalf, and bodies can speak in weird ways, through hysteria, for instance, in Freud's day, the modern equivalent of which might be addiction, anorexia, racism or various phobias.

Freud invented a new method of speaking, which involved two people going into a room together. One person would speak and the other would listen, trying to see in the gaps, resistances and repetitions what else, in the guise of the obvious, was being said. He would then give these words, translated into other words, back to the speaker.

Great individualists though they might be, both Wilde and Socrates, like Freud, used dialogue as their preferred form. Indeed, in another essay, Wilde replaces the Socratic imperative 'know yourself' with 'be yourself', which might become, in this version of 'being' – that of the language community – 'speak yourself'. The therapeutic couple is one method of seeing who you are by speaking, and it is an original and great invention. But there would be something odd, to say the least, about a society in which everyone was in therapy. Not that there isn't something already odd in the idea that only the wealthy can buy mental health.

Fortunately there has always been another place where the speaking of the darkest and most dangerous things has always gone on, which we might call a form of lay therapy. We know that this mode of speaking is useful because of the amount of prohibition it has incurred. It is sometimes called conversation, or the theatre, or poetry, or dance, the novel, or pop.

What is called creativity or culture might remind us of Freud's method because many artists have talked about the way in which words have the knack of speaking themselves. The writer is only there to catch them, organize them, write them down. Even the prophet Muhammad, around whose name silence is often required, was visited by an angel who gave him the law. Muhammad didn't make up these rules himself; they were spoken through him but came from elsewhere. Another instance of the death of the author, or the author at one side to himself, as secretary or midwife to himself, you might say, making a divine law that no human can modify or speak back to.

A culture is a midwife to images and symbolizations, a place where people speak to one another, where words matter and, because they are in the public domain, can be understood or used in a number of ways. It is also where one is forbidden to speak about certain things. It has, therefore, to be a place where the question of speaking and punishment is spoken about. The collective can have a conversation because artists like to loiter near the heat of the law, where the action is. If artists are considered to be on the edge, they are on the edge of the rules, close to punishment, and, like Beckett, not far from silence, where speaking has to be almost impossible if it is to be of value.

What Freud added, and the surrealists knew, along with the other artists who have formed our consciousness – Buñuel, Bergman, Joyce, Picasso, Woolf, Stravinsky, Pinter – was that if the unconscious was to be represented, there had to be new forms for it.

These artists knew that conventional talk and the conventional art which accompanied it had been turned into chatter. They knew that this worked as a block or filter to forms of knowledge which were essential if we were not to be silent, or if we were not to racially persecute and kill one another for reasons we couldn't understand. Therefore, if modern art and much of what has followed it has been the attempt to say the unsayable, some of these forms can only be ugly and disturbing. These forms have to be banned, dismissed and discouraged, partly because, like most forms of fantasy, they are subject to shame, itself a form of censorship.

To speak at all is to be aware of censorship. The first thing tyro writers come up against, when they uncap their pen, is a block – in the form of a prohibition. They may well find their mother's face floating into view, along with several good reasons why not continuing is a good idea. Freud, a prodigious writer himself, put it like this, 'As soon as writing, which entails making a liquid flow out of a tube on to a piece of white paper, assumes the significance of copulation, it will be stopped.'

This, you might say, is the imprimatur of good speaking – that there is a resistance which guarantees the quality of the utterance. There are, then, at least two voices called up here, the voice which needs to speak and the voice, or several voices, which refuse, which say these words are so exciting and forbidden that they are worthless. This is what makes any attempt at creativity a useful struggle. What makes it worthwhile is the difficulty, the possibility of a block.

Twentieth-century art has been fascinated by dreams and nightmares, by violence and sexuality, so much so that it might be termed an art of terrible fantasy. One begins to see splits, deep conflicts, terrors, hatreds and a lot of death in these art nightmares. These elements can be put together – somehow fused in a work of art – but they are not always reconcilable. However, irreconcilable parts may find a voice in some form of personal expression, which, partly, is why modern art has been so painful and difficult to look at, even now, and why any new art, to be of value, has to shock us. This is because it breaks a silence we didn't even know we were observing.

At least art brings us beauty as compensation for its message. But it is not, in the end, the favour it might be, because it can be an awful beauty, just as to tell the truth about sexuality might not be to talk about how good or hygienic it is for us, but to speak about how bad or painful it is for us.

Speaking, listening, being known and knowing others: we might say that at least, if everyone doesn't get much of a turn, we live in a representative democracy. This, at least, separates us from various fundamentalisms. We can vote; we believe we have politicians who can speak for us. Yet one of the reasons we despise politicians is that we suspect they are speaking on their own behalf while purporting to speak on ours. Our words, being handed on by our representatives, are not getting through and they never will. Our speaking makes not a jot of difference. One way of looking at globalization, for instance, is to say that it is a version of certain Orwellian authorities saying the same thing, over and over, the attempt being to keep new words, or any human doubt, need or creativity, out of the system.

Surely, then, if politicians cannot possibly do the trick, artists might do it. Speaking from themselves and sensibly refusing to do advertising, they do nonetheless speak for some of us, and they take the punishment on our behalf too. In the absence of other convincing figures, like priests or leaders, it is tempting to idealize artists and the culture they make.

Nevertheless, in the end, there is no substitute for the value of one's own words, of one's story, and the form one has found for it. Sartre, in his autobiography *Words*, says, 'When I began writing, I began my birth over again.' There is something about one's sentences being one's own, however impoverished and inadequate they might feel, which is significant, which makes them redemptive. If you wanted to tell someone you loved them you usually wouldn't get someone else to do it for you.

If there is to be a profusion, or multiculturalism, of voices, particularly from the margins of expression, then the possibility of dispute and disagreement is increased. The virtue and risk of real multiculturalism is that we could find that our values are, ultimately, irreconcilable with those of others. From that point of view everything gets worse. There is more internal and social noise and confusion, and more questions about how things get decided, and by whom. If the idea of truth itself is questioned, the nature of the law itself is altered. It can seem conditional, for instance, pragmatic rather than divine, or at least subject to human modification or intervention, if not control.

There are always good reasons not to speak, to bite our own tongues, as many dissidents, artists and children will testify. It will offend, it is dangerous, hurtful, frightening, morally bad, others will suffer or they will not hear.

But the good thing about words, sentences and stories is that their final effect is incalculable. Unlike violence, for instance, which is an unmistakable message, talking is a free form, a kind of experiment. It is not a description of an inner state, but an act, a kind of performance. It is an actor improvising – which is dangerous and unpredictable – rather than one saying lines which have already been scripted. 'The thought is in the mouth,' as

Tristan Tzara put it. It is not that we require better answers but that we need better questions. All speaking is a demand, at first for a reply, proving the existence of communication, but, ultimately, for an answer, for more words, for love, in other words.

You can never know what your words might turn out to mean for yourself or for someone else; or what the world they make will be like. Anything could happen. The problem with silence is that we know exactly what it will be like.

Free Speech: An Exchange

Adam Phillips with Lisa Appignanesi

LA: Free expression, offence, censorship – all these words move around not only in the public arena. They are also words which refer to the inner life and form part of psychoanalytic thinking. How do you understand free expression and censorship?

AP: *From a psychoanalytic point of view you would always be thinking of the difficulties of free expression, the resistances to speaking freely. You wouldn't be assuming that what people want to say is already there, and that the only question is whether they can get away with saying it.*

One tends to think of free speech in terms of people knowing what they want to say and judging whether it is acceptable or not, as though it was just a question of courage or of regard for other people. From a psychoanalytic point of view you would be saying that free speech also involves people actually surprising or offending themselves by what they say, not merely insulting others. So to be interested in free expression would be to be interested in just how fearful we are of it, and how ingenious we are at not speaking as freely as we might. It is strange, for example, that we tend to think of free speech in terms of offending others rather than of giving pleasure. Of offence rather than celebration. It is quite possible that we are more inhibited about celebrating people than about attacking them. So you have to think in at least two directions at once. So-called free speech is not only about saying the unacceptable thing to another person – many people can bear being criticized better than they bear being praised; it may also be about saying the thing that surprisingly is unacceptable to oneself as well.

Free speech means hearing what we ourselves have to say. At its best it is an invitation not to be narrow-minded. The great temptation to narrow our minds must be what democracy is supposed to offset. The aim, presumably, is to be surprised by oneself and others, rather than merely traumatized.

LA: But if you surprise yourself, that's a matter for the individual conscience. If you insult others . . . well, you might bump into religious sensitivity. What perplexes me about religion is that in the West, for the last two hundred years or so, we've thought of it largely as a matter for the individual conscience, but now it seems to be moving into the public arena with a punishing vengeance. What happens to the 'surprisingness' of free expression to the individual conscience, as it, too, moves into the public arena?

AP: *Well, you can imagine a situation, and perhaps this is caught most obviously in a racist or sexist joke, in which people who either don't think of themselves as racist or sexist, or are aware that they might be but don't want to be, find themselves amused by such a joke, told in the public arena. So what is an individual to make of that fact? Well, one thing it exposes is that one has views which are unacceptable to oneself, as well as being unacceptable to others. It seems to me that catching oneself out is unavoidable. Public morality is different from private: and if this is likely to be true, what do we do about it? What do we do with the fact that not simply do we know we think and feel and believe things that are unacceptable to other people, but that we don't have control over these things in the way we would wish? It seems to me that one of the things raised by this whole issue is not merely free speech but, as it were, free listening. The problem is often not so much in what is said, but in the way in which it is heard. One of the things we know is that the way something is heard is indeterminate. I cannot possibly know the consequences of my words. I might say something that to me is absolutely innocuous and to another person it could be heard as profoundly insulting. So one of the things that the free speech and censorship issue raises is: can we actually control the resonances, the interpretations, of our words? And the answer to that is: we can't. And I think in a way certain forms of censorship are acknowledgement of this anxiety. It's as though people are saying this is an area that can't be policed, so let's police it as much as we can.*

LA: Do you mean there's an over-compensation in terms of policing?

AP: *Yes. Or there's an excessive anxiety about the acknowledgement that words live a life of their own inside us. And outside us. The consequences of one's words are incommensurate with one's intentions. I may need to say something to you and you may hear it quite differently. And I then can't say to you, 'No, no, no! I didn't mean that!' because all that is saying is that I didn't intend that. I may or may not have meant it.*

LA: In other words, there's really no way, short of actually silencing everything and everyone, of ensuring that one will never cause offence.

AP: *No, we could never ensure it, but we could make attempts to regulate it. I think that those of us who believe in free speech need to think about what we don't want people to say to us, and what we don't want to hear people saying to other people, and why that is a problem. You could think if people just like the sound of people talking, free speech would not be a problem. I mean we don't talk about free music. But clearly the impact of words is so astounding. People have really strong beliefs about things.*

The free speech issue raises so many questions. One is: what's the nature of belief? Why if I'm interested in something would I be at all interested in it being contested? Why would I want to have a debate about it? Perhaps to believe something means you don't really need a debate about it. So it's as though once I've entered the realm of free speech, and start believing that people should say whatever they think to me, I've already somehow exposed that I've got lots of doubts about my beliefs. So much so that I need other people's beliefs to clash with mine to prove their validity. My beliefs might then be modified. All this might make people very anxious about what they actually do believe or how belief happens and how it works.

LA: What you're saying, if I've understood you correctly, is that believers, certainly believers in a group rather than individual believers, might want to stop free speech or to stop other people speaking because they already feel that their faith is under attack internally, from themselves.

AP: *Yes, exactly. A so-called psychological interpretation would be that they don't want to hear their own inner voices that dissent, that are sceptical. But that's only a psychological view. The other view would be – in one picture of belief – if I really believed something, in other words if it is a core belief, then who am I if there is a possibility that this core belief is subject to modification? Who am I if I want this belief to be contested? You would have to start thinking of your beliefs – even, or especially, your most cherished beliefs – as hypotheses; or as tools to secure yourself certain satisfactions. And as your pleasures change, so will your beliefs.*

LA: That's another way of saying 'Quiet out there'. Does that mean that in your view the only 'true' believers are the ones who don't mind the public arena being full of noise and free speech and attacks since these can't impinge on true belief? Are there believers like that?

AP: *Let's consider two versions of this. There is the democratic true believer who believes presumably that beliefs are formed in dialogue and debate. The other kind of true believer, whom we might think of* as a fanatic in a democracy, would be suffering from a form of superiority. In other words, they would enter the public arena so absolutely assured of their own convictions that they could take on all comers and remain untouchable. That would be a very worrying version of the free speech story: anybody can say anything they like because, actually, I am resolute and unchangeable.

I think one of the misleading things about the idea of free speech as a tag is that people do all sorts of things in the name of free speech: they have vested interests, engage in persuasive, rhetorical ploys. As a rule of thumb anything with a prefix 'free', isn't: free market, free association, free lunches, free speech.

LA: You mean normally isn't or can't be?

AP: I mean both. It's a way of signalling a sense of constraint. To call it 'free' is wishful. What would always be a question – and it might not be a debatable one – is: which of my views or which area of my preoccupations do I think is worth sharing, debating, contesting, conversing with other people about? And which are the areas where I have decided – and I might have decided, so to speak, unconsciously – there is no room for anybody else? This area is not available for debate. Let me give you an extreme psychoanalytic version of this. If I have what psychoanalysts call a sexual perversion, I may well really not be interested in somebody telling me a thousand explanatory stories about, say, spanking, because all I am aware of is the fact that this excites me and organizes my life. I may not want a conversation about it. Now I think that's a kind of analogy for what we've been talking about. My guess is that everybody's going to have areas where either they're going to be extremely resistant to debate or debate will literally be redundant for them. And those might be actually the most powerful, dangerous, energy-filled areas of their lives.

LA: But let's talk about your perversion migrating into public life. Let's say there's a society of spankers and one is not allowed to question the legitimacy of spanking in the public arena – if that's the right way of thinking about this! How do you contend with that? You want to grant the individual the freedom to spank or indeed to pray or eat particular foods, but you may not want to give the individual the freedom to hurt other people, that is, the person who's going to get spanked. And you might want to be able to write a book which contains the plea 'don't spank anyone in the public square'. So how does one work a society where you want to have the freedom to spank and also the freedom to say to people: 'You mustn't spank your child because this is harmful. It is, in fact, an expression of your perversion.'

AP: *Well, I guess you'd think there's rhetoric and then there's violence. People like us in the first instance believe that we will do everything we can to persuade people not to spank others . . . which of course brings with it something autocratic – the belief that we have shared criteria for persuasion. People like us will go along trying to persuade the other group of the value of our values. Finally, for reasons we very often don't understand, if this matters to us enough and the other people will concede nothing, we will force them. And that means violence.*

LA: By violence do you mean the constraint of the State or do you mean 'spanking' them?

AP: *Well, there's a whole spectrum of things. At one end of the spectrum, there's the public attacking paedophiles and feeling it's OK to take the law into their own hands; at the other end, there are people stopping people from having religious views, or indeed expelling people who have these views. We have a deeply held belief that an enemy is something we can get rid of.*

LA: We live in a plural society in which there are competing freedoms: freedom of religious expression and freedom of expression for artists, comics, psychoanalysts, politicians. Do you have any sense whether our particular world, in order to sustain itself, might need one freedom more than another? I mean can one speak of better or more important freedoms? For the individual? For the public sphere?

AP: *This is very difficult. You never know the consequences of these freedoms when and if they are achieved. People who talk about free speech are often saying, 'Well, we may not get the value of this now, but in the future, in some deferred future, it will be better if we've got this pluralistic array of views.' I think it's very likely to be too much of a strain on a lot of people – there being too many competing versions of things. It would be one of our better freedoms not to assume that everyone means the same thing by freedom.*

If you live in a supermarket of ideologies or religious beliefs there is a sort of overload. It can generate so much anxiety that people become violently intolerant of each other, rather than curiously interested, which is what liberal people want people to be. The problem with liberalism, the problem with a certain version of pluralism, is that it can underestimate just how strongly people feel about the things that matter to them, and just how unpredictable their feelings can be about those things they think of as mattering most. Liberalism wants to believe that everything is subject to rational debate, not acknowledging the fact that the very idea of rational debate is itself a specific cultural construct and not the kind of conversation that everybody wants to have. Not everybody believes in conversations.

We've got a clash of ways of going about things here. It's done in the context of a wish, a sort of cosmic wish, that there is global mutual understanding in the air if only we could find it. Well, it seems to me there isn't and that actually we are going to be faced with, and are indeed faced with all the time, things that are absolutely unacceptable to us. The question is what we do then. Not: how can we find ways of making everything in some way acceptable? But: how can we deal with the fact of unacceptability?

LA: And how *do* we deal with the fact of unacceptability?

AP: *I don't really think it's easy to translate from the microcosm – psychoanalysis – to the macrocosm – culture. But psychoanalysis must be thought of as a practice committed to the possibility of freer speech. So let's just pretend, for the sake of it, that we can do this even though we're both sceptical of the possibility. What happens it seems to me is that people in psychoanalysis evolve. It's not as though the category of the unacceptable is dissolved, it's that the category of the unacceptable changes. It's impossible to imagine an individual or a culture without the idea of the unacceptable, but the question becomes: how do you live with the unacceptable? Now, at one extreme you can scapegoat it – blame it, punish it, repudiate it and so on. At the other end of the spectrum you have some idea like 'you can only live by trading with the enemy'. So it's as though you have the belief that there really are possibilities of exchange, that there is something to be gained from some sort of acknowledgement of, or indeed even exchange with, the parts of oneself that are unacceptable. That the unacceptable is, in a certain sense, that which is needed.*

Now this is all very, very abstract. If we just make it more specific. Let's think of a psychoanalysis in which the person hates Jews. Consciously they've got all sorts of relatively benign, liberal feelings, and indeed idolize Jews, but what they find, the more they speak, is that they've got a lot of quite virulent prejudices as well. Now, as the analyst, you could think the point is to persuade them not to enact these things. So, in one version of the liberal premise you'd say: 'You can think whatever you like in the privacy of your own mind, but it's very important to me that you don't go out and start either killing these people or persecuting them.' The other version would be to persuade the person that they have 'invested' in what they are calling Jews: these Jews are repudiated parts of themselves. The question becomes how can they bear to acknowledge that this is a bit of themselves they find difficult, that they would rather see the all-too-familiar as alien.

This is where it all becomes hard to imagine. People use words like 'integration' or 'acknowledgement', as if once it's pointed out to people that this nastiness in themselves they call Jews is in fact within them, in a magical way everything will be resolved. These so-called Jews will become a part of the fabric of your being and you will become a less harmful, more tolerant individual. Well, it doesn't work like that. All the interesting problems start when persuasion breaks down.

LA: So how does it work?

AP: Well, it works in as many ways as there are people. Some people for some reason have the wish and the curiosity and the prior belief that it will be good for them to acknowledge these things in a certain way and not to enact them. If, for example, their hatred of Jews is based on the Jews' purported love of money, they may recognize that they are the mean ones who love money and the conversation will open out from there. So the progressive story will say: if only you can acknowledge the parts of yourself you cannot bear, you can reacquire the energy used in trying to repudiate them. That's the theory.

The practice is that it's extremely disturbing and frightening to acknowledge the really unacceptable parts of yourself. It really freaks you out. You might just over time develop some internal ironization of these things, some felt recognition. If I am the anti-Semite, I might be capable of ironizing this. A second thought might say to me, 'Come on, you know what you're really talking about. This hatred of yours is absurd.' This might be as good as it gets. You might even feel that, on the basis of this, you are freer, as it were, to mix with Jews. But I really think it's dangerous to be too optimistic here.

LA: You're talking about a relationship to money which we all share in some way, as your example of hatred against a group. But what if that hatred is based on something which is further afield, intolerable in a wider social sense – like murdering children in satanic rituals or enforced circumcision for grown women. Are there any 'objective' wrongs in the psychoanalytic world?

AP: *Yes, there are. But I would say that, from my point of view, you've used the word 'objectively' to enforce rhetorically the extent to which this is unacceptable to you. I would prefer to say it is really unacceptable, for me and my group, for people to commit satanic abuses. Absolutely, unnegotiably unacceptable. These are the people we aren't like. At a certain point you should say: this is actually the world I want to live in and beyond this I won't go. The question is: what distance is unacceptable? If there are people in my garden who are doing this, I will stop them. If there are people in Russia – I mean, how far does this go? And that seems to me to be the real dilemma, because we have to acknowledge that there really are what we call different cultures with radically different cosmologies, some of which will be unacceptable to us and which we might feel morally obliged to get rid of.*

LA: Can the psychoanalytic way of thinking about self and the world actually provide a transition from the individual to the social?

AP: *I think for some people, yes. Though it's a misleading model, because individuals are first of all individuals and not groups of people. One doesn't translate into the other. When I was training as a child psychotherapist, one of my supervisors said to me that if only there was more child psychotherapy, political problems would disappear. You can see the logic of this, but actually it's barmy. It isn't like that.*

LA: Why isn't it like that?

AP: *One of the things that isn't acknowledged enough within psycho-analysis is the intractable nature of people's histories: you are not going to dissolve hundreds of years of oppression and deprivation in a psychoanalytic conversation, however profound and moving and power-ful it is. People's histories are far stronger than their preferences and we just, I think, have to acknowledge that there are what psychoanalysts call trans-generational hauntings – a lot of people just call them* 'traditions' – which are so powerfully inside people that we more or less sleepwalk our way through these tribalisms. They're very difficult to modify.

LA: The free expression that we're talking about here is the free expression that grows out of a Western liberal tradition. Expression rather than just speech has something to do with acts of the imagination and works of the imagination. It's difficult as you said earlier to know how people will hear, listen and read any of them. Does this particular form of free expression have any kind of privileged status for you? Can it have a privileged status in our world?

AP: *Only for us. For people with our education, background and so on, the idea that you would not be allowed to write and publish a poem or a play is appalling, but on the other hand, if and when people publish racist, manifestly racist, books, tracts, plays or whatever and clearly want to incite people to humiliate other people, that, too, is unacceptable to me. I don't believe they should do this. I don't think righteous hatred should be promoted. But I don't think we should ever underestimate how frightened we are of other people.*

LA: Do you think there is a difference between inciting people to racial hatred, and inciting them to religious hatred? After all, religion is not race, religion is a set of beliefs, a system. I mean, if I insult Stalin, if I say, 'Fucking, child-murdering Stalin!' or, 'Stalin is a wanker!' is this an item which should be prosecutable in the same way as if I said blacks are bad or Jews are bad?

AP: *This is difficult, because we're back to the question of the strength of people's convictions or beliefs. Races, like religions, can be described in terms of core beliefs and core assumptions about how to live and who to be. So that it could be a false distinction. In one way or another, if one group is inciting its members to torment or abolish another group, that to me is unacceptable. Now that other group may be doing terrible things. Let's imagine the other group are Nazis. Like all liberals, I want to stop the Nazis tormenting the Jews but does that mean I then want to torment the Nazis? Because the risk always is symmetry here: that I do to the Nazis what the Nazis have done to the Jews. Well, that's presumably the move we want to avert. How to avoid turning trauma into triumph. Everyone somewhere in themselves believes that revenge works.*

LA: I want to get back to fiction. Let's take that recent classic case of *The Satanic Verses*. It's a work of the imagination which received a killing review of the kind many of us in the West find utterly unacceptable. But, if you like, it was a review based on a misunderstanding – that fiction can be read literally, as if it were fact and those facts were read as a provocative insult – though, of course, not by every Muslim.

AP: *That's a very optimistic account. There may be no misunderstanding. Ayatollah Khomeini reads* The Satanic Verses *and thinks, 'I, the Ayatollah, know what this book is about. It is about this . . .' We say to him, 'It's a work of fiction.' But can we say we have a privileged interpretation of it? We are the ones who believe in freedom of interpretation; well, here's his interpretation. It's as though we really want to believe that the consequences of our words are commensurate with our intentions. I write a novel and somebody else says to me, 'This is not a novel; this is actually inflammatory racist hatred.' I can't, I think, then legitimately say to them, 'No, no. You've got it wrong! It's a novel!' because I'm assuming that I have a privileged account of what I've done. But I don't. I mean, where does my privilege come from? Where does my authority come from to say, 'Look, this is actually a novel. It's very much like* Pride and Prejudice, *it's very like Tolstoy.' But then the other person could say, 'Well, actually, as I read this, it reminds me of* Mein Kampf.' *Books are only ever as good as their readers. The audience decides whether the joke is funny.*

LA: Would you then legislate not to allow this particular kind of discussion into the public realm? Would you institute laws which force people to self-censor?

AP: *What I would want is to legislate for procedures of dealing with such misunderstandings, if that's what they are, or dealing with conflicts when they arise. I don't want to produce a world without conflict. I want Salman Rushdie to be able to write* The Satanic Verses *and publish it, either with the intention of it being inflammatory or not. I don't know what his intention was, but it doesn't matter. He's written this book. I think what we need are not ways of pre-empting the problem by people not writing and saying things that matter to them. We need ways of dealing with the reception of and the negotiation of those differences. So I would want to legislate about what I can do when I have found myself reading my equivalent of* The Satanic Verses *and I'm appalled by it.*

LA: You could stop reading.

AP: *I could stop reading.*

LA: You don't have to go to the theatre.

AP: *I don't have to go and do any of those things. That's one option I have. And I could add to that as a liberal person: there could be a forum in which I meet with my author or my group meets with my author and his friends and I say, 'Actually this is the effect this has had on me. This is terrible.' So it's as if what we could call the conversation continues.*

LA: This is such a wonderfully idealized view, Adam. This is suggesting that people who use brickbats actually want to talk.

AP: *No, no. We know that they don't. It's not as though I really believe I can get the Ayatollah into a debating society. This is not* debating-society material. We have to say, 'What's unacceptable to me is not that Salman Rushdie wrote and published the book, it's the way people responded to the book.' That's what for me needs to be legislated against, from my group's point of view. I don't want a world in which Salman Rushdie mustn't do this. I want a world in which the people who hate the book can't do what they did. We shouldn't be trying to stop the hatred; we should be getting people to hate in acceptable ways.

LA: Now that would mean you'd be clearly against any form of censorship.

AP: *No, there would be things that I would want to censor. I would want to censor child pornography. I would want to censor extreme versions of incitement to racial hatred. But I would be unwilling to believe that child pornographers or racists by definition have nothing of value to say for themselves.*

LA: What does censorship mean in psychoanalytic terms? I mean, how does one *feel* censorship?

AP: *The interesting thing about censorship in psychoanalytic terms is that one doesn't feel it. It's invisible or it's unheard. You're not aware of what you can't say, you're just aware of what you do say every so often. So one of the things that psychoanalysis works to expose or bring to the light of day is how censorship works behind the scenes. I will have virtually no idea, no conscious sense of what this bureaucracy behind the scenes is doing to my thoughts, opinions and words, my feelings and desires. Sometimes one gets a belated sense of oneself.*

LA: What kind of person is this 'you' who isn't aware of the internal censorship?

AP: *Well, it makes me a person living under surveillance, broadly speaking. It makes me a person who is deemed by some part of myself* to be mad, bad and dangerous to know. And in need of censorship. So one thing a psychoanalyst can say is, 'We live as if we need censorship.' The next thought then is: what would we be like in some imaginary world without the censorship? Is this conceivable? And the answer is: no.

LA: The more censorship you have internally, does that make you prone to want more censorship externally? If I'm the kind of person who punishes bits of myself internally, will I want to punish other people?

AP: *Probably. Just like alcoholics need people to drink, I think that people who are living in very oppressive internal regimes will prefer, for want of a better word, similarly oppressive external regimes.*

LA: So if I were a believer who was tied with a great many rules and regulations and ritual activity, as part of that belief which my group, my society, followed, would I want more laws externally which would also tie people around me?

AP: *It's very unpredictable this, isn't it, because all forms of belief are based on exclusions. There's no way around that and so what you'd be looking at for an analogy would be things like conversion experiences in the nineteenth century or deconversion experiences. People losing their faith, for example. How does it happen that somebody is a powerful believer – they don't even necessarily think of themselves like that, they just think: this is the way the world is – then in some way, and often it's very surprising or indeterminate, an anomalous piece of information enters the system and they begin to wonder.*

These are experiences that liberals really value highly. They precisely value the ongoing metamorphosis of personal belief – living in a continual state of intellectual consideration in which your convictions are subject to reflection and modification. The interesting question is: how does this ever happen? How does a Maoist Red Guard begin to wonder about whether what he is doing is good? What's in the air?

Where do you pick things up from? Freud's model of dreaming is a good picture of what goes on here, because Freud's saying – You and I in this conversation might be very interested in what we are saying, we might think about it. Then tonight you might go away and dream about the buttons on my shirt. Were you to go to your analyst tomorrow and talk about this, this would disclose acres of potentially unknown personal history of belief, desire, thought and opinion. What this means is that quite unknown and unbeknownst to yourself, in the dream day you're picking up things that are really profoundly meaningful to you and you don't know it.

This to me is a much more convincing picture of how people change: the Red Guard or Stalinist isn't persuaded by reading anti-Stalinist tracts or criticisms of Stalinist ideology. It is much more unexpected and surprising: someone, in spite of themselves, is moved in some way or finds themselves haunted by a counter- or disturbing thought. Like a foreign body entering in – and then something begins to change.

LA: But isn't this precisely what the guardians of faith are worried about? Surely they're as wise as Freud in that sense. It's not the fact that someone might say, 'Oh dear! Your religion is bad,' that they're worried by, but the fact that the young move about in a society where things happen to them, where they read and see everything from Jane Austen to horror films. Where they may for a moment be metaphorically unveiled, where something will impinge on the parental view of life. And so they put up restrictions, insist on veiled purity.

AP: *Yes, you could say that it's the Stalins and the Maos and the religious puritans who profoundly understand the malleability of the human character, that it's so suggestible, so promiscuous in its potential abilities and allegiances. Because I, Mao, know that people are phenomenally changeable and suggestible, I'm going to brainwash them thoroughly. This very brainwashing is my acknowledgement of the fact that actually belief is endlessly inconstant. So it's as though there have* been massive acknowledgements of just how metamorphosable people are and this has terrified the daylights out of people. The question is: how can you have groups, how can you have religions, how can you have politics when people are so changeable and so suggestible? The idea of passion, paradoxically, made people believe in their capacity for commitment; modern people feel their fickleness.

LA: And the answer?

AP: *I don't know. I really don't know but I do think that the human problem at the base of all this is that people are suggestible. They're moved and changed and it's fantastically unpredictable.*

LA: What that suggests to me, and this may be fear speaking, is that we all end up locked up within boxes or behind walls of regulation so that the Maos can seal up our suggestibility.

AP: *Or we sit this out because we have an internal apprehension of just how changeable, how unfaithful we are so that we want to narrow our minds. There is a project to narrow one's mind.*

LA: But can one be unfaithful to plurality?

AP: *Well, you can be unfaithful to plurality by narrowing your mind, by becoming, as it were, an ideologue. You can become the emperor of one idea. I mean it could be that modern people are so freaked out by the complexity of their own minds (for want of a better word) that there is a very powerful unconscious wish to narrow them, to find what people call a belief system, a political ideology or a religion. It's like Sartre's story, the one where he describes the married couple. Every morning, the woman comes down, kisses her husband goodbye as he goes off to work, then sits by the window crying, only to perk up when he comes back. Sartre says the obvious interpretation of this is that she suffers from separation anxiety – he goes and she's bereft. The real interpretation is that when he goes, she's free. There are just too many options, so what she wants to do at that moment is curtail her freedom. That might be a very good picture of what we are talking about.*

LA: What do you think has brought us to this pass? Why do you think we're moving towards a more and more authoritarian, self-policing moment in our society? Is it that people actually want to narrow down from a world of too many choices?

AP: *Yes. Though not necessarily too many choices so much as an apprehension that we're infinitely seducible and that we don't have criteria by which to choose. That we are anybodies wishing to be somebodies.*

LA: Gloomy.

AP: *No, it's interesting. There seem to be at least two things going on currently. One is that we are beginning to have to acknowledge that the desires of modern people are prodigal and displaceable and assumed to be insatiable. That greed and self-interest are being taken for granted as the basic constituents of the version of human nature exposed and exploited by capitalism. That fellow feeling is becoming a repressed pleasure. That politics is for careerists, not idealists. And so on. And, secondly, that as it dawns on more and more people that there is no such thing as progress, progress is everywhere proclaimed as our great ideal. Free speech runs the risk of being a kind of advertising slogan, the brand name for progress and the so-called free market. There is, as Stanley Fish announced in a useful essay on the subject, no such thing as free speech; there is only the kind of speech that is more acceptable to some people than others. When free speech is invoked as an obvious and uncontroversial value, it is worth remembering not only what this putative freedom is freedom for and freedom from, but more importantly why we are inclined – whichever 'we' it is – to describe some kinds of speech as freer than others.*

Some people think now that what we can't say, and the reasons we can't say it, is more interesting – even possibly more valuable, more useful – than what we can say. That liberating their speech is tantamount to liberating people, that their words are where they are and that their unspoken words are where they might be. If the most difficult thing is to be able to speak relatively freely to another person, the second most difficult thing is knowing when and where to say what it is one wants to say. The question may not be of freedom of speech, or its censorship, but deciding what should be said where. And this involves acknowledging that our words are always something of an experiment. No amount of legislation is going to stop people hearing things in what is said.

It is important to keep in circulation the idea that, for better and for worse, people can choose their words.

Science and Islam

Pervez Hoodbhoy

On the morning of the first Gulf War in 1991, having just heard the news of the US attack on Baghdad, I walked into my office in the physics department in a state of numbness and depression. Mass death and devastation would surely follow. I was dismayed, but not surprised, to discover my PhD student, a militant activist of the Jamaat-i-Islami's student wing in Islamabad, in a state of euphoria. Islam's victory, he said, is inevitable because God is on our side and the Americans cannot survive without alcohol and women. He reasoned that neither would be available in Iraq, and happily concluded that the Americans were doomed. Two weeks later, after the rout of Saddam's army and seventy thousand dead Iraqis, I reminded him of his words. He had nothing to say.

But years later, soon after earning a reasonably good doctorate in quantum field theory and elementary particles, he quit academia and put his considerable physics skills to use in a very different direction. Today he heads a department that deals with missile-guidance systems inside a liberally funded, massively sized defence organization employing thousands to make nuclear weapons and missiles. Serving Pakistan and Islam, as he sees it, gives him a feeling of pride. Plus it pays about three times as much as a university job.

Technology is Very Welcome

In modern times every form of intellectual endeavour in Islam stands in poor health. Science, in particular, is almost nowhere to be seen. Nonetheless, several Muslim countries have aimed for nuclear weapons and the highest kinds of technology. As the little episode above illustrates, defence technology is accorded top priority and has been more successful than science. The emphasis is reflected not just in salaries but also in research funding and social status. The nexus between technology and defence is made at a student's early stages of development. For example, freshmen at the elite Lahore University of Management Sciences are introduced to the fundamentals of computer science with the following textbook preface: 'It is military prowess that bestows technical and economic superiority to nations, and it is not otherwise. The association of science and technology with ruling empires is, therefore, natural.'

Technological nationalism – the association of power and national greatness with technology – finds its expression in the yearly celebration of Pakistan's nuclear achievements. While Iraq, Iran, and Libya have actively sought to make nuclear weapons, Pakistan is the only Muslim country to have achieved this goal. Since May 1998 the Pakistani state has flaunted its nuclear potency publicly, proudly, and provocatively. Nuclear shrines, erected with Government funds, dot the country. One – a fibreglass model of the nuclear-blasted Chaghi Mountain – stands at the entrance to Islamabad, bathed at night in a garish, orange light. Officialdom has vigorously promoted nuclearization as the symbol of Pakistan's high scientific achievement, national determination, self-respect, and the harbinger of a new Muslim era. Pakistan's Islamic parties rushed to claim ownership after the nuclear tests, seeing in the Bomb a sure sign of a reversal of fortunes, and a panacea for the ills that have plagued Muslims since the end of the Golden Age of Islam many centuries ago. Their hero was (and largely remains) Dr Abdul Qadeer Khan, a metallurgist with intimate knowledge of uranium-enrichment technology acquired during his stint in Holland with URENCO, a European uranium enrichment consortium. Abdus Salam, winner of the Nobel Prize in theoretical physics, remains largely unknown.

Technology was surrounded by religious taboos in earlier times, but it is rapidly gaining acceptance in Muslim societies and earlier restrictions seem virtually incomprehensible to Muslims today. Public clocks had been banned in sixteenth-century Turkey under the Ottomans; the printing press was roundly condemned by the orthodox *ulema* in Muhammad Ali's Egypt; loudspeakers (even for the call to prayers) were once disallowed on religious grounds on the Indian subcontinent; and so forth. Some prohibitions still stand, but are rapidly weakening. Today prohibitions on blood transfusions and organ transplants are generally disregarded everywhere in the Muslim world in spite of orthodox restrictions. Television under the Taliban was severely restricted but has made its way into Muslim homes almost everywhere. In fact, technological innovation – even in matters relating to religious practices and rituals – is now welcomed by a growing consumerist middle class. Commercially available devices include Islamic screensavers and computerized holy texts, cell phones with GPS indicators indicating the direction towards *qibla*, prayer mats with sensors that keep count of the number of kneel-downs and head-downs for the forgetful; and electronically recorded voices that help in remembering the ninety-nine names of Allah.

Science Remains Problematic

Islam's relationship with science, on the other hand, is less comfortable. To remove possible ambiguities, let me define 'science': it is the process wherein knowledge about the physical world is acquired in a systematic and logically self-consistent manner by observation, experimentation, testing of hypotheses, and observer-independent verification.

Some Muslims bristle at the very suggestion that there might be a disjuncture between Islam and science. A common reaction is to point towards the debt owed by modern science to the achievements of their ancestors. Indeed, Muslim intellectual giants such as Omar Khayyam, Jabir Ibn Hayyan, and Alhazen, are rightly remembered for their front-ranking intellectual achievements. But this does not solve the compatibility issue: it is a mistake to think that modern science is simply a more advanced form of ancient science. The two are separated by fundamentally different goals and world views.

In ancient times, science was a matter of discovering curious and interesting new phenomena and facts. These would sometimes tickle the fancy of kings and caliphs, and make the scholar rich or famous. The relation of science with technology was a distant one – a scientific discovery would only rarely result in the creation of new implements or tools, weapons of war, or new architectural methods and designs. Most importantly, given the state of knowledge in pre-modern times, it was simply not possible to have today's view of the universe wherein every physical phenomenon is traceable to physical principles. Modern science insists that these laws are rationally comprehensible, and have validity far beyond the situation from which they were deduced. For example, the laws of physics governing the motion of a falling stone are identical to those that determine the motion of a spacecraft travelling to Venus. These very laws also determine the manner in which DNA replicates, cells divide, or electric signals communicate information inside a computer. In this modern view, the human body is undoubtedly an immensely complex mechanical and electrical system. However, every part can be fully understood in terms of biological, chemical, and physical processes.

Modern scientific thought clearly comes with a high price tag. Before the Lutheran Reformation, this provoked a bitter battle between its adherents and the Church. In contemporary Islam, where there is no formal centre of religious authority, the reactions have been more varied.

Fortunately, the dominant Muslim response to the issue of the compatibility of science with Islam is a rather sensible one – that of indifference. Most Muslims are quite content with a vague belief that there is consistency rather than conflict. This is helped by the generally held view that science is a conglomeration of techniques, formulae, equipment, and machines. At best, science creates new gadgets and even jobs. At worst, it is something technical, which is dreadfully boring and difficult to learn. In any case, the reasoning goes, it is better not to worry excessively over arcane matters.

But others will not let sleeping dogs lie. In recent years the applications, methodology, and epistemology of modern science have been severely criticized by growing numbers of Muslim academics. At one level, these are familiar postmodernist arguments: the development and application of a science that claims to be value-free is held to be the prime cause of the myriad problems facing the world today – weapons of mass destruction, environmental degradation, global inequities in the distribution of wealth and power, alienation of the individual, and so forth.

At another level, many orthodox Muslims reject the scientific method as well as the notion of science as knowledge. Knowledge for the sake of knowledge is declared to be dangerous and illegitimate; the only form of legitimate knowledge is that which leads to a greater understanding of the Divine. Daily television broadcasts and hugely popular Muslim websites and books resound with claims that exegesis of the Koran and a 'proper understanding' of the Arabic language can lead to every scientific discovery from human embryology and cerebral physiology to black holes and the expanding universe.

American universities are host to countless speakers who condemn modern science on Islamic grounds. Iranian-born scholar Seyyed Hossein Nasr, who commands five-thousand-dollar speaking fees, is often invited by campus Islamic groups. In a speech given at MIT that I found on the web, he argued that the Arabic word *ilm*, whose pursuit is a religious duty, has been wilfully applied to science and secular learning by Muslim modernists in an effort to make them more acceptable in Islamic societies. But science is subversion, he announces, 'because ever since children began to learn Lavoisier's Law that water is composed of oxygen and hydrogen, in many Islamic countries they came home that evening and stopped saying their prayers'. In 1983, Nasr advised the Saudi Government not to build a science museum because 'it could be a time bomb' and destroy faith in Islam.

A Widening Divide

My last Google keyword search on 'Islam and science' yielded 165,143 entries. These included hundreds of elaborately designed Islamic websites, some with counter hits running into tens of thousands. The one most frequently visited has a banner: 'Recently discovered astounding scientific facts, accurately described in the Muslim Holy Book and by the Prophet Muhammad (PBUH) 14 centuries ago.' Many seek to show that the birth of modern science would have been impossible but for Islam and Muslims. On the anti-science front there are familiar nineteenth-century arguments against Darwinism, with Harun Yahya of Turkey as the new Bishop Wilberforce.

I could not, however, find any websites dealing with the philosophical implications of the theory of relativity, quantum mechanics, chaos theory, strings or stem cells. Antiquity alone seems to matter. A visitor exits with the feeling that history's clock broke down somewhere during the fourteenth century and that plans for repair, at best, are vague.

In lieu of actual science, bizarre theories under the rubric of 'Islamic science' abound. Sometimes these are proposed by men with considerable technical skill. For example, Sultan Bashiruddin Mahmood, the first director of Pakistan's famous uranium-enrichment plant, the Kahuta Research Laboratory (KRL) near

Islamabad, the principal facility in the nuclear-weapons complex, was given a major national honour for his contribution. This includes having several nuclear-technology patents to his name. In addition, he was one of the chief designers of Pakistan's nuclear-weapons plutonium-production reactor at Khushab. For many years, Mahmood also ran the Holy Koran Research Foundation in Islamabad and drew up theories that he claimed to be founded in Islamic wisdom. He argued, for example, that capturing heavenly genies (said to be made out of fire by God) would provide the ideal fuel for solving Pakistan's energy problems. Mahmood and I had an acrimonious public debate in 1988 after he published his book *Mechanics of Doomsday and Life after Death*, in which he discussed the physics of souls and their electromagnetic properties. After 9/11, he shot into worldwide prominence upon the discovery of his contacts with the Taliban and Osama bin Laden.

It is not just science that stands in such poor health today. In a stunning indictment of the state of the Arab world, the *Arab Human Development Report 2002*, written by Arab intellectuals and released in Cairo, concluded that Arab societies are crippled by a lack of political freedom and knowledge. High-quality, mind-opening education is virtually non-existent. Half of all Arab women cannot read or write. The facts point to a bleak situation: 'The entire Arab world translates about 330 books annually, one-fifth the number that Greece translates,' says the survey. It adds that in the thousand years since the reign of the Caliph Maa'moun the Arabs have translated as many books as Spain translates in just one year.

The 2003 report was no less scathing: 'Almost all Arab countries have relinquished important knowledge-intensive aspects of oil production to foreign firms,' say the authors. 'The consequences of this abdication are severe.' They note that the divide between Arab countries and knowledge-based societies continues to widen.

Closer to home: in Pakistan, the commonly referred to 'crisis' of higher education understates the situation. Pakistan's public (and all but a handful of private) universities are intellectual rubble; their degrees of little consequence. With a population of 150 million, Pakistan has fewer than twenty computer scientists of sufficient calibre even to have a chance of getting tenure-track faculty positions at some B-grade US university. In physics, even if one roped in every good physicist in the country, it would still not be possible to staff one single proper department of physics. Mathematics is yet more impoverished: to claim that there are even five able mathematicians in Pakistan would be exaggerating their numbers. According to the Pakistan Council for Science and Technology, Pakistanis have succeeded in registering only eight patents internationally in fifty-seven years. The state of the social sciences is scarcely better.

Not surprisingly, the teaching of modern science in schools and universities in Muslim countries (Iran, Turkey, and Malaysia are exceptions) is generally very different from that in Western countries. Students are brought up to respect authority uncritically, and efficiently memorize and reproduce formulae and facts, as if they were scripture. (For some, this is their only skill.) Many of my department's graduate students write the magical inscription '786' on their exam sheets; others spend long hours praying before examinations. The general ambience in educational institutions has become progressively more conservative. A first-time visitor to my university's physics department in Islamabad (reputedly the best in Pakistan) innocently asked me if this was the Islamic studies department. He had good reason to be confused: young burqa-clad women students were chanting something (actually, formulae for a physics test) with only their eyes visible from behind all-enveloping black shrouds. Instructions affixed to the walls specify the proper prayer to use while ascending and descending the stairs; sayings of the Prophet have been posted all around; and there is scarcely anything related to physics on the noticeboards.

Iran and Turkey offer some relief in an otherwise bleak situation. Their universities and schools appear to be qualitatively better, and scientific research more fruitful and advanced. Nevertheless, flipping through scientific journals one seldom encounters a Muslim name. Muslims are conspicuous by their absence from the world of ideas and scholarship. Professor Abdus Salam became a notable exception when, together with Americans Steven Weinberg and Sheldon Glashow, he won the Nobel Prize for physics in 1979. Salam was a remarkable man, in love with his country and religion. But although he was born a Muslim, he died a non-Muslim because the Ahmadi sect to which he belonged was expelled from Islam by an act of the Pakistani Parliament in 1974.

The frequent exhortations and unprecedented attention to science and technology in Pakistan, as well as some parts of the Muslim world, are welcome. But will they work?

Noticeably absent is the call for critical thinking, scepticism, and the scientific method. But here lies the crux of the problem: science is about ideas, the flight of the imagination, and the unsparing rigour of logic and empirical testing. It is not primarily about resources for laboratories and equipment. The most powerful engines of science – mathematics and theoretical physics – are also the most parsimonious and undemanding of resources. Yet, with only modest exceptions, theoretical and foundational science is all but gone from Islamic lands. It is already evident that the huge science budget increase in Pakistan is also leading to massive wastage. Clearly money and resources are a relatively small part of the solution. We need to probe deeper.

A Brilliant Past That Vanished

Unlike the native peoples of South America or Africa, Muslims have a rich history of contributing to science and, to an extent, technology as well. Martians visiting Earth in the Golden Age of

Islam, between the ninth and thirteenth centuries, would surely have reported back to headquarters that the only people doing decent work in science, philosophy or medicine were Muslims. Muslims not only preserved the ancient learning of the Greeks, they also made substantial innovations. Science flourished in the Golden Age because of a strong rationalist and liberal tradition, carried on by a group of Muslim thinkers known as the Mutazilites. To the extent that they were able to dominate the traditionalists, progress was rapid. But in the twelfth century, Muslim orthodoxy reawakened, spearheaded by the Arab cleric Imam Al-Ghazali, who championed revelation over reason, and predestination over free will. Al-Ghazali damned mathematics as hostile to Islam; an intoxicant of the mind that weakened faith. Caught in the iron grip of orthodoxy, Islam eventually choked. The bin Ladens and Mullah Omars of antiquity levelled the impressive edifice of Islamic cultural and scientific achievements. For petty doctrinal reasons, zealots persecuted and hounded those very Muslim scholars to whom Islamic civilization owes much of its former brilliance and greatness. Al-Kindi was whipped in public by a fanatical sultan and blinded; Al-Razi and Ibn Sina escaped numerous charges of blasphemy and attempts upon their lives; and Ibn Rushd was exiled and had his books burned. It was also the end of tolerance, intellect, and science in the Muslim world.

Meanwhile, the rest of the world moved on. The Renaissance brought an explosion of scientific enquiry in the West. This owed much to translations of Greek works carried out by Arabs, as well as original Muslim contributions in science, medicine, and philosophy. But the age of Arab cultural vitality and military dominance was on the way out. Mercantile capitalism and technological progress drove Western countries, in ways that were often brutal and at times genocidal, to colonize the Muslim world rapidly from Indonesia to Morocco.

The Rise and Fall of Muslim Modernization

The nineteenth and early-twentieth centuries saw a modest revival of efforts to bring science back into Islam. It had become clear, at least to a part of the Muslim elites in colonized countries, that they were paying a heavy price for not possessing the analytical tools of modern science and the associated social and political values of modern culture. Therefore, despite resistance from the orthodox, the logic of modernity found nineteenth-century Muslim adherents. Modernizers such as Mohammed Abduh and Rashid Rida of Egypt, Sayyed Ahmad Khan of India, and Jamaluddin Afghani (who belonged everywhere) wished to adapt Islam to the times, interpret the Koran in ways consistent with modern science, and discard the Hadith (ways of the Prophet) in favour of the Koran. Others seized on the modern idea of the nation state.

When new nation states emerged in the twentieth century, not a single leader was a fundamentalist. Turkey's Kemal Atatürk, Algeria's Ahmed Ben Bella, Indonesia's Sukarno, Pakistan's Muhammad Ali Jinnah, Egypt's Gamal Abdel Nasser, and Iran's Mohammed Mosaddeq all sought to organize their societies on the basis of secular values. However, Muslim and Arab nationalism, part of a larger anti-colonial nationalist current across the developing world, included the desire to control and deploy national resources for domestic benefit.

The conflict with Western greed was inevitable. Indeed, America's foes during the 1950s and 1960s were precisely these secular nationalists. Mosaddeq, who opposed Standard Oil's grab at Iran's oil resources, was removed by a CIA coup. Sukarno, accused of being a communist, was overthrown by US intervention, with a resulting bloodbath that consumed about eight hundred thousand lives. Nasser, who had Islamic fundamentalists like Sayyid Qutb publicly executed, fell foul of the USA and Britain after the Suez Crisis. On the other hand, until 9/11, America's friends were the sheikhs of Saudi Arabia and the Gulf states, all of whom practised highly conservative forms of Islam, but were strongly favoured by Western oil interests. Pressed from outside, corrupt and incompetent from within, secular Muslim governments proved unable to defend national interests or deliver social justice. Such failures left a vacuum that Islamic religious movements grew to fill – in Iran, Pakistan, and Sudan, to name a few. The times had begun to change, but what was only a trot became a gallop in 1979 when Ronald Reagan's America entered a final stage of Cold War hostilities with the Soviet Union, aided by Pakistan and Saudi Arabia, who helped bring in some of the fiercest, most ideologically hardened Islamic warriors from around the Arab world.

After the Soviet Union collapsed, the United States walked away from an Afghanistan in shambles. The Taliban emerged; Osama bin Laden and his Al-Qaeda made Afghanistan their base. September 11th followed. The subsequent vengeance extracted by the USA against Afghanistan, Iraq, and Palestine was radically to change the relationship of Islam with the West. The two Gulf Wars, televised in exultant detail, revealed the Arabs as a crippled, powerless mass.

When Israeli bulldozers levelled entire neighbourhoods of Jenin and Rafah, and American soldiers tortured and sexually abused the inmates of Abu Ghraib, Arabs could do no more than impotently rail at their enemies. The lure of Islamic fundamentalism provided an escape from bitter realities and the promise of ultimate victory. The modernization and secularization of Muslim countries, which had seemed inevitable just a half-century ago, has been indefinitely postponed in the wake of 9/11, and particularly the latest conflict in Iraq. Many in the Muslim world ascribe these reversals solely to America's imperial actions (and, earlier, those of Europe). But this is only one contributing factor, albeit an important one. The extreme difficulty of adapting to a post-Renaissance, knowledge-based society is also due to a belief system that is remarkably resistant to change.

Will it Rain if you Pray?

Questions hovering over science and Islam will not go away. Take the issue of miracles: does God suspend the laws of physics in response to the actions of human beings? Following the lead of Renaissance thinkers, Muslim reformers of the nineteenth century, such as Sayyed Ahmad Khan, argued that miracles must be understood in broad allegorical terms rather than literally. Following the Mutazilite tradition, they insisted on an interpretation of the Koran that was in conformity with the observed truths of science, thereby doing away with such commonly held beliefs as the Great Flood and Adam's descent from heaven. It was a risky proposition, and one that has been wilfully forgotten in our times.

Miracles of all sorts continue to be sought. For example, whenever there is a drought in Pakistan, every head of state from General Zia-ul-Haq to General Pervez Musharraf, together with their governors and chief ministers, have joined with the *ulema* in asking the public to come out in large numbers and perform the prescribed *namaz-i-istisqa* (prayer for rain). Millions comply.

My allusion to this issue in a seminar where I described rain as a physical process uninfluenced by divine forces drew an angry reaction from a professor who is also an influential religious authority at the Lahore University of Management Sciences, possibly the most liberal university in Pakistan. All students received an email, part of which is reproduced below:

The fact that rainfall sometimes is caused in response to prayers is a matter of human experience. Although I cannot narrate an incident directly, I know [this] from the observations of people who would not exaggerate. The problem is that Dr Hoodbhoy has narrowed down his mind to be influenced by only those facts that could be explained by the cause-and-effect relationship. That's a classic example of academic prejudice . . . our world is not running on the principle of a causal relationship. It is running the way it is being run by its Master. Man has discovered that, generally speaking, the physical phenomena of our world follow the principle of cause and effect. However, that may not always happen, because the One who is running it has never committed Himself to stick to that principle.

I responded with the following points:

1. Dr Zaheer admits that he has never personally witnessed rainfall in consequence to prayers, but confidently states that this is 'a matter of human experience' because he thinks some twenty-one others have seen unusual things happen. Well, there are people who are willing to swear on oath that they have seen Elvis's ghost. Others claim that they have seen UFOs, horned beasts, apparitions, and the dead arise. Without disputing that some of these people might be sincere and honest, I must emphasize that science cannot agree to this methodology. There is no limit to the power of people's imagination. Unless these mysterious events are recorded on camera, we cannot accept them as factual occurrences.

2. Rain is a physical process (evaporation, cloud formation, nucleation, and condensation). It is complicated, because the atmospheric motion of gases needs many variables for a proper description. However, it obeys exactly the same physical laws as deduced by looking at gases in a cylinder, falling bodies, and so forth. Personally I would be most interested to know whether prayers can also cause the reversal of much simpler kinds of physical processes. For example, can a stone be made to fall upwards instead of downwards? Or can heat be made to flow from a cold body to a hot body by appropriate spiritual prompting? If prayers can cause rain to fall from a blue sky, then all physics and all science deserves to be trashed.

3. I am afraid that the track record for Dr Zaheer's point of view on rain is not very good. Saudi Arabia remains a desert in spite of its evident holiness, and the poor peasants of Sind have a terrible time with drought in spite of their simplicity and piety. Geography, not earnestness of prayer, appears to be the determining factor.

4. Confidence in the cause-and-effect relationship is indeed the very foundation of science and, as a scientist, I fully stand by it.

Press the letter 'T' on your keyboard and the same letter appears on the screen; step on the accelerator and your car accelerates; jump out of a window and you get hurt; put your hand on a stove and you get burned. Those who doubt cause and effect do so at great personal peril.

5. Dr Zaheer is correct in saying that many different people (not just Muslims alone) believe they can influence physical events by persuading a divine authority. Indeed, in the specific context of rain-making, we have several examples. Native Americans had their very elaborate dances to please the Rain God; people of the African bush tribes beat drums and chant; and orthodox Hindus plead with Ram through spectacular *yagas* with hundreds of thousands of the faithful. Their methods seem a little odd to me, but I wonder if Dr Zaheer wishes to accord them respect and legitimacy.

Can Islam and Science Live Together Again?

The reader who wishes to get to the bottom line will be disappointed. There is no universally accepted answer, and there cannot be one. Unlike Christianity, in Islam there is no Vatican and no Pope. In the absence of a central authority, Muslims have greater flexibility to decide on theological and doctrinal issues.

The questions posed above can be asked of any religion. For

purposes of discussion, it is useful to split every religion into four components. Science has no problem with the first three – they are matters of faith and individual choice:

1. *Metaphysical:* This relates to the particular beliefs of religion. Every faith has specific positions on issues such as monotheism and polytheism, death and reincarnation, heaven and hell, prophets and holy men, and rituals and relics.

2. *Ethical and moral:* Religions have a specific prescription of how individuals are expected to order their lives and why they have been brought into being. Conversely, science offers no guidance in determining right from wrong, and does not provide a reason for the existence of individuals or the human race. It is silent on eugenics or cloning, and polygamy or polyandry.

3. *Inspirational and emotional:* Marmaduke Pickthall, who translated the Koran into English, wrote of how the melody of its verses could move men to tears. Abdus Salam, transfixed by the symmetry of Lahore's Badshahi Mosque, said that it inspired him to think of the famous $SU(2) \times U(1)$ symmetry that revolutionized the world of particle physics.

4. *Beliefs about the physical world:* There is a definite problem here: taken literally, the texts of all religions lead to a description of physical reality that belongs to antiquity and is definitely at odds with modern science. The issues are well known: the origin of life, non-material beings such as spirits and genies, geocentricity, the nature of comets and meteors, and miracles such as the Great Flood and the parting of the Red Sea.

Let us provisionally accept the argument that the religious impulse propelled science in Muslim civilization in its Golden Age through requirements such as accurate determination of prayer times, sightings of the moon, directions of the *qibla* and of Mecca, quantitative application of Muslim inheritance laws, and so forth. But in the age of the globalized positioning system, atomic clocks, and computers, it is difficult to point to religious imperatives for scientific progress.

If Muslim societies are to escape their ice age then they must accept modernity – which should not be confused with Westernization – as desirable, and welcome the role of science, reason, and universal principles of law and justice in the arbitration of human affairs. Scarcity of material resources is not the primary issue and cannot be used as an excuse for arrested development. It will be crucial to allow dogmas to be challenged without incurring the charges of heresy and blasphemy. Muslims must understand that there is no alternative now to respecting personal freedom of thought, encouraging artistic and scientific creativity, cultivating a compulsive urge to innovate and experiment, and making education a vehicle of change.

Is a Muslim Renaissance Around the Corner?

'Now Muslim leaders are planning [science's] revival and hope to restore a golden age,' says Ziauddin Sardar, writer on Islam and contemporary cultural and scientific issues, in an optimistic article published recently in the *New Statesman*. Brave words, but I can see no visible evidence of significant collective activity, much less steps towards a 'golden age'. Visiting the websites of the Islamic Academy of Sciences (IAS), the Islamic Education, Scientific and Cultural Organization (ISESCO) and the Organization of the Islamic Conference Standing Committee on Scientific and Technological Co-operation (COMSTECH), one learns that the sum of their combined activities over the last decade amount to sporadic conferences on disparate subjects, a handful of research and travel grants, and pitifully small sums for repair of equipment and spare parts. Lavish conferences have become an annual feature in Islamabad, with routine exhortations to develop science and technology for the *ummah*.

At the level of individual countries, there is more promise. An extraordinarily dynamic individual, Dr Atta-ur-Rahman, when he was Pakistan's Minister for Science and Technology, was able to persuade the Government to increase his ministry's budget over a three-year period by a whopping factor of 60 (6,000 per cent) and the higher education budget by 12 (1,200 per cent). In consequence, a large human-resource development plan for training teachers and researchers has been launched; internet connectivity in Pakistan has been substantially expanded; infra-structural improvements in universities and research institutions have been made; and a huge increase in faculty salaries is in the pipeline. Pakistan may well be unique: when I asked Dr Rahman, who also heads COMSTECH, if any of his ministerial counter-parts in other Muslim countries felt a similar sense of urgency, he sadly shook his head.

Creationism: No Offence?

Andrew Berry

Surveys show that some hundred million Americans think that humans appeared, more or less fully formed, sometime in the past ten thousand years. There's no doubting that the creationist movement has been spectacularly successful in foisting its cocktail of medieval theology and modern anti-intellectualism on to a supposedly educated public. From my perspective as an evolutionary biologist, this is first and foremost simply bewildering. How is it possible for so supremely irrational a world view to flourish in the face of mountains of simple, clear, and unambiguously contradictory evidence? But it's also deeply disturbing. It reveals both the deficiencies of American science education and the power and extent of a movement whose message goes far beyond a simple denial of Darwin. Creationism is part of a package of 'family values' that promotes discrimination – homophobia, for example – and lies at the heart of America's ongoing we-know-what's-best-for-you experiment in imperialism.

The US is famously good at exporting itself – think of Japanese teenagers wearing 'Coke is It' T-shirts on their visit to the Hiroshima Memorial. And there are alarming signs now that creationism is entering its export phase. Fundamentalism – and the holy-book literalism that comes with it – is after all not just an American phenomenon: creationism has pan-fundamentalist appeal. In Turkey, for example, a well-funded creationist organization proselytizes, via glossily produced translations of the American anti-Darwin literature, effecting in the process a surprising alliance between fundamentalist Christianity and Islam. (The same

Turkish organization also puts out Holocaust-denial tracts.) At the end of a public lecture on Darwinism in Istanbul, I was once asked, 'Dr Berry, why have you dedicated your life to a lie?' Europe, which happily seems to have expended most of its religious anti-science venom in the Copernicus/Galileo era, is a tougher nut for creationism to crack. But, despite the traditional British suspicion of America's enthusiasms, creationism is making inroads even in the UK. And there's a danger that the import process will be massively aided by the proposed 'Incitement to Religious Hatred' legislation. Creationists, as will become clear below, are adept at exploiting the smallest of legal loopholes, but the incitement law hardly qualifies as a loophole: it's an invitation. Will there come a day when my teaching the basics of evolutionary biology is construed, by the law, to be an incitement to religious hatred?

When I first crossed the Atlantic years ago to begin postgraduate work in evolutionary biology, part of the thrill actually lay in the prospect of encountering real live creationists. They seemed exotic. We didn't have them in the UK – at least, not in the educational mainstream I came from. So I made a point of listening to the stories told by more experienced colleagues – tales of clashes, often in the middle of a lecture, between creationist students and their biology lecturers. Some students, I learned, are primed and ready, coming to lectures clasping bibles. Some prefer not to rely on biblical authority but trot out instead the latest creationist 'research' – like the fossils that supposedly show that dinosaurs and antediluvian humans once trod the earth side by side – that 'disproves' evolution.

Others are genuinely taken aback: so sheltered has their Bible-belt upbringing been that they have no idea that alternatives to the Genesis account exist. Some form of backlash follows. Some come out of their corner swinging, thumping notional bibles and insisting on the authority of the Word of God. Others suffer a quiet theological meltdown. They have been raised both to view the Bible as the only source of unimpeachable truth and, in good conservative fashion, to respect the wisdom of their teachers. This isn't a problem when the teachers and the source of unimpeachable truth are in agreement with each other, which, remarkably, is often the case until the students reach university. Then comes the parting of the ways. The reconciliation of the conflict can be tough. Some find themselves questioning the authority of the Bible – if its opening salvo is demonstrably *wrong*, then maybe the rest of it is equally dubious – and suddenly their entire moral universe is in tatters. There's something mildly surreal about the scene. With those plastic flip-down seats and the banks of quietly buzzing fluorescent lights, science lecture theatres are inappropriate venues for anti-spiritual epiphanies. And academic evolutionary biologists are definitely inappropriate mentors for those struggling to cope with the moral and theological fallout entailed by a catastrophic loss of faith. The lecture drones on – more detail on the action of natural selection on the wing colour of moths – as a young woman in the middle of the audience weeps.

It is the fundamentalists who promote the unnecessary either-every-word-of-the-Bible-is-literally-true-or-none-is dichotomy that is so painfully apparent to our weeping student. The irony is that the creationist position actually harms the institutions it aspires to defend. By courtesy of her encounter with a set of simple scientific facts, our young woman may disavow her faith altogether. Had she instead been raised in the more accommodating traditions characteristic of Christianity in Europe (in 1996, even that icon of social conservatism John Paul II gave evolution a limited papal thumbs-up), her faith would have survived. Science is fatal to belief only when belief is brittle.

Sad to say, my vision of grappling heroically on the frontline of science versus bigotry was way off the mark. For a start, I have taught mainly at academically elite east coast universities where creationists tend to be sparse and to favour a low profile. Second, universities, even in the Bible belt, are not on the frontline: it's high-school science teachers who are Darwin's foot soldiers, not high-falutin' university lecturers. As in the UK, you typically learn about evolution in the US in school. What's remarkable is the number of students who make it all the way through high school in certain regions of the US *without* being taught about the central principle of all biology – the principle that glues together the diverse and complex strands of a science that embraces everything from the biochemistry of bacteria through to the nature of human consciousness. Maybe the science teacher is a creationist and decides not to teach the material; maybe the local school board, a set of elected officials usually with no particular expertise in education, has decreed that evolution should not be taught; or maybe – and I think this is the overwhelming cause of evolution omission in American classrooms – pressure, whether from school administrators or from parents and pupils, on teachers results in the topic being skipped.

The extent to which American science teachers are bearing the brunt of the creationist onslaught is revealed by a recent poll conducted by the National Science Teachers Association. Some thirty per cent of teachers 'feel pressured to include creationism, Intelligent Design [a currently voguish form of creationism], or other alternatives to evolution in their science classroom' and/or to 'de-emphasize or omit evolution or evolution-related topics from their curriculum'.[1] And that pressure can be nasty. One teacher reports a typical experience: 'I had a parent come in and basically said I was going to spend an eternity in hell, if I taught her kids about evolution.'[2] Creationists are not averse to strong-arm tactics, and will happily resort to physical intimidation should it

1 National Science Teachers Association, reported in *USA Today*, 23 March 2005: http://www.usatoday.com/news/education/2005-03-23-evolution_x.htm
2 PBS *Newshour*, 28 March 2005: http://www.pbs.org/newshour/bb/education/jan-june05/creation_3-28.html

become necessary – after all, theirs is the highest calling and all means are justified in pursuit of so exalted an end. Ian Plimer, an Australian geologist, recalls in his exposé of creationism, *Telling Lies for God*, a lecture in Sydney on Noah's Ark. The organizers had brought their own security personnel to deal with hecklers. One sceptical scientist was successfully evicted after trying to ask a question. Then 'the curator of palaeontology at the Australian Museum, Dr Alex Ritchie, attempted to ask a question and, again, the black-shirted goons moved in and tried to remove him. Dr Ritchie enjoys a generous physique and, despite physical violence from the hired thugs, he was immovable . . . the meeting erupted into chaos.'[3]

Pressure can be indirect as well. In the US, Imax big-screen movie theatres are typically associated with science centres and are therefore heavily involved in public education. But even public science education must bow before Mammon, and operators must balance educational and commercial considerations. As a result, a number of Imax films, notably recent ones on volcanoes and on the Galapagos, are not carried by some theatres because the films mention the 'E word', evolution, and this is known to impair box office performance.[4] I suspect this form of economic boycott – which got an early outing in the mid-nineties when the Disney Corporation did the unthinkable in extending insurance benefits to employees' same-sex partners – will become an ever more popular tactic with the religious Right over coming years.

The heart and soul of creationism lies in America's southern and central reaches – what, since the 2004 presidential election, we know as the red states. The statistics are extraordinary: a 2001 poll reports that 48% of Americans identify themselves as

3 Ian Plimer, *Telling Lies for God: Reason vs Creationism*, Random House, Australia, 1994, p. 178.
4 Cornelia Dean, 'A new test for Imax', *New York Times*, 19 March 2005.

creationists; only 28% consider themselves evolutionists; the remainder, in true poll style, are 'undecided'.[5] Mr Bush himself thinks that 'children ought to be exposed to different theories about how the world started.'[6] That other prominent Texas Republican Tom DeLay declared after the Columbine High School massacre that he had identified the cause of the moral decay of American society: '. . . our school systems teach our children that they are nothing but glorified apes who have evolutionized out of some primordial soup of mud, by teaching evolution as fact.'[7]

In general, non-Americans are much less creationism-prone. In other industrialized countries, 80% typically accept evolution, with most of the remaining 20% taken up with 'not sures'. Even a socially conservative, Catholic country like Poland can boast a 75% evolution-acceptance rate.[8] But, as we've seen, creationism is definitely on the march, struggling to gain a foothold in the world beyond those red states. Even the UK is these days not immune. *Private Eye*, not traditionally the friend of the loony religious, recently published a letter from a creationist sent in response to a review of a book by Richard Dawkins.[9]

The factors underlying this triumph of anti-science are many and complex – a messy mix of sociology and history. There are, however, a couple of institutional considerations which I think have played important roles: the decentralized nature of Ameri-

5 Raja Mishra, 'Evolution foes see opening to press fight in schools', *Boston Globe*, 16 November 2004.
6 Cited at: http://www.interventionmag.com/cms/modules.php?op=modload &name=News&file=article&sid=933
7 Cited in: Chet Raymo, 'Darwin's Dangerous De-Evolution', *Boston Globe*, 6 September 1999.
8 Cornelia Dean, 'Evolution takes a back seat in US classes', *New York Times*, 1 February 2005.
9 *Private Eye*, 26 November 2004.

can government, and creationism's ability to evolve in response to legal and other challenges.

A lot of American educational policy is set at the regional level: individual towns may, for example, prescribe their own curricular priorities through an elected school board. To be elected to the school board, you don't have to have credentials as an educator or even a working knowledge of curricular requirements; it's essentially just another political position. School boards pop up regularly with a creationist axe to grind. They will mandate 'equal time' teaching (evolution taught on an equal footing with alternatives) in their schools. They will require that biology textbooks carry a sticker proclaiming that evolution is 'just a theory'. They will insist that the anodyne 'change over time' is used in class as a substitute for the 'E word' . . .

More often than not, it's the oldest failing of democracy in the book that's responsible: rule of the motivated few over the apathetic many. Because – courtesy of the either-every-word-of-the-Bible-is-literally-true-or-none-is syndrome – the issue is of such supreme importance to fundamentalists, they are willing to invest the time and effort required to succeed in local elections. The rest of us? Well, we hardly pay attention to the school-board election; we've got plenty of other things to worry about. It's only once the school board is elected and in place that apathy gives way to activism in the non-creationist ranks. Creationist-dominated school boards are typically not re-elected, even in the deepest reaches of the Bible belt. But by then the damage has been done: curricular changes initiated, publicity for the movement garnered. Across the US in 2004 alone, there were ongoing challenges to the teaching of evolution in *thirteen* states. It's these repeated brush fires – plenty of smoke, even if the curriculum ultimately emerges unscathed, though perhaps a little sooty – that inspire and stoke the fundamentalist cause. They give creationists across the country a sense of belonging to a grand, heroic movement.

A Pennsylvania Republican senator, Rick Santorum, tried to insert an anti-evolution rider into the Bush administration's federal education bill, dubbed 'No Child Left Behind'. Santorum's language was mild by the standards of local- or state-level creationist initiatives but it nevertheless provoked a furious response, with more than eighty science-advocacy groups decrying the effort.[10] A non-scientific science-education policy might play well on the local stage, but it is unlikely to thrive in the bright lights of centre stage.

Also critical to the success of creationism in the US has been its ability to 'evolve'. Legal setbacks have necessitated changes of tactic and a movement whose *raison d'être* is an inflexible insistence on what in fundamentalist circles is termed 'biblical inerrancy' has proved remarkably protean. Indeed, creationists might consider adopting as their motto 'Adapt or Die'.

Key to creationism's ability to adapt is the diversity of beliefs the movement enfolds. It's not monolithic; rather, it's weirdly pluralistic. Young Earth creationists, for example, believe the earth is less than ten thousand years old (for believers, the most reliable estimate of its actual age is derived from totting up the ages of all the Old Testament patriarchs). Flood creationists think that Noah's flood is responsible in one cataclysmic stroke for the fossil and geological records. Steady-state creationists doubt that there has been any turnover in the species inhabiting earth, assuming that fossils are, each one, mineralogical miracles unrelated to actual life forms. Old Earth creationists are willing to admit that the earth is older than ten thousand years but may still insist on the fixity of species – the Earth is old but everything on it is exactly as it was created.

During the seventies and eighties, much of the creationist emphasis was on 'equal time', the argument that 'alternative' theories of creation and evolutionary ones deserve equal time in

10 See http://www.pfaw.org/pfaw/general/default.aspx?oid=3636&print=yes

the classroom. That was until 1987, when, in the landmark case of *Edwards* v. *Aguillard*, the US Supreme Court struck down a 1981 Louisiana law mandating equal time for 'creation science'. The court's rationale was simple: creation science isn't science, it's religion. And the separation of Church and State that is so central to US constitutional law prohibits the teaching of religion in state schools. This was a major blow to the US creationist movement, but not a fatal one. Time to evolve. Creationists seized on a statement in the legal opinion delivered with the decision: that broaching 'a variety of scientific theories' about evolution was within the law when there is 'clear secular intent of enhancing the effectiveness of science instruction'. Hence the latest incarnation of creationism, intelligent design (ID). 'Secular' means that there can be no mention of God, and the theory must at least *look* 'scientific'. IDism rose from the ashes of creationism's most stinging recent defeat. Now that ID is being peddled widely by creationists – most of those thirteen 2004 challenges to evolution were ID-based – it too will eventually be defanged by the law. Then creationism will evolve again.

ID is decried by many old-school creationists on the grounds that it lurches too close for comfort to generic Darwinism. ID's careful non-mention of God allows it to pretend to be science. A flimsy claim to sciencehood, admittedly, but it is definitely more scientific-seeming than some of its predecessors in the pantheon of creationism's torch-bearers. ID does not, for example, indulge in lengthy and convoluted attempts to reconcile the biblically specified size of Noah's ark with the tricky problem of accommodating two of all of creation. The argument nevertheless is an old one, one addressed by Darwin in *On the Origin of Species*: that it's difficult to conceive scenarios whereby certain complex characteristics evolved. If evolution isn't up to the job, then a Designer (aka God, but you'd never catch an IDist using the G word) must by default be responsible. For Darwin, the test case was the eye: what use is half an eye? Given that an eye cannot plausibly evolve by Darwinian means in a single mega-evolutionary step, Darwin's question is an important one: how can a complex and obviously useful organ evolve if incomplete versions of itself – evolutionary intermediates – are useless? It turns out that an incomplete eye – incomplete, that is, from the perspective of the fully evolved vertebrate eye – is in fact not useless. It can be a very useful thing for organisms that don't need the full functionality of our eye. Some species, for example, need only to be able to detect the presence of light; others need only to be able to detect movement. IDists prefer to focus on the molecular level – dealing with biochemical pathways, not eyes – but the argument is exactly the same as the one that Darwin addressed. And the solution to the problem – that intermediates are (or were, in the evolutionary past) adaptive – is equally applicable.

For a long time, creationism was very marginal indeed in Britain. For twenty years from the mid-fifties, the wonderfully named Evolution Protest Movement run by Albert Tilney, who has been described as 'a theologically dogmatic and scientifically illiterate schoolmaster and pastor', was very much 'a one-man band'.[11] Things, however, have moved on since the Revd Tilney's demise in 1976. The success of the evangelical movement has seen a resurgence of biblical literalism. The efforts of the Thatcher and Blair Governments to encourage entrepreneurial investment in education, through business–government partnerships, have permitted the intrusion of American-style creationism into some British classrooms. The Blair scheme, City Academies, seems to involve giving more control of a school's curriculum and practices to sponsors than is warranted by the size of the investment alone. Presumably, the sponsors have to feel they are getting something

11 Ronald L. Numbers, *The Creationists: The Evolution of Scientific Creationism*, Knopf, 1992, p. 323.

for their money – and the cheapest and easiest thing to let them have is the hearts and souls of the pupils. As the *Guardian* put it, 'The idea is roughly this: for a fee of £2m – payable in random instalments – private benefactors are handed effective control of brand-new state schools, although the taxpayer meets the lion's share of both building and running costs.'[12]

Sir Peter Vardy, a millionaire car-dealer and fundamentalist Christian based in the North-East, has seized upon the opportunity to convert his cash into cohorts of indoctrinated school-children. The schools his foundation funds are required to follow the national curriculum, but they may also teach additional material as stipulated by each school's governors (themselves largely appointed by Vardy). There is nothing in British law that prohibits the teaching of creationism and creationism is taught in the Vardy schools.

It's possible that the Vardy experiment will remain just that, and creationism will never gain a significant foothold in the UK. Two factors, however, currently hint at the possibility that it is the beginning of something significant – and disturbing.

Whatever success the forces of the Enlightenment have had in damping down the fires of creationism in the US has typically depended upon an American constitutional peculiarity not shared with the UK. The separation of Church and State is fiercely defended in the US, and has traditionally provided the legal wherewithal for cleansing the classroom (State) of creationism (Church). No such legal recourse exists in the UK, so in principle a concerted creationist campaign will be more difficult to stop here than in the US. Second, the anti-incitement legislation may make creationism a protected species in the eyes of British law. If my religion insists that God created the planet and all its habitants over the course of a week in October 4004 BC (as has been computed from biblical evidence), and you go around

12 John Harris, 'What a creation . . .', *Guardian*, 15 January 2005.

claiming that the planet is in fact rather older and that species are related to each other genealogically, aren't you inciting religious hatred? You're certainly upsetting me, and, with access to the right kind of slick fundamentalist lawyer, I reckon I could convince a court that you're inciting my classmates to sneer at my religion . . . to religious hatred. This might all sound far-fetched, but, as we've seen, a key feature of the creationist movement is its ability to widen and exploit the smallest of chinks in a legal dyke. Today we are dealing with the outcome of one of those opportunistic exercises in chink-widening: the flood of IDism is born of the creationist response to the Supreme Court's *Edwards* v. *Aguillard* decision. Creationism – true to its Adapt or Die credo – has adapted.

Blair's anti-incitement legislation, however noble its intentions, is a gift to the creationists. It would create a legal climate positively conducive to the movement's growth. Before we know it, British courts will find themselves revisiting the American experience of fundamentalist-sponsored legal challenges to the teaching of evolution. Only there will be a difference: British courts will not be able to invoke legislation mandating the separation of Church and State and will find themselves additionally hamstrung by anti-incitement laws hijacked by creationists for their own purposes. Fundamentalism – whether Bush-style or Osama-style – is blighting our world. Creationism is a core part of the either-every-word-of-the-Bible-is-literally-true-or-none-is fundamentalist package, and we should make every effort to thwart its agenda as it tries to worm its way into our classrooms. But the anti-incitement legislation promises to do exactly the reverse: to promote and protect the worst kind of dogmatic, irrational, and divisive bigotry.

Free Speech, Religious Freedom and the Offence of Blasphemy

Anthony Lester, QC[1]

A Moscow court yesterday convicted the director of the Sakharov Museum of inciting religious hatred by organizing a controversial exhibit condemned by the Russian Orthodox Church. Yuri Samodurov was fined $3,600 (US) by the Tagansky district court . . . The 2003 exhibit – titled Caution! Religion! – featured works by about 40 artists, including a Russian Orthodox-style icon with a hole instead of a head where visitors could insert their faces. Another featured a Coca-Cola logo with Jesus Christ's face drawn next to it and the words: 'This is my blood.' [Samodurov] told the Ekho Moskvy radio that the exhibit had provoked an official backlash because 'many of the artists had a critical attitude towards the behaviour of the Russian Orthodox Church.'

(*Toronto Globe and Mail*, 29 March 2005)

It remains our firm and clear intention to give people of all faiths the same protection against incitement to hatred on the basis of their religion. We will legislate to outlaw it and will continue the dialogue we have started with faith groups from all backgrounds about how best to balance protection, tolerance and free speech.

(*New Labour's Election Manifesto*, April 2005)

1 The author is grateful to Alison Hayes, Parliamentary Legal Officer of the Odysseus Trust, for her assistance.

Bringing Human Rights Home

When I came to the Bar, some forty years ago, there was no legally enforceable right to free expression in this country. Free speech was a hallowed British political value, but as a matter of law it had an inferior status, occupying the space left by manifold legal restrictions protecting official secrecy, personal reputation, confidential information, copyright, public decency, public order and the right to a fair trial. Free speech was a weak residuary legatee of the English legal system, an exceptional freedom rather than a positive right.

The legal restraints on free speech are contained both in Acts of Parliament and in the judge-made common law. Until very recently, in the absence of a constitutional Bill of Rights protecting the right to freedom of expression, there was no legally binding standard against which to interpret restrictions upon free speech either in the laws themselves or in the wide powers of censorship vested in ministers and state authorities.

English courts gave too little weight to free speech and too much weight to the restrictions on free speech; and Parliament was indifferent to the lack of effective legal protection and a fair balance. There were no effective remedies for many breaches of the rights of writers, newspapers, broadcasters and the public. English law was ethically aimless because there was no statutory framework to guide the courts in human rights cases. The way the courts gave new life and coercive force to the obsolete crime of blasphemy was a classic example of an outmoded approach to freedom of speech.

In 1966, the Wilson Government decided that complaints of breaches of the European Convention on Human Rights by public authorities of the United Kingdom could be made to the European Commission and Court of Human Rights. I was fortunate to be instructed to use this new forum on behalf of media and other complainants. In free speech cases we relied upon enlightened American Supreme Court case law under the First Amendment to the US Constitution.

We successfully challenged restrictive decisions of the Law Lords trumping free speech unnecessarily: for example the *Sunday Times* prevented by contempt law from publishing articles on the 'Thalidomide' tragedy attributing negligence to the manufacturers and distributors of the drug which caused gross foetal abnormality;[2] Harriet Harman found guilty of contempt for giving the *Guardian* Home Office documents about prison conditions that had been read out in open court;[3] and the press for publishing in breach of government confidentiality extracts from *Spycatcher: The Candid Autobiography of a Senior Intelligence Officer* alleging wrongdoing by MI5. The Law Lords restrained the press from publishing in the UK even though the book was freely available in the United States.[4] We also obtained a ruling from the European Court that the award of £1.5 million damages against Count Nicholai Tolstoy Miloslavsky for a libel on Lord Aldington was excessive.[5] A pamphlet written by Tolstoy and entitled 'War Crimes and the Wardenship of Winchester College' had been circulated to parents, boys, staff and former members of the school as well as to MPs. It accused Lord Aldington of being a major war criminal for his role in 1945 in the handing over to the Soviet Union of some seventy thousand Cossack and Yugoslav prisoners of war and refugees, most of whom were subsequently massacred. In other landmark cases the Strasbourg Court limited Home Office powers of censorship of prisoners' correspondence with the outside world; for example, an Orthodox Jew prevented from seeking dietary guidance from the Chief Rabbi, and a prisoner prevented from writing letters to his mother

2 *Sunday Times* v. *United Kingdom* (1979) 2 EHRR 245.
3 *Harman* v. *United Kingdom* (Application 10038/82) 38 DR 53 (1984) (E.Com HR).
4 *Sunday Times* v. *United Kingdom (No. 2)* (1991) 14 EHRR 14.
5 *Tolstoy Miloslavsky* v. *United Kingdom* (1995) 20 EHRR 442.

because they contained rude language;[6] and prevented criminal and civil libel laws from unnecessarily inhibiting public discussion and debate on issues of public importance.[7]

These cases influenced the Strasbourg jurisprudence favourably, and, in turn, these and other European judgments illuminated the legal philosophy and technique of a new generation of British judges, unhappy at their inability to give direct effect to Convention rights, but willing to do so indirectly. Gradually English courts gave more latitude to free speech and interpreted restrictions on free speech more narrowly. In striking a balance between freedom of expression and competing rights and interests, they referred to case law not only from the Strasbourg Court of Human Rights but also from the Supreme Court of the United States (interpreting the right to free speech in the First Amendment to the US Constitution) and Commonwealth courts in Australia, Canada, India, New Zealand and South Africa.[8]

Most notably, in the *Derbyshire* case,[9] where the local council tried to use libel law against the media, the English Court of Appeal had regard to European, Commonwealth and United States case law in concluding that the Derbyshire County Council, like government departments (as distinct from individual public officers), could not invoke libel law to vindicate their so-called 'governing reputation'. The *Spycatcher* case[10] was another example of English courts using the Convention as a prism through which to view the common law (in that case protecting the

6 *Silver and Others* v. *United Kingdom* (1983) 5 EHRR 347.

7 *Lingens* v. *Austria* (1986) 8 EHRR 407 (criminal libel by a journalist for criticizing Austrian Chancellor Bruno Kreisky's coalition with right-wing parties); *Bladet Tromsø and Stensaas* v. *Norway* (1999) 29 EHRR 125 (civil libel by a Norwegian newspaper for alleging brutal and unlawful conduct by seal hunters).

8 *Reynolds* v. *Times Newspapers Ltd* [2001] 2 AC 127 (HL).

9 *Derbyshire County Council* v. *Times Newspapers Ltd* [1992] QB 770 (CA); [1993] AC 534 (HL).

10 *A-G* v. *Guardian Newspapers Ltd (No. 2)* [1990] 1 AC 109 (HL).

secrecy of government information) to prevent government from unduly limiting freedom of information and debate. The courts began to recognize that public authorities were constitutionally obliged not to interfere unnecessarily with the right of the media to communicate and the right of the public to receive information and opinions on matters of legitimate public concern and importance, especially concerning the workings of government.

But because of the doctrine of parliamentary supremacy, in the absence of any parliamentary mandate for the judicial use of the Convention, there were limits beyond which our courts refused to go. That was especially so where Parliament had delegated broad discretionary powers of censorship to ministers. In *Brind*'s case,[11] we failed to persuade the Law Lords to require the Home Secretary to have regard to the Convention right to free expression when deciding whether to ban broadcasting by Sinn Fein. Since Parliament had not made the Convention part of UK law, the Law Lords decided that they would be usurping Parliament's role in incorporating Convention rights through the back door, when the relevant legislation had given the Home Secretary sweepingly broad powers.

The *Brind* case illustrated the pressing need for a Human Rights Act that would make the Convention rights part of our law and enable our courts to give effective remedies. I campaigned for such a measure for over thirty years, from 1968 onwards. Nineteen sixty-eight was the year in which an executive-controlled Parliament enacted, as an emergency law, a racially motivated statute depriving British Asians who had been made refugees in East Africa of their right to enter and live in the UK. It was a shocking example of John Stuart Mill's description of 'the tyranny of the majority' – a group of citizens used their public powers to

---

11 *R* v. *Secretary of State for the Home Department, ex p. Brind* [1991] 1 AC 696 (HL); but see *R* v. *Secretary of State for the Home Department, ex p. Simms* [2000] 2 AC 115 (HL).

deprive another group of citizens, on racial grounds, of a basic right of citizenship. The victims of this gross abuse of political power had to seek redress in Strasbourg for want of the kind of constitutional remedies available in almost all other democracies.[12] It showed the need to reform our Victorian constitution.

Thirty years later, as part of John Smith's political legacy, Tony Blair's New Labour Government introduced what became the Human Rights Act 1998. That measure is no ordinary law. It gives direct effect to the Convention rights in UK law. It requires all existing and future legislation, so far as possible, to be read and given effect in a way compatible with the Convention rights. It places all public authorities (except the Westminster Parliament) under a duty to act compatibly with the Convention rights. Courts are included in that duty in interpreting and applying both statute law and common law, and are empowered to grant effective remedies against the public authorities of the State.

Freedom of Expression and Religious Freedom Without Discrimination

The Convention rights include both the right to freedom of expression, protected by Article 10, and the right to religious freedom, protected by Article 9. Given the value added by the Convention to the legal protection of free speech in this country, and the successful use of the Convention to strengthen free expression, one might have expected the British media to be among the most enthusiastic supporters of the Human Rights Act. But the Convention also protects the right to respect for private life, and powerful sections of the media campaigned to prevent the Human Rights Act from being used to develop a right of privacy. They even sought a specific immunity to shield themselves. Their campaign resulted in the inclusion of section 12,

12 *East African Asians* v. *United Kingdom* (1973) 3 EHRR 76, E Com HR.

which, happily, gives no immunity but requires the courts to have particular regard to the importance of freedom of expression and the need to avoid unnecessary restrictions by the courts. The tabloids and some right-wing broadsheets have continued to mount ill-informed and unjustifiable attacks on the Human Rights Act, aided and abetted by their suitors in the Conservative Party.

Church organizations also sought special protection against the impact of the Human Rights Act. They persuaded the House of Lords (contrary to the Government's wishes) to approve amendments giving special protection to religious beliefs because of concern that the Bill might otherwise compel churches and their members to engage in acts contrary to their religious principles: for example, in relation to whom they would marry in church, or whom they would employ. The amendments were neither necessary nor appropriate, and were removed by the Commons. Instead, section 13 was included to meet the churches' concerns without compromising the integrity of the Human Rights Act. It sends a signal to the courts that they must pay regard to the rights guaranteed by Article 9, including, where relevant, the right of a church to act in accordance with religious belief.

Article 9 protects the right to freedom of thought and conscience as well as religion. It includes the right to change one's religion or belief and freedom, whether alone or in a community with others, to manifest one's religion or belief in worship, teaching, practice and observance. Freedom to manifest one's religion or belief is subject only to such limitations as are prescribed by law and are necessary in a democratic society in the interests of public safety, for the protection of public order, health or morals, or for the protection of the rights and freedoms of others.

The values of Article 9 are closely related to the right to freedom of expression and freedom of assembly and association. They are at the foundations of a democratic society. The Strasbourg Court has observed of Article 9: 'It is, in its religious dimension, one of the most vital elements that go to make up the identity of believers and their conception of life, but it is also a precious asset for atheists, agnostics, sceptics and the unconcerned.'

Article 10 guarantees the right to freedom of expression, including the right to hold opinions and to receive and impart information and ideas without interference by a public authority. The exercise of these freedoms may be subject to exceptions prescribed by law and those necessary in a democratic society for various purposes including: the prevention of disorder or crime; the protection of health or morals; and the protection of the rights of others (including the right to religious freedom protected by Article 9). Article 10 protects the expression not only of information and ideas which are favourably received but also expressions which would be regarded as offensive and which would offend, shock or disturb the State or any sector of the population.

Article 14 guarantees the enjoyment of Convention rights, including the right to free expression and the right to freedom of thought, conscience and religion, without discrimination.

Two main legal principles are used by the European Court of Human Rights, and now by our own courts, in striking a fair balance between these competing rights and freedoms: the principle of legal certainty and the principle of proportionality. The principle of legal certainty requires the law to be accessible so that the citizen has an adequate indication of the legal rules that apply in a given case.[13] The principle of proportionality requires that:

(a) the aim of a restriction must be sufficiently important (to meet 'a pressing social need') to justify limiting a fundamental right;

13 Lester and Pannick, *Human Rights Law and Practice*, LexisNexis Butterworths, 2nd ed., 2004, paragraph 3.14.

(*b*) the means employed to meet that aim must not be arbitrary or unfair; and

(*c*) the means employed must be necessary to achieve that aim – the more severe the detrimental effects of a measure, the more important the objective must be if the measure is to be justified in a democratic society.[14]

The Offence of Blasphemy – Dead or Alive?

The leading English case on the common law crime of blasphemous libel was decided by the Law Lords in 1979, in the *Gay News* case. By a majority of three to two, and without the benefit of the framework of the Human Rights Act 1998 or full argument on the free speech issues, the Law Lords breathed new life into what had been regarded as an anachronistic and arbitrary relic of Tudor and Stuart times, when draconian powers of censorship had been exercised by the Ecclesiastical Courts and the Court of Star Chamber, until they were taken over by the common law courts. As Lord Diplock (one of the dissenters in the *Gay News* case) observed:

In the post-Restoration politics of seventeenth- and eighteenth-century England, Church and State were thought to stand or fall together. To cast doubt on the doctrines of the established Church or to deny the truth of the Christian faith was to attack the fabric of society itself: so blasphemous and seditious libel were criminal offences that went hand in hand.

Mrs Mary Whitehouse brought a private prosecution against the editor and publishers of *Gay News* alleging that they had 'unlawfully and wickedly published ... a blasphemous libel

14 Ibid., paragraph 3.10.

concerning the Christian religion namely an obscene poem and illustration vilifying Christ in His Life and in His crucifixion'. For the previous fifty years the offence had disappeared from the criminal calendar and was regarded as having become obsolete.

The *Gay News* defendants were tried at the Old Bailey and convicted. The editor was sentenced to nine months' imprisonment, suspended for eighteen months, and fined £500, and the publishers were fined £1000. The Court of Appeal dismissed their appeal, as did the House of Lords.[15]

The poem by James Kirkup was entitled 'The Love that Dares to Speak its Name'. It was accompanied by a drawing illustrating its subject matter. It purported to describe in explicit detail homosexual acts with the body of Christ immediately after his death and to ascribe to him during his lifetime promiscuous homosexual practices with the apostles and other men. Each of the judges who decided the case expressed his profound disgust at the poem's offensive and obscene content.[16]

15 Viscount Dilhorne, Lord Russell of Killowen and Lord Scarman (Lord Diplock and Lord Edmund-Davies dissenting) *R* v. *Lemon* [1979] AC 617 (HL). On 7 May 1982, the European Commission of Human Rights declared an application made by the editor and publisher of *Gay News* to be inadmissible: *Gay News Ltd and Another* v. *United Kingdom* (Application No. 8710/79) 5 EHRR 123. In spite of the Court's repeated reference to the demands of 'pluralism, tolerance and broadmindedness' in a democratic society, this is an area in which the Strasbourg jurisprudence lacks those qualities. For example, in *Otto Preminger Institut* v. *Austria* (1994) 19 EHRR 14, the Court held that the seizure and banning of a film which was potentially offensive to Christians was justified as pursuing the legitimate aim of protecting the religious rights of others. In *Wingrove* v. *United Kingdom* (1996) 24 EHRR 1, the Court found that the refusal by the British Board of Film Classification was a justifiable interference with freedom of expression with the legitimate aim of protecting the rights of Christians: see further, Nash, *Blasphemy in Modern Britain*, Ashgate, 1999, pp. 265–73.

16 The text has been published by Annoy.com (see http://annoy.com/history/doc.html?documentID=100045) without threat of prosecution. The Crown Prosecution Service decided not to charge the Lesbian and Gay Christian Movement for committing the same offence as in the *Gay News* case, after

The appellants' counsel in the *Gay News* case did not argue that blasphemous libel as a crime was unenforceable. With hindsight that is regrettable, because the Irish Supreme Court recently decided that the same common law offence should not be recognized in Irish law because of its lack of sufficient legal certainty.[17] Nor did they contend that the offence was incompatible

---

receiving a complaint by religious conservatives over a hypertext link to the poem on the Movement's website. In 1995 a priest and university student created a website for the Lesbian and Gay Christian Movement (LGCM). For about six months the website contained a hyperlink to another site which contained the offending poem. The police received complaints from three individuals, including from the evangelical pressure group Reform. The student and the general secretary of LGCM were twice interviewed by police under suspicion of having 'aided and abetted the distribution of a known blasphemy'. The threat of prosecution was lifted eighteen months later.

17 *Corway* v. *Independent Newspapers (Ireland) Limited* [2000] 1 IRLM 426. In 1995, in the wake of the divorce referendum, the *Sunday Independent* carried an article by Dr Conor Cruise O'Brien on the implications of the referendum. Associated with the article was a cartoon that depicted on the right a plump and comic caricature of a priest. The priest was holding a host in his right hand and a chalice in his left hand. He appeared to be offering the host to three prominent Irish politicians, but they appeared to be turning away and waving goodbye. At the top of the cartoon were printed the words 'Hello progress – bye bye Father' followed by a question mark. The words were meant to be a play upon a phrase used during the election campaign by some of the campaigners against divorce, that is to say, 'Hello divorce – bye bye Daddy'. The prosecution was brought in the name of John Corway, a carpenter living in Dublin. He complained that he and others had 'suffered offence and outrage by reason of the insult, ridicule and contempt shown towards the sacrament of the Eucharist as a result of the publication'. The Supreme Court noted that the Irish Constitution is secular, and guarantees the right to freedom of conscience, freedom of religion and freedom of expression. It found it difficult to see how the mere act of publication of blasphemous matter without proof of any attempt to blaspheme would be reconciled with a Constitution-guaranteed freedom of conscience and the free profession and practice of religion. It commented that, if the Church of England had been disestablished and if England had introduced a similar Constitution, it is highly probable that the debate in the *Lemon* case would have taken 'a very different course'. It decided that it was 'impossible to say of what the offence

with the Convention and common law right to free speech. Instead it was argued that blasphemy should not be regarded as an offence of strict liability, and that modern criminal jurisprudence required proof of a specific criminal intent to commit blasphemy. The only question in the appeal therefore was whether the mental element is satisfied by proof only of an intention to publish material which in the opinion of the jury is likely to shock and arouse resentment among believing Christians or whether the prosecution must go further and prove that the accused, in publishing the material, in fact intended to produce that effect upon believers. Astonishingly, a majority of the Law Lords ruled that the offence is one of strict liability and that guilt does not depend on the accused having an intention to blaspheme.

The appellants did argue that the Law Lords should allow continued use of what they termed an 'obsolescent crime' only so long as it complies with Article 9 of the Convention by including a requirement of specific intent. But no reliance appears to have been placed by them on the right to free expression in Article 10.

The only member of the Appellate Committee who referred to the Convention right to free expression was Lord Scarman, who explained why he wished not only to give new life to the offence but also to extend its reach to protect all religions. In the Irish Supreme Court's judgment in *Corway* they referred to what they described as Lord Scarman's 'remarkable' rationale for the existence of an offence of blasphemy. Lord Scarman said this:

. . . I do not subscribe to the view that the common law offence of blasphemous libel serves no useful purpose in the modern law. On the contrary, I think there is a case for legislation extending it to protect

---

of ''blasphemy'' consists. In the absence of legislation and in the present uncertain state of the law the Court could not see its way to authorizing the institution of a criminal prosecution for blasphemy'. Leave to prosecute was therefore refused.

the religious beliefs and feelings of non-Christians. The offence belongs to a group of criminal offences designed to safeguard the natural tranquillity of the kingdom. In an increasingly plural society such as that of modern Britain it is necessary not only to respect the differing religious beliefs, feelings and practices of all but also to protect them from scurrility, vilification, ridicule and contempt . . . I will not lend my voice to a view of the law relating to blasphemous libel which would render it a dead letter, or diminish its efficacy to protect religious feelings from outrage and insult. My criticism of the common law offence of blasphemy is not that it exists but that it is not sufficiently comprehensive. It is shackled by the chains of history.

The previous trial for blasphemy had taken place fifty years before, in *Gott*'s case.[18] John William Gott was indicted for having published a blasphemous libel by selling to the public two pamphlets, entitled, 'Rib Ticklers, or Questions for Parsons' and 'God and Gott' satirizing the biblical story of the entry of Jesus into Jerusalem (Matt. 21: 2–7), which is based on a literal interpretation of the prophecy that the King of Zion would come 'riding upon an ass, and upon a colt the foal of an ass' (Zech. 9: 9). One man in the crowd said, 'You ought to be ashamed of yourself'; one woman said, 'Disgusting, disgusting!' Nothing further occurred. Gott was convicted and sentenced to nine months' imprisonment with hard labour, even though he was suffering from an incurable disease.

In dismissing Gott's appeal, the Lord Chief Justice, Lord Hewart, said:[19]

18 *R* v. *Gott*, 16 Cr.App.R.87.
19 Two years later, Lord Hewart famously described it as being of 'fundamental importance that justice should not only be done, but should manifestly be seen to be done'. *R* v. *Sussex Justices, ex p. McCarthy* [1924] I KB 256, 259. In 1936, he told the Lord Mayor's banquet that 'His Majesty's Judges are satisfied with the almost universal admiration in which they are held', R. M. Jackson, *The Machinery of Justice in England*, 7th ed., 1977, p. 475.

The appellant has been three times before convicted of publishing blasphemous libels, and he had ample knowledge of what he was doing. It does not require a person of strong religious feelings to be outraged by a description of Jesus Christ entering Jerusalem 'like a circus clown on the back of two donkeys'. There are other passages in the pamphlets equally offensive to anyone in sympathy with the Christian faith . . . Such a person might be provoked to a breach of the peace . . . If the appellant is in ill-health, the hard labour will not be enforced so as to injure him. In fact, a sentence of hard labour will cause the prison authorities to pay even greater attention to his health than they would otherwise do.

The harsh sentence aroused great public indignation, with strong criticism in the press and condemnation by a number of clergymen. But there was no condemnation or criticism by any of the Law Lords in the case of *Gay News*. Indeed, Lord Scarman described as 'relevant to British society today' Home Secretary Edward Shortt's statement, when pressed to remit Gott's sentence:[20]

The common law does not interfere with the free expression of bona fide opinion. But it prohibits, and renders punishable as a misdemeanour, the use of coarse and scurrilous ridicule on subjects which are sacred to most people in this country. Mr Shortt could not support any proposal for an alteration of the common law which would permit such outrages on the feelings of others as those of which Gott was found to be guilty.

Lord Scarman also described as relevant to British society today the fact that Macaulay's Indian Penal Code 'protected the religious feelings of all'. It is regrettable that Lord Scarman did

20 Quoted in Kenny, 'The Evolution of the Law of Blasphemy' (1922) 1 C.L.J. 127.

not have the benefit of the well-informed views of Soli Sorabjee, SC, until recently the Attorney-General of India, that:[21]

experience shows that criminal laws prohibiting hate speech and expression will encourage intolerance, divisiveness and unreasonable interference with freedom of expression. Fundamentalist Christians, religious Muslims and devout Hindus would then seek to invoke the criminal machinery against each other's religion, tenets or practices. That is what is increasingly happening today in India. We need not more repressive laws but more free speech to combat bigotry and to promote tolerance.

In the wake of the *Gay News* case, the Law Commission undertook a review of the subject. After detailed study and consultation, its report was published twenty years ago, in June 1985.[22] It recommended the abolition of the common law offences of blasphemy and blasphemous libel. The report identified three main defects in the common law:[23]

(i) 'The law is to an unacceptable degree uncertain.'

(ii) 'In so far as the law requires only an intention to publish the offending words and not an intention to blaspheme, the offence is to an undesirable extent one of strict liability.'

(iii) 'In the circumstances now prevailing in England and Wales, the limitation of the offence to the protection of Christianity and, it would seem, the tenets of the Church of England cannot be justified.'

21 Quoted in the report of the House of Lords Select Committee on Religious Offences in England and Wales, HL Paper 95–1, 10 April 2003, paragraph 52.
22 *Criminal Law: Offences against Religion and Public Worship*, 18 June 1985 (LAW COM. No. 145).
23 Ibid., paragraph 2.18.

The Report noted that:[24]

> If there is no argument which may properly be regarded as sufficiently powerful to justify the derogation from freedom of expression which any offence of blasphemy must occasion, that offence, whether it be the present common law or some statutory replacement of it, should have no place in the criminal law.

Three of the five Law Commissioners, including Brenda Hoggett (now a Law Lord, Baroness Hale of Richmond), recommended the abolition without replacement of the common law offences. Two Law Commissioners were unable to agree that the common law offence of blasphemy should be abolished without enactment of a new offence, because of what they saw as 'the duty on all citizens, in our society of different races and people of different faiths and no faith, not purposely to insult or outrage the religious feelings of others'.

In *Choudhury*'s case,[25] a challenge was made with the support of many Muslims to the publication of Salman's Rushdie's novel, *The Satanic Verses*, seeking to prosecute Rushdie and his publishers, Viking Penguin, for blasphemous libel and seditious libel. Reliance was placed upon Lord Scarman's judgment in the *Gay News* case, and upon the Convention right to the enjoyment of religious freedom without discrimination, to persuade the courts to extend the common law offence of blasphemy to protect Islam against alleged insult. I acted for Viking Penguin. It was a painful experience, illustrating the danger of retaining blasphemy as a criminal offence, because it encourages followers of other faiths to seek a blasphemy law to protect their faith against gross insult. One religion's faith is blasphemy to another religion. The Divisional Court rejected the application and the Law Lords refused leave to appeal.

24 Ibid., paragraph 2.20.
25 *R* v. *Chief Metropolitan Magistrate, ex p. Choudhury* [1991] 1 QB 429 (DC).

The Divisional Court agreed that extending the law of blasphemy would pose insuperable problems, and that the Convention does not demand the creation of a law of blasphemy for the protection of Islam. The European Commission of Human Rights subsequently declared that a complaint that the Convention was being breached was inadmissible[26] because Article 9 of the Convention does not guarantee a right to bring proceedings against those who, 'by authorship or publication, offend the sensitivities of an individual or group of individuals'.

In April 2003, the House of Lords Select Committee on Religious Offences in England and Wales published its Report.[27] The Committee's appointment had its origins in the Anti-Terrorism, Crime and Security Act 2001, in particular, Parliament's decision not to agree to a proposed offence of incitement to religious hatred. It considered two main questions:

1. Should existing religious offences (notably blasphemy) be amended or abolished?

2. Should a new offence of incitement to religious hatred be created and, if so, how should the offence be defined?

On the first question, the Report noted that no blasphemy case has been prosecuted in England and Wales since the passage of the Human Rights Act 1998, but 'it is a reasonable speculation that, as a consequence of that legislation, any prosecution for blasphemy today – even one which met the known criteria – would be likely to fail or, if a conviction were secured, would probably be overturned on appeal.'[28]

26 *Choudhury* v. *United Kingdom* (Application No. 17439/90). Decision of 5 March 1991.
27 HL Paper 95–1, 10 April 2003. The select committee was chaired by Viscount Colville of Culross.
28 Ibid., paragraph 20.

On the second question, the Committee expressed its belief that 'there should be a degree of protection of faith, but there was no consensus among us about the precise form that it might take. We also agree that in any further legislation the protection should be equally available to all faiths, through both the civil and the criminal law.'[29]

The Home Office, by contrast, does not regard the offence of blasphemy as dead. In its view, 'If material or conduct is gratuitously offensive to Christians, and is prosecuted as such, a finding of blasphemy may be the appropriate response by a court to ensure that the rights of others under Article 9 are protected.'[30]

Such an official statement can only encourage bodies like Christian Voice and the Christian Institute in their bigoted campaign against the BBC and regional theatres to prevent public performances of *Jerry Springer – The Opera*.

I believe that, if a suitable case were now to come before the courts, such as a private prosecution brought or threatened by the Christian Institute or by Christian Voice against the BBC or a theatre for allowing the public to see *Jerry Springer – The Opera*,[31] the Law Lords would now be likely to overrule the *Gay News* decision. They would find persuasive the Irish Supreme Court's decision holding that blasphemous libel is so lacking in legal certainty that it is no longer an enforceable criminal offence. They would also be likely to decide that the offence sweeps too broadly in interfering with free speech, and that it is discriminatory in protecting only Christianity.

29 Ibid., paragraph 133.
30 669 HL Official Report, Written Answer 226 by Baroness Scotland of Asthal of 24 February 2005; and 670 HL Official Report, Written Answer 40 by Baroness Ashton of Upholland of 3 March 2005.
31 According to press reports on 16 June 2005, a High Court judge refused to grant an evangelical group, the Christian Institute, permission to call for a judicial review of the BBC's decision to broadcast *Jerry Springer – The Opera*.

In spite of the uncertainty about its current legal status, and even though its removal would secure equality before the law and remove a legitimate source of grievance among British Muslims and others, successive Governments have refused to abolish the offence of blasphemy. To be true to New Labour's election-manifesto commitment 'to give people of all faiths the same protection against incitement to hatred on the basis of their religion' the Government would need to legislate to bury the offence. But the Home Office has merely agreed to 'keep the issue under review, particularly as the benefits of the new provision against incitement to religious hatred are realized',[32] but that is to put the cart before the horse.

The Government's Political Crime of Stirring Up Religious Hatred

The new New Labour Government, like its predecessor,[33] proposes to introduce a series of offences involving stirring up 'hatred against a group of people by reference to religious belief or lack of belief'.[34] An earlier attempt was rejected by Parliament when passing the Anti-Terrorism, Crime and Security Act 2001. During the Second Reading debate in the Lords on the Serious Crimes and Police Bill, the Government's proposals were criticized from all sides.[35] The Government agreed to the removal of the offences from the Bill, without giving any opportunity for the House of Lords to debate amendments, supported across the House, to abolish the offence of blasphemy, prevent the misuse of religion as disguised racism, and protecting freedom of expression. New Labour blamed the Opposition parties and promised British

32 669 HL Official Report, Written Answer 98 by Baroness Scotland of Asthal of 8 February 2005.
33 In Clause 124 of the Serious Organized Crime and Police Bill read with Schedule 10.
34 New Labour Election Manifesto, April 2005.
35 670 HL Official Report, 14 March 2005, cols. 1077–93; 1100–97.

Muslims in particular that, if returned to office, it would ram the proposals through Parliament.

The proposed offences are 'political' in two senses. First, they would punish or deter vigorous public criticism of the beliefs and practices of faith organizations and their supporters of a political nature. Secondly, the Government's determination to create these offences was politically motivated – a targeted bid to woo British Muslim support for New Labour in marginal constituencies where hostility to the illegal invasion of Iraq had alienated many Muslim and other potential voters from Labour to the Liberal Democrats.

The political motivation was made plain when the Home Secretary, Charles Clarke MP, wrote to the mosques at the outset of the election blaming the Liberal Democrats and the Conservatives (in that order) for blocking the legislation. The letter described the Opposition parties as bearing 'full responsibility' and urged 'you and other members of the Muslim community' to 'take very careful note of that, particularly the opposition of the Liberal Democrats on this issue.' The *Muslim News* reported[36] Fiona Mactaggart MP, a Home Office Minister of State, as having told the paper's editor that the New Labour Government would, if re-elected, use the Parliament Act if necessary to force through its proposals, in spite of assurances in New Labour's manifesto that they would 'continue the dialogue we have started with faith groups from all backgrounds about how best to balance protection, tolerance and free speech'.

Objections to New Labour's Proposals

New Labour's plans suffer from the twin vices of vagueness and uncertainty and over-breadth and a lack of proportion. Ministers

36 *Muslim News* press release, 15 April 2005.

have claimed that 'the proposed measure is not an extension of the law on blasphemy – it is about protecting people – not beliefs.'[37] But ministers acknowledge that there is an 'understandable tendency to link the two' and that the public debate has 'led to some unrealistic expectations'.

Like the offence of blasphemy, the proposed crimes lack legal certainty because of the link made between protecting groups of people and protecting their beliefs. It is that linkage which creates the expectation that the proposals are akin to a blasphemy law writ large. It is a measure of public confusion that David Blunkett MP published an article in the *Observer* (12 December 2004) as Home Secretary under the title 'Why we'll outlaw persecution of belief', in which he asked: 'Can it be right that hatred based on deliberate and provocative untruths about a person's *religion* remains unchallenged?' (emphasis added). So Mr Blunkett, the original Home Office architect of the proposals, believes that the offences are designed to protect beliefs rather than groups of people against what he terms 'untruths'. In a similar vein, in a Commons debate,[38] Mr Khalid Mahmood MP was apparently under the impression that the new offences would enable Salman Rushdie to be prosecuted for publishing his novel *The Satanic Verses*, for stirring up religious hatred against beliefs as a statutory extension of blasphemy law.

Because I strongly believe in the equal protection of the law, I have long campaigned for comprehensive equality legislation to tackle religious and other forms of invidious discrimination and harassment. That is why I would also support a declaratory amendment to Part III of the Public Order Act 1986 to make clear that, where what is ostensibly an attack on a group of persons by reference to their religion or belief is in fact an attack

37 670 HL Official Report, Written Answer 147 by Baroness Scotland of Asthal of 17 March 2005.
38 430 HC Official Report, 7 February 2005, col. 1216.

on them because of their ethnicity, the offence of inciting racial hatred is committed. That would make clear what is in reality the present position. Contrary to a widespread misunderstanding, the law in fact treats Jews, Sikhs and Muslims equally as regards racial-incitement law.[39] The only inequality of treatment is in relation to the protection of Christianity by blasphemy law.

The legislation on racial discrimination and incitement to racial hatred and racially aggravated offences defines a protected 'racial group' very broadly by reference to 'race, colour, nationality (including citizenship) or ethnic or national origins'. The courts have made it clear that a wide and non-legalistic approach must be given to the meaning of 'racial group'. It includes, for example, multiple 'racial' identities, and references to being 'non-British', or 'immigrant', or 'Indian' are within the protection of the law.[40] When members of a 'racial' group are also members of a religious group because they share a common religion, it is a question of fact whether adverse treatment against the group is based on 'race' or 'religion'. Jews and Sikhs have been treated by the courts under the Race Relations Act 1976 as belonging to racial and

---

39 Discrimination and harassment on the grounds of religion or belief in employment and vocational training were made unlawful under the *Employment Equality (Religion or Belief) Regulations* 2003 (SI 2003/1660). Protection from *discrimination* on the grounds of religion and belief would be further extended in the Government's proposed Equality Bill to the provision of goods, facilities, services (e.g., the sale of books to the public). This would mirror the Race Relations Act 1976. However, because of legitimate concern about the threat to freedom of speech, the Government is not intending to mirror the racial *harassment* provisions by making religious harassment unlawful in the provision of goods, facilities and services. It is difficult to understand why it should be regarded as legitimate to read across from race to religion in criminalizing incitement to hatred while adopting a more proportionate approach in relation to the civil law on harassment.

40 *Attorney-General's Reference No. 4 of 2004*, Court of Appeal (Criminal Division), 22 April 2005.

ethnic as well as to religious groups.[41] The same applies to the definition of what is meant by a 'racial group' for the purpose of Part III of the Public Order Act 1986. If their religious beliefs or practices are used as a device to attack their race or ethnicity, Jews and Sikhs are protected by the offence of stirring up racial hatred. Equally, if attacks on the religious beliefs or practices of Islam are used as a device to attack the race or ethnicity of British Muslims, most of whom are members of a 'racial group', they too are protected by the offence of stirring up racial hatred. By contrast, if religious beliefs or practices of Jews, Sikhs or Muslims are attacked not on racial but on religious grounds, then they are not protected by the offence of stirring up racial hatred. There is equal protection or lack of protection for Jews, Sikhs and Muslims, whereas the religious beliefs and practices of Christians alone are protected by blasphemy law.

Instead of sweepingly broad new offences of stirring up religious hatred, we need a carefully tailored provision that makes it clear that individuals sharing a common racial or religious identity (to which I would add a common sexual identity) are equally protected when hatred is stirred up against them because of their actual or perceived group identity. The new offences

41 The treatment of Sikhs as an ethnic group results from the Law Lords' decision in *Mandla* v. *Dowell Lee* [1983] 2 AC 548 (HL), which reversed the unanimous decision of the Court of Appeal that Sikhs are a religious rather than an ethnic group: [1983] QB 1. An independent school in Birmingham had a rule forbidding the wearing of turbans. In my view, the Court of Appeal rather than the House of Lords reached the correct conclusion in that case. I agree with Kerr LJ that 'Sikhs can only be described as a "racial group" in the wider sense of colour; or by reference to descent from the peoples of the Indian sub-continent or (predominantly) from what is now the Republic of India; or, possibly, by reference to the region or State of the Punjab or the Punjabi people.' The Court of Appeal invited counsel to put the plaintiffs' case on this basis but he declined. In my view, that is the correct approach. Unfortunately, when the case came before the Law Lords it was argued by the headmaster in person, unaided by counsel.

need to break the link between verbal attacks on a faith group (for example, Muslims as Muslims) and verbal attacks on the beliefs or practices of a faith group. Let us hope that this can be achieved when the Bill reaches the House of Lords, and that the Government withdraw their threat to ram the Bill through using the Parliament Act.

Free speech is the lifeblood of democracy, and another objection to the proposed offences is that their adverse impact on freedom of expression is unnecessary and disproportionate. They involve using a steamroller to crack a nut. Although the Government says that these offences are designed to protect *people*, the definition expressly links people with their religious belief or lack of religious belief. 'Religious belief' plainly includes belief in the teachings or practices of a religion or its followers. 'Religious' means concerned with religion, and religion may include a multitude of belief systems, old and new, the theistic but also non-theistic, as well as sects within religions and cults.

'Religious hatred' means hatred against a group of persons 'defined by reference to religious belief or lack of religious belief'. 'Hatred' is not defined. The proposed offences are not confined to hate crimes akin to violence, nor do they deal, for example, with stirring up hatred against people because of their sexuality, even though that is also a serious social evil more akin to racism than hatred based on religion.

Hatred is not an activity; it is an emotion or a state of mind. The deliberate stirring up of hatred, that is, the intense dislike, of members of a *racial* group is an offence even though it creates no immediate risk of stirring up violence. That is an acceptable use of the criminal law because criminalizing incitement to racial hatred does not normally threaten the right to freedom of expression. A verbal attack on members of a *racial* group is an attack on their common humanity and ethnicity.

But a verbal attack on members of a *religious* group, expressing intemperate criticism of, or hostility to, the beliefs, teachings or practices of their religion, is not an attack on their common humanity, unless in reality it involves an attack on their ethnicity, their origin and biology;[42] for example when it uses a religious attack to stir up racial hatred against Jews, Sikhs, Hindus or Muslims of Asian descent. Subject to narrowly construed exceptions, the right to free speech applies not only to information and ideas that are favourably received or inoffensive, but also to those which offend, shock or disturb.

The proposed offences are sweepingly broad in their reach. They would make it an offence to stir up religious hatred by using threatening, abusive or insulting words or behaviour, or by displaying or publishing written material which is threatening, abusive or insulting, or by publicly performing a play or distributing, showing or playing a recording, or broadcasting a programme involving the use of such words or behaviour. They would also make it an offence to be in possession of religiously inflammatory material intended for publication.

These offences would be committed not only if the defendant deliberately intended to stir up religious hatred but also where religious hatred is 'likely in all the circumstances' to be stirred up. The offences could be committed in a public or a private place. They would be punishable on conviction on indictment by up to seven years' imprisonment or a fine, or both.

There is already a wide range of offences that incur higher penalties if they are motivated or aggravated by religious hostility. One is the offence in section 4A of the Public Order Act 1986, which involves using threatening, abusive or insulting words or behaviour or disorderly behaviour, or displaying any writing, sign or other visible representation which is threatening, abusive

42 'The validity of the declaration that all men are created equal in dignity and rights does not depend upon a permit from the biologists that has to be renewed at regular intervals.' Michael Banton, *Race Relations*, Social Science Paperback, 1967, p. 4, quoted in Anthony Lester and Geoffrey Bindman, *Race and Law*, Penguin Books, 1972, p. 75.

or insulting, with the intention and the effect of causing someone harassment, alarm or distress. Section 5 covers similar conduct within the sight or hearing of a person likely to be caused harassment, alarm or distress. These offences cover *all* forms of harassment, not only racial or religious harassment. The Protection from Harassment Act 1997 also creates a criminal offence in addition to providing civil remedies for the victims of harassment, including alarming a person or causing distress to that person.

In an attempt to explain the vague and ambiguous language of the proposed incitement offences, the Home Office made a statement explaining that it would not be unlawful to criticize the beliefs, teachings or practices of a religion or its followers by claiming that they are false or harmful, or to express antipathy or dislike of particular religions or their adherents. It is unclear why such activities would not be unlawful under the Government's proposals if done with the intention of stirring up religious hatred or in circumstances where the stirring up of religious hatred is likely. The apparent mismatch between the statutory language and the Home Office statement is difficult to reconcile. Such uncertainty is dangerous. Not only would it have a chilling effect on free expression, but also the campaign led by a section of the Muslim community for these offences to become law takes place amidst an atmosphere of heightened 'unrealistic expectations'.

The Home Office asks the public to place their faith in the Attorney-General since he alone can authorize a prosecution. But, as the present Attorney-General told the Colville Committee, it is for Parliament itself, and not the Attorney-General, to decide where the balance should be struck between freedom of expression and unlawful conduct. The effect of enacting these offences would be to require the police to log and consider every complaint of an offence. The Attorney-General's decisions to authorize or refuse consent to prosecutions would be a source of mischief-making and resentment by extremists and troublemakers, whether they are fundamentalist and militant Christians, religious Muslims, devout Hindus, Sikhs or the BNP. No doubt a wise Attorney-General would only rarely consent to a prosecution. Between 1993 and 2003, there were no prosecutions for incitement to religious hatred in Northern Ireland (where it is unlawful), and there was only one prosecution for distributing written material that would incite religious hatred. But the Attorney-General's refusal to consent would be twisted by extremists as evidence of the discriminatory operation of the law, and it would leave embittered those whose expectations were not fulfilled.

The Home Office has identified the perceived gap in the law that the offence of incitement to religious hatred is intended to close.[43] It is a very narrow gap surrounded by a wide array of existing criminal offences against the person or property and involving harassment or incitement.[44] The Home Office examples

43 Letter of 4 March 2005 to the author and accompanying note.
44 '[O]ften the problem is that those engaging in hate speech do not incite their followers to commit specific crimes, but rather encourage them in more general terms to hate members of a particular race or religion. It is this conduct that Part III of the Public Order Act 1986 is designed to deal with. However, that offence applies only to the stirring up of racial hatred. This means "hatred against a group of persons defined by reference to colour, race, nationality (including citizenship) or ethnic or national origins". The definition follows closely the definition of "racial group" in the Race Relations Act 1976. In light of *Mandla* v. *Dowell Lee* [1983] 2 AC 548 (HL) it is accepted that this definition includes Jews and Sikhs but does not include Muslims or Christians. It is irrelevant how hate of a racial group is stirred up and the words or behaviour need not be racist in a strict sense. For example the offence applies to the stirring up of hatred against Jews as a race, Judaism as a religion or indeed any other factor.

'Inciting hatred of religious groups other than Jews and Sikhs is not caught by Part III of the Public Order Act 1986. If no particular crime is incited then common law incitement does not apply. Furthermore, if the conduct is not likely to cause anyone present harassment, alarm or distress, then section 5 of the Public Order Act 1986 will not apply. For example, the existing law does

of the leader of a far-Right group who speaks to his followers in the back room of a pub encouraging his supporters to hate Muslims or the radical Islamist preacher who circulates his tapes to his followers encouraging hatred of Christians do not begin to justify what has been proposed.[45]

Fiona Mactaggart MP described the proposal (letter to *The Times*, 9 March 2005) as tackling a 'small but serious problem of extremists whose efforts have a disproportionate and corrosive effect on communities and were the background to the riots in northern towns in 2001'. That is certainly a serious problem, but there are plenty of criminal offences and police powers in place to enable effective action to be taken against extremists. There are formidable weapons in the existing criminal code to tackle verbal and physical attacks whether against or by racial and religious groups.[46] We need not new laws but the effective enforcement of existing laws by the police and prosecutors.

---

not cover the leader of a far-Right group who gives a speech in the back room of a pub that encourages his followers to hate Muslims; neither does it cover the radical Islamist preacher who circulates his tapes to his followers encouraging hatred of Christians. In both situations religious hatred is likely to be stirred up with all the negative consequences that brings, but at present there is nothing the law can do to prevent that. That is why an offence of religious hatred is required.'

45 Prosecution is pending against three members of the British National Party charged with offences of using words or behaviour intended or likely to stir up racial hatred. These are in relation to undercover filming of BNP activists talking at a private meeting. The Chairman of the BNP was taped apparently condemning Islam as a 'vicious, wicked faith'. The outcome of this prosecution may well be relevant as regards whether there is a gap in the law as suggested by the Home Office.

46 Including, for example, the ugly violent demonstrations by Sikh militants in December 2004 against the showing by the Birmingham Repertory Theatre of Gurpreet Kaur Bhatti's play *Behzti* (*Dishonour*) resulting in the closure of the production. Gurpreet Kaur Bhatti was forced to live in hiding for a while, on police advice. No one has been prosecuted for the serious offences that were committed.

Justice Holmes once said: 'We should be eternally vigilant against attempts to check the expression of opinions that we loathe . . .'[47] Making incitement to religious hatred a criminal offence in the way the Government has proposed is not the way to tackle the serious and sensitive problems of religious discrimination, harassment and incitement in this country.

47 *Abrams* v. *United States* 210 US 616 (1919).

Postscript

Helena Kennedy, QC

Two alarming trends are currently coalescing in Britain: the willingness of Government to abandon legal principle and obliterate civil liberties and the politics of religious identity.

Globalization is creating a slew of anxieties and citizens within our disturbingly uncertain world are seeking areas of certainty. The idea of the nation is being reclaimed with enthusiasm all over the world; people are seeking the comfort of national and religious identity, retiring into smaller and smaller groupings, exhibiting what the political commentator Michael Ignatieff calls, after Freud, 'the narcissism of minor differences'. In the absence of other ideologies to provide a sustaining vision of our human purpose and because of the world's uncertainties, we have seen an increasing assertiveness of religions. Religion has replaced politics as a dominant form of identity and 'taking offence' is a way of refusing to be passive.

Many citizens are easily alarmed by the idea that barbarians are at every gate, including their own, in the form of asylum seekers, illegal immigrants and criminals. As a result they are prepared to sacrifice a significant level of freedom in exchange for greater security. The Government has been reading these expressions of public fear and the willingness of people to make sacrifices as giving them carte blanche to rewrite underlying principles of law. The erosions of civil liberties have been breathtaking and while many people will have been aware of the most egregious assaults on rights – such as the internment of non-citizens without trial in Belmarsh prison on suspicion of terrorist links, or the suspension of habeas corpus – the catalogue of inroads extends far beyond control orders and house arrest. It includes the undermining of jury trial and the presumption of innocence, lowering of the standard of proof, severe limitations on the right to silence, attacks on the judiciary, subversion of new technologies like telecommunications and DNA for undeclared ends, erosion of the double-jeopardy principle, curfews and anti-social behaviour orders. The list is long and continues to grow.

The events of 11 September 2001 added the new dimension of Islamic fundamentalist terrorism to the public's fears. Since then, the Muslim community in Britain has been at the receiving end of greatly increased harassment from fellow citizens as well as racist attack. Muslims have also been the focus of extensive police and intelligence activity, with a sixteen-fold increase in stop and search, hundreds of arrests (of which few lead to charges of any kind), efforts to recruit informants and many house raids – the numbers of the latter will not be released by the Home Office on the pretext that each police force keeps its own statistics and the resource outlay in collating the figures could not be justified.[1]

One of the Home Office Ministers, Hazel Blears, has made it clear that the Islamic community will have to accept such targeted policing as a necessary feature of the war on terrorism.

Not surprisingly, the recent election has shown that British Muslims are seriously alienated from Government and feeling understandably beleaguered. The war in Iraq has added considerably to their belief that new rules are being created where Muslims are concerned, both nationally and internationally.

In such circumstances the Government is looking for ways to generate some goodwill and build bridges. Directing attention towards remedies for abuse, which come from the British National Party or other chauvinist elements, distracts attention

1 The London bombings in July 2005 have aggravated the situation H. K. describes [ed.].

from the abuses which will continue to be perpetrated by the State. The erosion of freedom of expression will have barely caused a moment's reflection because it fits with the overall pattern of trade-off when it comes to civil liberties.

We should be clear, for all the reasons contained in this book, that the creation of an offence of 'inciting religious hatred' will have a chilling effect on free speech. The mere existence of such an offence will rarely inhibit ugly displays of xenophobic hostility, but it will make people uncertain of the law and fearful about crossing the line.

New paradigms of state power are created with every erosion of civil liberty.

It is important not to minimize the fact that Muslims are experiencing insult and abuse at a heightened level. Most of it is racism in new clothes as Anthony Lester has described. What do you do, I am asked, when a dead Muslim woman lying in the morgue has bacon rashers placed on her body, as happened recently in London? I have to point out that this law of inciting religious hatred will not deliver any remedy. What you do is sack the attendant who is responsible. You disgrace him or her publicly, making clear our abhorrence at such defilement. The criminal law is not the only answer to disgraceful conduct. Societies have other sanctions which they can bring to bear.

Existing anti-racist legislation already covers most insult and offence directed at individuals. Indeed the whole raft of public order legislation already in existence around the use of threatening words and behaviour covers the acts and words that Muslims describe when asked to give examples of what they experience and what they want to prevent. Unfortunately, what Muslims also think the legislation will do is prevent critics of their religion from saying things which are offensive to the word of the Prophet in the Koran or of the Prophet himself. Religious conservatives the world over – and this includes Christian fundamentalists and extreme Orthodox Jews – often seek to silence others and to impose on society not merely tolerance of their beliefs but actual acceptance of them. Nothing should make us willing to accept the abuse of the human rights of another, but unfortunately religious texts are often used to do precisely that.

The Home Office creators of the proposed legislation insist that the Bill will only outlaw an offence directed at followers of a religion not the tenets of the religion itself. They agree that religion, like any other ideology, should be tested in the market-place of ideas and even ridiculed. However, what Muslims and others want and believe they are getting is a blasphemy law such as Christians have. It suits community leaders to encourage this belief because it suggests to their own people that they have wrung potent concessions from the Government and extends their authority. However, the law will not only leave minority communities unrequited when it fails to produce their desired outcomes but it will also affect the willingness of people to address the most pernicious aspects of religious practice.

Over the years I have had a close association with the women's organization Southall Black Sisters, which includes Asian women of Sikh, Muslim and Hindu backgrounds. They have been struggling for many years against attempts to silence their voices in relation to violence against women. They are clear in their opposition to the proposed new law on incitement to religious hatred because it would support and encourage the culture of intolerance that already exists in all religions. Challenge has to be offered to religions particularly over human rights issues affecting women and they have no doubt that this law would be used as a weapon to suppress dissent within their communities, particularly crushing those who are more vulnerable and power-less. They point out that increasingly it is women who are being silenced. Men in community leadership positions try to close down debate about abuses of power. It happened in the Catholic Church over child abuse and priests fathering children.

The issues depicted in the Birmingham Rep play *Behzti* – rape and corruption – need to be exposed, however shaming it is for the communities involved. Southall Black Sisters point out that in the mid nineties a Sikh woman was raped by a Sikh priest but when she found the courage to proceed with criminal charges she was subjected to a sustained campaign of vilification. Ramanathan Samanathan, a Hindu priest, was jailed for twelve years in February 2005 for rape of a vulnerable woman in a temple in Croydon, south London. Minority religious communities hate the exposing of their dirty linen because they already feel so marginalized. Taslima Nasrin, a Bengali novelist, had a fatwa created against her in 1993 because one of her books, *Shame*, criticized Islamic texts which are used to oppress women.

Censorship can kill and maim for, when people draw a cloak of secrecy over their actions, gross abuse can happen with impunity.

I was brought up in the Catholic community of Glasgow where the regular taunts of 'Fuck the Pope' and 'Fenian bastards' followed us to school. My identity remains strongly linked to my background and I am very conscious of the ways that obscenities and prejudice can disfigure people's lives. People within communities can be torn between their loyalty to their tribe and the desire to be freed from the stranglehold of dogma. True confidence of one's place in the wider polity comes when you can comfortably laugh at aspects of your belief system and see them from the perspective of the other. But perhaps that laughter only comes easily when your sense of belonging has become secure.

I particularly remember the liberation of laughter when Tom Lehrer sang his 'Vatican Rag' in the sixties, although it gave the clergy and my mother heart failure. For many he was utterly sacrilegious but, by being way out there in the scurrilous zone, he and other satirists lifted a taboo and made more space for dissent about contraception, women's reproductive freedom and the authoritarianism of the Church.

One of the first lessons that all citizens should learn is that ill-considered laws of this kind often have unintended consequences. Feminists in Canada persuaded the Canadian legislature to introduce censorship laws to deal with pornography only to find them used against homosexual authors, a radical black feminist (who was accused of stirring up race hatred against white people) and Andrea Dworkin, the feminist anti-porn activist. In Eastern Europe and the former Soviet Union, laws against defamation were used to stifle criticism of the communist regimes. A Polish satirist, Jerzy Urban, was in early 2005 convicted and fined in a Warsaw court for mocking the late Pope over his poor health. The law used was normally directed at maintaining international relations. In Turkey defamation laws were used against Ismail Besikci for exposing human rights abuses of Kurds. In South Africa during apartheid, race-hate laws were used against the victims of the State's racist policies. Even Alex Haley's novel *Roots* was banned on the grounds that it would 'polarize racial feelings'.

The first people to be prosecuted under this offence are likely to be extremist young Muslims who are members of groups like al-Mujaharoun or Hizb ut-Tahrir, which are highly critical of Israeli policy, and who often fall into abusive language about Jews.[2] Instead of reducing religious antagonisms, they are likely to be fuelled. As religious intolerance rises, dialogue and democracy are the most effective tools to combat hatred rather than laws designed to silence.

The liberties which have been hewn into our democracy are there by dint of hard struggle and scalding lessons. My clients have taught me why they matter. Individual pain is the clearest point of entry into understanding their importance. The women in minority communities for whom I act are unlikely to be served well if their experience within a patriarchal hierarchy is denied

2 H. K.'s predictions have come to pass [ed.].

expression. Telling the truth to power, whether that of the State or that of religions, is a vital way of securing human rights.

The Government again says: 'Trust us. This law will not be used to close down debate or hush voices of legitimate dissent or silence satirists or the artistic community.' No Government can ever speak for those who will step into their shoes hereafter. Free speech is one of the core values in a democracy and it should be championed with a vengeance.

Bannings, Burnings and Suppressions

c. **411 BCE**   Aristophanes' *Lysistrata* was condemned by Plutarch in AD 66, although Plato said of him that 'the graces chose his soul for their abode'. *Lysistrata* was also banned by the Nazi Occupation of Greece in 1942 and again by the military Junta in 1967; as well as the US customs and mails between 1867 and 1930.

c. **1 BCE**   Ovid's *The Art of Love* and other work earned him his exile in AD 8. In 1497, Savonarola burned his works on his great bonfire of the vanities, because they were 'erotic, impious and tending to corrupt'. In 1599, the Archbishop of Canterbury condemned Ovid's *Elegies* in translation to the flames, for 'immorality'. US customs banned import of *The Art of Love* in 1929.

12th–17th centuries   The Talmud, the main (and cumulative) source of rabbinical teaching, disputations and Jewish lore, was burned, banned, and confiscated repeatedly by the Catholic Church in various parts of Europe. It was also the subject of various papal bulls.

1409   The Bible in translation was banned by the Synod of Canterbury. In 1525, the New Testament, the first printed book in England, translated by William Tyndale, was banned. He was imprisoned, then burned at the stake along with copies of his Bible in 1536. In 1624, Luther's Bible was condemned in Germany by papal authority.

1542   The Koran was seized and confiscated by Protestant authorities in Basel, then released at Martin Luther's intervention.

1559 Pope Paul IV instituted the *Index auctorum et librorum prohibitorum*, the first in a long line of papal indexes of forbidden books. He censored Boccaccio's *Decameron*, banned Dante's *De Monarchia* (for claiming that the monarch's authority came directly from God and not the Pope) and the complete works of Calvin and Erasmus.

1633 Galileo's *Dialogue on the two Great World Systems* was banned by Pope Urban VIII. Other works were burned.

1644 Milton's *Areopagitica* was condemned by Cromwell for its advocacy of press freedom.

1649 Bacon's entire works were banned by the Spanish Inquisition.

1664 Molière's *Tartuffe* was banned under Louis XIV from public (though not court) performance.

A Few of the Works and Authors Placed on the Papal Index

1673 Descartes, *Méditations métaphysiques*.

1676 Montaigne, *Essais*.

1697 Spinoza, *Tractatus theologico-politicus*.

1720 Defoe, *Robinson Crusoe*.

1734 Locke, *An Essay Concerning Human Understanding* (French translation).

1753 Diderot, D'Alembert, Holbach, *L'Encyclopédie*.

1789   Pascal, *Pensées*.

1792   Paine, *The Rights of Man* and other works (also prosecuted in England).

1819   Sterne, *A Sentimental Journey*.

1827   Kant, *Critique of Pure Reason* (Italian translation).

1834   Hugo, *Notre-Dame de Paris*; 1864 *Les Misérables*.

1836   Heine, various works.

1841   Balzac, *Contes drolatiques* and other works.

1863   Dumas, all his love stories, including *La Dame aux camélias*.

Other authors include Sand, Flaubert, d'Annunzio, Addison and Steele, Swedenborg, Rousseau, Zola, Bergson and Sartre.

Some Books Banned and Prosecuted by Other Authorities

1856   Flaubert was prosecuted for *Madame Bovary*.

1857   Baudelaire, author of *Les Fleurs du mal*, and his printer and publisher were prosecuted and fined.

1859   Darwin's *On the Origin of Species* was refused by Cambridge University Library.

1912   James Joyce's *Dubliners* was suppressed in Ireland and elsewhere. In 1918 several instalments of *Ulysses* were seized by US postal authorities, resulting in a ban on the novel and a series of obscenity trials. The novel was only finally published in the US in 1934. In 1922, five hundred copies of the whole book in its London edition were burned by the New York Post Office. The book was banned in the UK between then and 1936.

1915   D. H. Lawrence published *The Rainbow*: 1011 copies were seized during a police raid on the London offices of Methuen and burned on grounds of obscenity – though this was an anti-war novel. The police solicitor told Bow Street magistrates that the book's obscenity was 'wrapped up in language which I suppose will be regarded in some quarters as artistic and intellectual effort'.

1928   D. H. Lawrence had the first edition of *Lady Chatterley's Lover* privately printed in Florence; it was seized by British customs. Only in 1960 did the book finally find a publisher in Penguin who fought the obscenity trial which followed in November. E. M. Forster and Raymond Williams testified for the defence. The book was also banned in Australia and the United States.

1929–53   In the Soviet Union under Joseph Stalin, scores of writers were censored, tortured, murdered, exiled, amongst them Babel, Osip and Nadezhda Mandelstam, Pasternak, Akhmatova, Zoshchenko and Solzhenitsyn.

1933   On 10 May, just a few months after seizing power, the Nazis organized book burnings in Germany's major cities, in an attempt to purify the nation of 'degenerate' ideas. In Berlin on the Opernplatz, in a great illuminated spectacle, they threw some twenty thousand books, culled from libraries and bookshops, into the flames, while chanting their manifesto for the purification of German literature and thought. Some of the authors were Jewish – Marx, Freud, Einstein, Kafka; others, like Thomas Mann, were married to Jews; others were simply deemed degenerate –

Rilke, Kastner, Jack London, Hemingway, Sinclair Lewis and Erich Maria Remarque.

1948 Several of William Faulkner's novels were banned in Philadelphia.

1953 Alfred C. Kinsey's *Sexual Behaviour in the Human Female* was banned in US Army Post Exchanges.

1959 Naguib Mahfouz, the great Egyptian Nobel Prize-winning author of *Children of Gebelawi*, earned a fatwa for apostasy from Omar Abdul Rahman. Many of the novelist's works have been banned in the Middle East. In 1994, thirty-five years after the fatwa was issued, Mahfouz, at the age of eighty-three, was stabbed in the neck by two extremists outside his Cairo home.

1988 Salman Rushdie's *The Satanic Verses* was banned in India on 5 October, ten days after its UK publication. It was then banned in South Africa.

1989 On 14 January, *The Satanic Verses* was burned in Bradford. Muslim protests took place in Hyde Park. In February there were riots in Pakistan and Kashmir in which the book figured.

1989–99 On 14 February 1989 Iran's Ayatollah Khomeini proclaimed a fatwa against Salman Rushdie and his publishers, Penguin. A price was put on his life. The writer went into hiding. There were bannings of the book and protests in India, Turkey and elsewhere. The Japanese translator of the book was killed. A special paperback edition of the book came out published – in solidarity with Penguin and the author – by a group of publishers.

1993 Taslima Nasrin, the Bengali novelist, poet, journalist and doctor, had a fatwa declared against her in Bangladesh for the novel *Shame*, which described the plight of a Hindu family under attack by Muslim fundamentalists. She escaped death threats by fleeing to Sweden. In 1998, she surrendered to the Bangladeshi high court, but after further death threats she had to flee once more. In many of her writings, Nasrin describes the plight of women under sharia law.

1995   Mark Twain's *Huckleberry Finn* was removed from classes in various US schools.

1997   Gunter Grass's *The Tin Drum* was published in 1959. The later film version was banned in Oklahoma City for child nudity.

2004   Theo van Gogh, Dutch film-maker, was murdered for his film *Submission* by Mohammed Bouyeri, who left a letter with jihadist slogans on his body. Somalian-born Dutch politician Ayaan Hirsi Ali, who wrote the script for *Submission*, went into hiding after threats and lives under police protection. In 2005, a court in The Hague rejected a petition from a Muslim group to bar her from making a sequel to the film, which is about the treatment of women under Islam.

A Few of the Writers Persecuted for Their Work in Their Home Countries, from the PEN Case List (December 2004)[1]

Ardeshire Gholipou	Australia
Salah Uddin Shoaib Chaudhury	Bangladesh
Yury Bandazhevsky	Belarus
Chen Yanbin	China
Gao Qinrong	China

1 A full case list may be viewed on International PEN's website (www. internationalpen.org.uk).

He Depu	China
Huang Jinqiu	China
Lu Zengqi	China
Yu Dongyue	China
Jesús Alvarez Castillo	Cuba
Pedro Argüelles Morán	Cuba
Victor Rolando Arroyo Carmona	Cuba
Mijaíl Bárzaga Lugo	Cuba
Carlos Brizuela Yera	Cuba
Adolfo Fernández Saínz	Cuba
Miguel Galván Gutiérrez	Cuba
Julio César Gálvez Rodríguez	Cuba
José Luis García Paneque	Cuba
Normando Hernández González	Cuba
Said Abdelkader	Eritrea
General Ogbe Abraha	Eritrea
Yusuf Mohamed Ali	Eritrea
Emanuel Asrat	Eritrea
Dawit Habtemichael	Eritrea
Medhanie Haile	Eritrea
Hamid Himid	Eritrea
Dawit Isaac	Eritrea
Saleh Idris Kekia	Eritrea
Mahmud Ahmed Sheriffo	Eritrea
Abbas Abdi	Iran
Reza Alijani	Iran
H. H. Y. Eshkevari	Iran
Amir Abbas Fakhravar	Iran
Akbar Ganji	Iran
Hossein Ghaziyan	Iran
Ensafali Hedayat	Iran
Siamak Pourzand	Iran
Taghi Rahmani	Iran
Khalil Rostamkhani	Iran

Hoda Saber	Iran
Said Sadr	Iran
Nasser Zarafshan	Iran
Fawwaz Muhammad al-Awadhi Bessissu	Kuwait
Ahmed Ibrahim Didi	Maldives
Ibrahim Moosa Luthfee	Maldives
Fathimath Nisreen	Maldives
Naushad Waheed	Maldives
Mohamed Zaki	Maldives
Aung Myint	Myanmar
Aung Pwint	Myanmar
Aung San Suu Kyi	Myanmar
Ko Aung Tun	Myanmar
Khin Zaw Win	Myanmar
Kyaw Sein Oo	Myanmar
Myo Htun	Myanmar
Ohn Kyaing	Myanmar
Sein Hla Oo	Myanmar
Thaung Tun	Myanmar
Win Tin	Myanmar
Zaw Thet Htwe	Myanmar
Ali Al-Domaini	Saudi Arabia
Matrouk Al-Faleh	Saudi Arabia
Iñaki Uria	Spain
Nu'man Ali Abdu	Syria
Abdul Aziz Al-Khayer	Syria
Abdel Rahman Al-Shagouri	Syria
Aref Dalila	Syria
Emine Senlikoglu	Turkey
Leyla Zana (writer in exile)	Turkey
Muhammad Bekzhon	Uzbekistan
Mamadali Makhmudov	Uzbekistan
Yusif Ruzimaradov	Uzbekistan
Thich Quang Do	Vietnam

Nguyen Dinh Huy	Vietnam
Thich Huyen Quang	Vietnam
Le Chi Quang	Vietnam
Nguyen Dan Que	Vietnam
Abdel Karim Al-Khaiwani	Yemen

Case Statistics for 2004

Killed	12
Killed: Investigation	22
Disappeared	12
Main Case (imprisoned)	169
Under Investigation (imprisoned)	71
Judicial Concern	12
Under Judicial Process	220
Non-custodial Sentence	59
In Hiding	6
Brief Detention	153
Death Threat	89
Other Threat/Harassment	62
Attacked/Ill-treated	76
Kidnapped	13
Deported/Expelled/Fled	20
Total	**996**
Released	73

Notes on Contributors

Monica Ali's first novel, *Brick Lane*, an epic saga of a Bangladeshi family in London, was shortlisted for the Booker Prize in 2003.

Yasmin Alibhai-Brown is an award-winning journalist and columnist with the *Independent*. She is the author of several books, including the recent *Some of My Best Friends Are . . .* and has written and performed in her play, *Nowhere to Belong*. In 2005, she was voted the tenth most influential black / Asian woman in the UK in a local poll.

Lisa Appignanesi's books include the novels *The Memory Man, Sanctuary*, and *The Dead of Winter*; the acclaimed family memoir, *Losing the Dead*; as well as *Freud's Women* (with John Forrester), *Simone de Beauvoir*, and *The Cabaret*. She is Deputy President of English PEN. She broadcasts regularly and recently made *Freudian Slips* for Radio 4.

Rowan Atkinson is an actor, writer, comedian and producer, famous for his *Blackadder* and *Mr Bean* series, amongst much else.

Andrew Berry is an evolutionary biologist and research associate at Harvard University's Museum of Comparative Zoology. He is a regular contributor to the *London Review of Books*, co-author, with James Watson, of *DNA*, and the editor of a collection of the writings of the Victorian biologist Alfred Russel Wallace, *Infinite Tropics*.

Gurpreet Kaur Bhatti's first play *Behsharam* (*Shameless*) broke box office records at the Soho Theatre and the Birmingham

Repertory Theatre in 2001. Her second play *Behzti* (*Dishonour*) played to packed houses at the Birmingham Rep, but was sensationally closed after violent protests in December 2004. *Behzti* won the prestigious Susan Smith Blackburn Prize in 2005 for the best English language play written by a woman. Bhatti has recently written *The Cleaner*, a film for BBC1, and her first feature film, *Pound Shop Boys*. She is now working on commissions for the Royal Exchange, Manchester, the National Theatre and Kali Theatre as well as developing a primetime drama series for BBC1.

Ian Buruma has written widely for the *Guardian*, the *New York Times* and the *New York Review of Books*. His many books include *Occidentalism: The West in the Eyes of Its Enemies* (with Avishai Margalit), *Voltaire's Coconuts*, *Bad Elements* and *The Wages of Guilt*.

Frances D'Souza has taught at both the London School of Economics and Oxford Brookes University. She was the Founder Director of an independent research group focusing on applying systematic evaluation methods to development and emergency aid and collaborated in original research on the economic origins and alleviation of famine. She was for over nine years the Executive Director of Article 19, a human rights organization devoted to promoting freedom of expression. She is a governor of the Westminster Foundation for Democracy. She was awarded a CMG in 1998 for services to human rights and appointed as an independent peer in 2004.

Julian Evans wrote and presented BBC Radio 3's twenty-part series on the European novel, *The Romantic Road*, and the BBC4 film *José Saramago: A Life of Resistance*. He is the author of *Transit of Venus*, an account of a journey to the heart of the US's nuclear-missile testing programme in the Pacific Ocean, and is currently researching a biography of the writer Norman Lewis.

Moris Farhi is the author of the critically acclaimed novels *Young Turk* (2004), *Journey through the Wilderness* (1989), and *Children of the Rainbow* (1999). His poems have appeared in many British, US and international publications and in the anthology of twentieth-century Jewish poets *Voices Within the Ark*. For many years, he has been an active campaigner on behalf of persecuted writers for English PEN, as well as being a Vice-President of International PEN.

Timothy Garton Ash is Professor of European Studies at the University of Oxford, a *Guardian* columnist, and the author, most recently, of *Free World: Why a Crisis of the West Reveals the Opportunity of Our Time*.

Philip Hensher's most recent novels are *The Fit*, *The Mulberry Empire* and *Kitchen Venom*. He is also a columnist for the *Independent*.

Pervez Hoodbhoy is Professor of Physics at Quaid-e-Azam University, Islamabad, as well as a Visiting Professor at MIT. He has won many awards for his scientific work, as well as being a commentator on South Asian politics. He is the author of *Islam and Science: Religious Orthodoxy and the Battle for Rationality*.

Nicholas Hytner has been Director of the Royal National Theatre since 2001. Apart from many plays, he has also directed several films including *The Crucible* and *The Madness of King George*.

Michael Ignatieff is Carr Professor of Human Rights Practice at the Kennedy School of Government, Harvard University. He is the author of many books, most recently *Empire-Lite*, *Isaiah Berlin: A Life*, and *The Lesser Evil: Political Ethics in an Age of Terror*, as well as novels. He served on the International Commission on

Intervention and State Sovereignty. He is a frequent contributor to the *New York Times* and the *New York Review of Books*.

Howard Jacobson's acclaimed novels include *The Making of Henry*, *The Mighty Walzer*, *No More Mr Nice Guy*, and *Peeping Tom*. He is a columnist for the *Independent*, has made films for television and is the author of various non-fiction works, including *Seriously Funny: From the Ridiculous to the Sublime*, and *Roots Schmoots*.

Helena Kennedy, QC, was Chair of the British Council and chairs the Human Genetics Commission. She is the author of *Just Law* and *Eve Was Framed*, a member of the Bar Association's International Task Force on Terrorism, and a Labour peer.

Hari Kunzru is the author of the novels *The Impressionist* and *Transmission*. In 2003 Granta named him one of its Best of Young British Novelists. He is a member of the Executive Council of PEN. A selection of his writing and photography may be found online (www.harikunzru.com).

Hanif Kureishi's many works for page, film and stage include *My Ear at His Heart*, *The Body*, *Love in a Blue Time*, *The Buddha of Suburbia*, *My Son the Fanatic*, *Intimacy*, and *My Beautiful Laundrette*. His most recent film is *The Mother*.

Anthony Lester, QC, is a practising member of Blackstone Chambers. He has argued many leading free speech cases before English courts and the European Court of Human Rights, including several referred to in his essay. He is a Liberal Democrat life peer (Lord Lester of Herne Hill).

Adam Phillips's books include *Going Sane*, *The Beast in the Nursery*, *Darwin's Worms*, *Promises, Promises: Essays on Poetry and Psycho-*

analysis, and *On Kissing, Tickling and Being Bored*. He is a practising psychoanalyst and general editor of the Penguin Freud.

Philip Pullman is the author of some twenty books, most notably the trilogy *His Dark Materials*, beginning with *Northern Lights* (1995), then *The Subtle Knife* (1997) and *The Amber Spyglass* (2000). These have received many prizes including the Whitbread Book of the Year, the first time the award was given to a children's book. His work has been instrumental in blurring the dividing line between children's and adult fiction.

Salman Rushdie's latest novel is *Shalimar the Clown*. Others include *Fury*, *The Ground Beneath Her Feet*, *The Moor's Last Sigh*, *Haroun and the Sea of Stories*, *The Satanic Verses*, *Shame*, and *Midnight's Children*, which won the Booker of Bookers. Ten years of his non-fiction is collected in *Step Across This Line*. *The Satanic Verses* caused what was the first modern 'global' persecution of an author. In 2004, he became President of American PEN.

Madhav Sharma made his acting debut with the Shakespeareana International Company touring India, Singapore, Malaysia and Hong Kong. He has appeared in Gurpreet Kaur Bhatti's *Behzti* and in Tom Stoppard's *Indian Ink*, as well as in film and on television, including *Dr Who*.